UNDERSTANDING FACE-TO-FACE INTERACTION

*Issues Linking
Goals and Discourse*

COMMUNICATION TEXTBOOK SERIES

Jennings Bryant—Editor

Language and Discourse Processes
Donald Ellis—Advisor

TRACY • Understanding Face-to-Face Interaction: Issues Linking Goals and Discourse

UNDERSTANDING FACE-TO-FACE INTERACTION

Issues Linking Goals and Discourse

Edited by

Karen Tracy
University of Colorado

LEA LAWRENCE ERLBAUM ASSOCIATES, PUBLISHERS
1991 Hillsdale, New Jersey   Hove and London

Lawrence Erlbaum Associates, Inc., Publishers
365 Broadway
Hillsdale, New Jersey 07642

Library of Congress Cataloging-in-Publication Data

Understanding face-to-face interaction : issues linking goals and
　　discourse / edited by Karen Tracy.
　　　　p.　cm. — (Communication textbook series. Language and
　　discourse processes)
　　　　Includes indexes.
　　　　ISBN 0-8058-0538-9 (c.) — ISBN 0-8058-0907-4 (p.)
　　　　1. Interpersonal communication.　2. Goal (Psychology)　I. Tracy,
　　Karen. II. Series.
　　BF637.C45U53　1990
　　153.6—dc20　　　　　　　　　　　　　　　　　　90-39526
　　　　　　　　　　　　　　　　　　　　　　　　　　　　CIP

Printed in the United States of America
10　9　8　7　6　5　4　3　2　1

CONTENTS

CHAPTER 1

Introduction: Linking Communicator Goals with Discourse

Karen Tracy
University of Colorado-Boulder

The assumption that communicative action is strategic and goal-oriented is virtually a given starting point of communication research (e.g., see recent volumes by Cody & McLaughlin, 1990; Daly & Wiemann, in press; Tracy & Coupland, 1990) as well as its most influential disciplinary neighbor: psychology (Frese & Sabini, 1985; Giacalone & Rosenfeld, 1989; Jones & Pittman, 1982; Schank & Abelson, 1977). The purpose of this book is *not* to challenge the reasonableness of the assumption—it is unimaginable that accounts of communicative action could be adequate without recognizing that people are purposeful and use talk to accomplish "goals"—but rather to challenge the simplistic way in which that assumption has typically been understood.

For the purposes of this introduction, I use *goal* as a general concept that references a family of concepts: goal, purpose, concern, intention, and want. Whether we should make more distinctions within that family of concepts is but one of the issues that this volume addresses (see especially chapter 9). The typical practice, however, is for researchers to *not* specify very precisely which meaning is intended when the concept is used (Craig, 1986, 1990).

Not all study of face-to-face interaction starts with an "intentional actor" assumption. Most notably, "discourse" studies (Bilmes, 1986; Gumperz, 1982a, 1982b; Tannen, 1981, 1984), studies that begin with naturally occurring talk, have attempted to sidestep the assumption in some interesting, although not completely successful, ways (see Tracy & Coupland, 1990, for a review). In this chapter, I restrict my focus to "communicator goals" approaches to face-to-face interaction, the approach type dominant in communicative and social psychological research. I argue that assuming that communicator goals relate to discourse in simple transparent ways is neither empirically warrantable nor theoretically wise.

As initial evidence of the complexity of the relationship between discourse and goals, consider one example of a "simple" exchange. Two friends have been conversing, and the first friend (A) says, "There was flooding in Harrisburg." It is now the second friend's (B's) turn to talk; how should he or she respond? What did A mean by the comment? B's ability to respond appropriately depends on B understanding A's intended goal, which is inferred from the discourse in light of background knowledge (Schank et al., 1982). As illustration of the potential difficulty, consider the following four responses and how each suggests B inferred markedly different goals motivating A's comment:

R1:   Is your brother OK?

R2:   Yeah, I was lucky this time. We closed the sale on our property a little over a month ago.

R3:   Yeah, we've certainly had obnoxious weather this Fall.

R4:   What's your point?

Response 1 is a sensible one if friend A has a brother in Harrisburg. It will demonstrate that B cares about what A cares about; it will also show that B recognizes that a general event (weather/flooding) has emotional significance for A and that B recognizes that A was not bringing it up just because weather is an acceptable topic for general talk. Put another way, R1 suggests that Friend B took A's comment about Harrisburg as a bid for interest and sympathy.

In R2, B interprets the goal motivating the Harrisburg comment quite differently. In essence, B treats the comment as an expression of interest and concern from friend A to self. R2 would be a sensible next comment for B to make if he or she has property in Harrisburg and knows that A knows that fact. Stated with words, A's point would be something like, "I'm telling you this piece of information because I know it affects you and I notice and keep track of things that affect you."

The third response is the most general; Schank et al. (1982) labeled it a "general interest" point. General interest points presume that the speaker's goal was to say something that is generally of interest for people to talk about—in this case, weather and disasters. That is, there was not a more specific goal that motivated the comment; it is merely a topic to talk about to pass time and avoid awkward silences.

Where the first three responses presume that the speaker had friendly intentions, R4 does not. R4 is the kind of response that makes sense if, for example, A had warned B not to buy property in Harrisburg but B had gone ahead and done it anyway. In this case, B might be inferring A's goal in commenting about Harrisburg to be a way to say, "I told you so." The goal of Speaker *B* in responding with R4, then, could be to challenge *A* to be openly critical and self-righteous, a move that *B* might expect *A* to not want to do. In this last case, then, the point of the Harrisburg comment is for *A* to criticize *B*, and R4 is *B*'s response to that criticism.

There are many more goals than the four exemplified here that a speaker could have in making a single simple comment. The four, however, are sufficiently diverse to illustrate why being able to link discourse to goals is essential in understanding face-to-face interaction. This need to have methods for linking goals and discourse becomes even clearer when we start from the opposite vantage point—that of the speaker who has a goal. Imagine a speaker who had one of the following four communicative goals: (a) to express interest in another; (b) to make a bid for another to show interest in self; (c) to keep talk going and avoid awkward silences; (d) to criticize another's judgment. How would these different goals be expressed in talk? As I have shown already, these goals could be expressed in an identical discourse form. Obviously, however, each goal could be expressed in a myriad of ways. A speaker interested in expressing interest in another, for example, could (a) ask a question ("What's going on in your life?"); (b) give a compliment ("That was a good movie you selected."); (c) demonstrate his or her attentiveness to the other's past talk ("I was thinking about what you said yesterday, and . . ."); or (d) make a comment about something that affects the other ("There was flooding in Harrisburg.").

If the same discourse form can indicate different goals, and different forms can express virtually the same communicative goal, then we are going to need good conceptual frameworks (theoretical distinctions, guiding ideas) to discover and construct how goals and discourse are (or should be) linked in any particular case. This example points to the complexity of relations between discourse and goals. All of the chapters in this volume consider issues involved in understanding how goals and discourse expression can be linked. In the remainder of the chapter, I do three things: (a) evidence the degree to which the assumption of simple transparency is widespread; (b) show how untenable such an assumption is in one kind of face-to-face interaction—intellectual discussion among faculty and graduate students in an academic department; and (c) overview the contributions that each of the chapters makes to conceptualizing more adequately how goals and discourse are linked.

ASSUMPTION: GOALS AND DISCOURSE ARE TRANSPARENTLY LINKED

The assumption that goals and discourse are transparently linked rests on two interconnected premises. The first is that the goals that undergird communicative action are a small, easily defined set. The goals in this set, moreover, are assumed to be related to each other in a straightforward manner. The second premise is that, if the links between a goal (get compliance) and functional message strategies (make a request, be rational, be friendly) are identified, then the interesting part of the goal–discourse relationship has been explained. That is, it is presumed that the extension to discourse is unproblematic and easy to do.

Premise 1: There is a Small, Easily Defined Set of Goals

The assumption that the goals undergirding communication are a small, easily defined set is seen in much theorizing. For instance, Clark and Delia (1979), in their now much-cited article, suggested that interactants have three main types of goals: a task or instrumental one, a self-presentational, identity one, and a relational one. Each of these goals is present in every social situation, they argued, but specific situations differ in the salience of each. Others have made similar arguments about the general goals of face-to-face encounters (Forgas, 1983; Graham, Argyle, & Furnham, 1980; McCann & Higgins, 1984; O'Keefe & Delia, 1982). Theoretical formulations such as these suggest that (a) the goals that people possess for specific types of interaction could easily be placed in one of three categories; and (b) the goal priorities that people will have is given, or at least strongly suggested, by the nature of the social situation.

When we look at research that investigates how people pursue a particular kind of communicative goal, we find the implications of these theoretical typologies drawn out explicitly. This is especially well illustrated in research on face-to-face persuasion, a research tradition typically labeled *compliance-gaining* or *social influence*. Study of social influence is based on the assumption that there are a large set of situations in which getting compliance is the obvious goal (Bisanz & Rule, 1990; Dillard, 1990; Rule & Bisanz, 1987; Smith, Cody, LoVette, & Canary, 1990).

Take, for instance, a much-studied situation (Marwell & Schmitt, 1967; Miller, Boster, Roloff, & Seibold, 1977; Seibold, Cantrill, & Meyers, 1985): getting one's son to do his homework. This situation *could* be primarily a compliance-gaining situation, but there are many other goals that could be central. A parent could be concerned with motivating a son to take responsibility for his behavior. In this case, getting one's son to do homework would be only part of a broader goal. Thus, if a parent saw the conversation with a son turning into a situation where the son seemed to perceive the situation as a compliance-gaining one, that is, one where the parent was trying to impose his or her preferences on the child, a parent might abandon attempts to get the son to do homework. In this case, although the parent might prefer that his or her son study more, the parent's concerns to recognize that the son is a mature decision maker (relational goal?) and that he or she is able to give his or her child independence (identity goal?)

might lead a parent to avoid the subject entirely or broach it in an indirect manner ("We're going to Aunt Sarah's for dinner on Sunday. You'll need to plan around that in doing your homework."). In such a situation, where compliance-gaining is not the central goal, we would expect a parent to speak in different ways than when it was (treat the situation as an information-giving one, for example). My point is that face-to-face situations do not come with easily prespecified goal packages.

Many researchers do recognize that situations have more than a single goal influencing action (see Tracy & Coupland, 1990, for a review); but, nonetheless, how these multiple goals are to be related is treated as self-evident. By and large, more attention is given to goal hierarchy than to goal multiplicity. The goal of compliance-gaining, for instance, is conceived as a midrange goal: on the one hand, an instantiation of a task goal (Dillard, 1990); on the other, a general category of more specific action. For instance, Cody, Canary, and Smith (in press) have identified 10 more specific goals of compliance-gaining, including such concerns as obtain permission, gain assistance, give advice, change relationship, change opinion. Others have specified slightly different compliance-gaining goal typologies (Dillard, 1989; Rule & Bisanz, 1987).

Of those studying compliance-gaining, Dillard (1990) has been especially sensitive to the fact that interaction involves multiple goals. But even he argued that, in compliance-gaining situations, compliance-gaining will be the primary goal, and other concerns (e.g., self-presentational, relational) will be secondary—that is, ones that shape how a speaker accomplishes the primary one. The difficulty with this is, as I argued earlier, is that face-to-face situations do not come tagged by type (e.g., "This is a compliance gaining situation."). Rather, the speaker is faced with figuring out how important any single goal is in light of his or her other existing goals. The simplicity of goal conceptions interacts with a second assumption: that there is no need to look at discourse.

Premise 2: If We Understand What Communicators Do at the Level of Message Strategies, There is No Need to Look at Discourse

Although the specific issues of interest in communication research are quite diverse, most conceptual discussion about face-to-face interaction is at the level of message strategies or tactics detached from discourse expression. Message strategies specify a general type of action that another might take. For instance, in compliance-gaining situations, people might use threats, direct requests, promises, and ingratiation. By and large, the treatment of discourse expression as inconsequential is not argued for explicitly; rather, it is an assumption embedded in research practice (Potter & Wetherell, 1987; Robinson, 1985). That is, when researchers interested in "affinity-seeking" (Bell & Daly, 1984; Berger &

Bell, 1988), comforting (Burleson, 1983, 1984), relationship termination (Baxter, 1982), compliance-gaining (Seibold et al., 1985) the management of embarrassing moments (Cupach, Metts, & Hazelton, 1986) sexual harassment (Bingham & Burleson, 1989), and so on neither look at actual interaction nor defend why, in the particular case, it is reasonable to omit looking at actual interaction, they are taking for granted the inconsequentiality of that type of information.

However, if one believed that studying discourse could significantly alter the conclusions drawn about the nature of face-to-face interaction, there would be no warrant for ignoring discourse. That conclusions can be markedly different is illustrated in a study (Hopper & Drummond, 1990) that compares ideas about relational termination developed through study of self-reports with those garnered through study of a telephone exchange in which a couple breaks up.

To summarize, much communicative research assumes that (a) social situations come with obvious and easily identified goals; (b) the goals will relate to each other in ways that can be specified a priori; and (c) looking at discourse expression will not yield much new information useful for understanding face-to-face exchanges. I have generally suggested that this is untenable; let me further illustrate the inadequacy of these assumptions in a particular kind of interaction, which I label *intellectual discussion*.

CASE STUDY: AN INTELLECTUAL DISCUSSION

One type of interaction that has received intensive philosophical consideration but little observational study is intellectual discussion (cf. Grimshaw, 1989). I became interested in this type of talk because what participants said in one intellectual discussion group in which I participated often seemed strange and convoluted—at least from any simple vantage point. Moreover, as a social actor in this situation, it was not uncommon for me to find myself thinking about what I "should" say. Reflection suggested that the situation was likely to involve multiple complex goals for interactants; as such, study of an ongoing discussion group seemed an ideal place to examine how goals and discourse were linked. Over a period of a year, Sheryl Baratz and I collected audio-tape, interview, and observational data about this group.

The "intellectual discussion" we studied was a weekly departmental colloquia in a PhD communication program. A typical colloquium involved a speaker giving a 40-minute presentation, followed by an equally long discussion. The discussion usually, although not always, focused on the speaker's claims. Attendance varied from week to week, usually numbering about 20 people, with the attendants consisting of faculty and graduate students in the department and visitors from other departments and universities.

Our first project involved analyzing the in-depth interviews we had conducted with 10 regular participants (Tracy & Baratz, 1989). We were interested in understanding how people perceived the institutional and individual goals in the colloquia. We asked participants what their own concerns were and what they thought others' concerns were when in the roles of presenter and discussant. As data we used not only what participants told us directly but also what they implied about goals through their comparisons, criticism, and complaints.

Study of the interviews revealed two sets of goals that individuals oriented to in the situation. The first goal set was intellectual display/community membership display. Participants were concerned with displaying themselves as intellectually able or, at least, not intellectually inferior. As presenters, this meant that people worked to show their position to be interesting and reasonable. As discussants, they were concerned to ask tough challenging questions, point out problems, and show the limitations of other's viewpoints. Participants also wanted to demonstrate themselves to be "good community members." Being a good community member meant knowing about and being interested in other's work, not deliberately hurting or humiliating another, and helping others accomplish the intellectual work goals they pursued—that is, giving advice that was helpful, was supportive, and took account of others' skill level.

We argued (Tracy & Baratz; 1989) that the relationship between the goals, and even within the different parts of the single goal of being a good community member, was far from a simple one and was influenced by many things, particularly the relative equality of the participants (graduate students, faculty). In summarizing our conclusions about the meaning of the community goal we concluded (Tracy & Baratz, 1989):

> We are left, then, with a complex picture of what it means to be a good member of community—one in which people are expected to be considerate, gentle and tactful but one in which they show that they take the other seriously by criticizing and challenging; a community in which people are expected to play the game with all the skill they possess yet recognize that not all players are equally skilled. (p. 9)

The second set of goals that participants oriented to concerned the nature of the relationship between self and ideas. Participants reported having both the goal of demonstrating their distance from ideas (not getting defensive) and demonstrating their involvement (showing investment with ideas). Although the involvement issue seemed primarily tied to the initial choice to talk, it also surfaced in comments about the ideal manner of discussion; people were both praised and criticized for getting emotionally involved.

The goals that were identified for this intellectual discussion, then, were complex ones that involved at least partial contradictions. They do not easily map into the abstract categories that prior theorizing has identified (task, identity, relational). Rather, each goal seems a complex combination whose salience we could expect to shift over the course of an exchange.

Consider now an excerpt of "intellectual discussion" and what insights would be forfeited if we did not examine actual discourse. The exchange that follows occurred between a speaker (Pat) and another member of the department (Lee). Pat had given a presentation soon after the 1988 presidential election about campaign strategies and had made a number of claims about why Governor Dukakis had lost and how he could have avoided losing. After about 20 minutes of discussion, Lee asked how Pat could be so certain about something that was said about Walter Mondale, referring to Pat's ideas as speculation. Pat did not accept the label "speculation" and instead used "theory." The following discussion ensued:[1]

01 Lee   Oh the theory is, I'm sure it's not speculative ( ) whether it can be applied in the given case to reach your desired results

02 Pat   Well in that sense I'm a little bit like uh like the rest of us, right? We do communication studies, we do discourse analyses, we do rhetorical criticism; where's the evidence?

03 Lee   Well we don't forecast or we don't prophesize ( )

04 Pat   Well what makes what makes that better?

05 Lee   Looking at it after its happened?

06 Pat   Yeah.

07 Lee   As opposed to before?

08 Pat   Right.

09 Lee   It would, it would seem more difficult. It would be turning into a prophecy somehow

10 Pat   Ok but in 19 uh 88 in July, uhm in early August I was at University X and I said to my students Bush is gonna win. Dukakis was at that point, was at that point 17 points ahead. I operated off a theory of campaigning and uh now that theory is being supported. I, you, Well I can say what a wonderful clairvoyant I am or what a great prophet I am or what a wonderful theory I have. No I couldn't have predicted that it would be this bad but I did have some ideas about how this thing was going to fall that were counter intuitive, counter empirical at the time and then gave reasons to kinda support this trajectory that I had

11 Lee   There, counter intuitive and counter empirical

12 Pat   Well counter most people's intuitions because the intuitions at the time from the pundits was that it was going to be a Dukakis victory. But uh, but I had, I had a theory of what was going on uh that uh, that began with the observation that the democratic party was riddled with contradictions and

---

[1]Punctuation in this transcript was added to aid readability.

that what plays well in primaries doesn't play well in election campaigns and so on, this then substantially supported by the evidence. One good thing about forecasting rather than being a Monday morning quarterback is that you gotta lay things out on the line, you gotta say beforehand uh this is where I'm making my bets uh and uh, there's a certain kind of uh uh uh scientific character to that unlike the rhetorical critic who always gives the retrospective analysis.

13 Lee   Jean Dixon came out in the New York times a couple weeks ago. She forecasted Bush would win and I'm sure it's based upon a theory.

14 Pat   Right. But what's your point?

15 Lee   Well I'm wondering how you how you're drawing ( )

16 Pat   How is it different? Well Jean Dixon, Jean Dixon looks at the stars or uh looks at people's palms and does her forecasting on that basis. I don't know that there's very much uh evidence in support of her uh, methods; uh, the question comes down to method and and here uh what we know methodologically suggests that that there are other ways of reading the future than reading palms.

17 Lee   What would you have said if if Dukakis had done X, and Y would have been the result How can you possibly know?

18 Pat   I don't know it.

19 Lee   How come you have confidence ( )

20 Pat   But notice, notice now your false dichotomy. We either have to know it or we have to not talk about it not speculate about it

21 Lee   Oh no we should recognize what it is. It's kinda a loose, a speculation, kind of a nice fun exercise but it doesn't mean much. It it doesn't doesn't tell us much. ( ) It's been fun talking about it but that's as far as it goes and there's a function to that. I mean we should have fun when we talk I mean having fun is worthwhile
(laughter from group)

22 Lee   ( ) I mean what's better than that? It doesn't cost anything

23 Pat   Ok, I guess, I guess I would hafta hafta give up on an awful lot of what I rely on in a course of a day, uh any day in uh a week if I bought into your theory. I would rarely make judgments, uh unless I absolutely had all of the evidence and I never do. Uh I wouldn't simply say to myself I'm not gonna make a judgment uh today I do it as a policy uh I I wouldn't know how to vote on a tenure candidate, on a promotion, on what sorta judgment to make in the way of promoting policy for the department

24 Lee   Voting on a tenure candidate is a long way from ah saying If Dukakis had said X, Y would have resulted. A long way. Are those those no different? I don't know how you ever could ever ( )

25 Pat   Well in both cases, in both cases I'm saying we're involved in what might be
          called an art of judgment. It's not a science of judgment, it's an art of
          judgment. Uh we are, we are finding out ways uhm to connect our best
          inferences, our best interpretations with uh, some implications for action uh
          it's

26 Lee   on the one hand

27 Pat   It's rarely the case, it's rarely the case that we have evidence sufficient on its
          own terms to make those sorts of judgments

28 Ted   It takes it takes no art to judge that we are past four o'clock. Well I think it can
          be continued but some of us, some of us must go.

Features of Intellectual Discussion Suggested by Examination of the Discourse

Let me highlight two aspects of this exchange that shed light on possible
relationships between intended or attributed goals and discourse moves. The
first issue concerns the way intellectual attack and refutation are carried out; put
another way, the kinds of discourse strategies used to present one's own position
as reasonable and the other's as unreasonable (Tracy, 1990). As was gleaned
from the interviews, the goal of displaying one's own intellectual ability was seen
to involve presenting one's own claims as reasonable and the other's as unreasonable. Study of this exchange revealed that one way of displaying another's
"unreasonableness" is by characterizing the other's position in terms that the
community can be understood to evaluate negatively. Consider Lee's characterization of Pat's position as prophesizing (utterances 3, 8), as being the same as
what Jean Dixon does (13–16), loose speculation, and a fun exercise (21). In an
academic community, which can be presumed to put considerable weight on
thinking that is serious, careful, and rigorous, Lee can be seen as attempting to
portray Pat's position as unreasonable.

Pat also used this strategy to portray Lee's position as unreasonable and his
own as reasonable. Toward the end of the interchange (25), Pat characterized his
position regarding the similarity between predicting who will be president and
deciding if a faculty member should be tenured as "an art of judgment," not a
"science of judgment." Pat's characterization of the two positions implicitly
presented his reasonableness and suggested Lee's unreasonableness. In describing the two positions this way, he called on the community's understanding
that "the process of judgment" is inherently an imprecise activity and that
"science" is a precise activity. By implication, then, a person who advocates a
science of judgment is unreasonable, mixing things that do not go together.

The subtlety of these kinds of characterizing moves is further evidenced in
another of Pat's uses of the term *science*. Whereas, in the prior example, he
called on one aspect of science to attempt to make Lee's position seem unreasonable, in utterance 12, he associated his own position with science to make it

look reasonable. Pat drew on slightly different connotations of science in each exchange. Lee had just characterized Pat's position as "prophesizing" (9). Pat then countered this framing, suggesting that what he does has a "certain kind of scientific character." Science in this contrastive context implies the activities of prediction and hypotheses testing—desirable activities, not the undesirable kind: nonrational, fuzzy, religious ones that the academic community could be counted on to associate with prophesizing. To summarize, one strategy of being "reasonable" and showing the other to be unreasonable is to characterize one's own and others' positions in ways that the community can be expected to have strong positive or negative reactions to.

A second interesting issue surfaces around the goal of defensiveness. The interviews indicated that presenters were concerned about being "nondefensive" in their responses to comments and criticisms. In essence, presenters cared that others regard their handling of potentially difficult questions as appropriate. We could ask whether speakers always orient to the goal of being nondefensive and whether audiences always evaluate presenters' "defensiveness." I suggest that they do not. Instead, I argue, speakers (and audiences) orient to the management of defensiveness when the questions asked are "difficult" ones for a speaker.

Consider how Pat, the presenter, responded to several potentially difficult questions from Lee. I offer my reactions as a participant in the group—reactions that, while undoubtedly having an idiosyncratic component could also be expected to have points of similarity to others in the audience. During most of the exchange (the end is the exception), the issue of defensiveness seemed not to be relevant. Why was this the case? As an audience member, I initially saw Lee's questions as "tough" ones that called into question the basic nature of Pat's intellectual work. Pat's reactions altered my initial characterization. Rather than treating Lee's comments as difficult, Pat treated Lee's comments as naive and not demanding serious intellectual engagement. Consider how that was accomplished.

In the exchange between Lee and Pat where Lee suggested that Pat's activities are similar to Jean Dixon's (13–16), it seemed likely that Lee's comment that Jean Dixon forecasted Bush winning was meant as a sarcastic comment, a highly tinged negative evaluation about what Pat was claiming. Pat (14), however, did not respond to it as such. Rather, he explicitly asked Lee what his point was. In asking Lee what his point was, Pat can be seen as relying on Lee's likely reluctance to verbalize that he had an explicit goal of making Pat look stupid. Thus, in response to the direct question, we see Lee partially at a loss for words, unable to formulate his concern (15). Pat turned Lee's loss for words into a specific question that he presumed Lee was trying to formulate. (How are Pat's ideas about forecasting presidential elections different from what Jean Dixon does?) This question seems a ludicrous one—one that is hard to imagine taking seriously. In fact, the only imaginable grounds for the question not to be dismissed out of hand would be if it was asked by a naive, unsophisticated

person. A serious answer, then, implicitly casts the asker as naive and unsophisticated. Pat addressed the question seriously: "Jean Dixon looks at the stars, or
uh looks at people's palms and does her forecasting on that basis. I don't know
that there's very much, uh, evidence in support of her, uh methods." We are left,
then, with the impression that Pat did not take Lee seriously, because he treated
Lee's question "seriously."

Thus, although the goal of avoiding defensiveness might generally be relevant for presenters, it did not seem to be relevant in this particular segment of
discussion. It was not the case, however, that the issue of defensiveness was
irrelevant the entire time. Pat's reactions lost their "I'll try and be reasonable
with you tone" when Lee succeeded in eliciting laughter from the group at Pat's
expense (21–22). In his next turn (23), rather than trying to characterize the
limitations of Lee's position delicately, as was seen in the reference to Jean
Dixon's "methods," Pat used extreme formulations—Lee's position, Pat stated,
would lead him to "rarely make judgments, uh, unless I absolutely had all the
evidence, and I never do." Such a framing strongly challenged the reasonableness of Lee's position.

In this last section, then, in contrast to the earlier ones, Pat responded to Lee
as a serious intellectual opponent. And, although the thrust of Pat's comment
was to show that Lee's position was wrong, because the response was strong and
emotional, it implied that the question was tough, it supported Lee's identity as
intellectually able, and it made relevant to the audience the question of whether
Pat was being "defensive."

Study of this exchange suggests that goal attributions about defensiveness
become relevant when a speaker treats a tough question as tough. If a speaker
belittles a question, treats it as naive, ill-informed, or irrelevant, the focus of
observers' attributional attention moves away from the speaker's question
handling toward the questioner's intellectual ability.

If the preceding analyses are persuasive, it becomes reasonable to conclude
that the discourse moves that realize the interactional goals that people have in
intellectual discussion—to be perceived as reasonable, to handle tough questions
well, and so on—are extremely complex and are dependent on a large web of
taken-for-granted assumptions in light of connotations made salient by specific
discourse formulations. Thus, if we are to adequately understand how people
accomplish their communicative goals, we cannot ignore discourse expression.
Let me describe, next, how each of the chapters in this volume enhances
understanding of goal–discourse relationships in face-to-face interaction.

OVERVIEW OF THE VOLUME

The chapters in the volume focus on particular exchanges, situations, and
relationships, unpacking actor's goal concerns and the way these concerns are

expressed in specific types of face-to-face exchange. The chapters also grapple with issues that cut across situations, offering conclusions about the nature of goals and how they relate to discourse generally. Many chapters do both of these things; but each chapter gives priority to one. The volume is organized in terms of this specific/general priority. Chapters in the first half give their main attention to issues within specific contexts (the courtroom, divorce mediation, therapy) or relationship types (intergenerational, friendship). Chapters in the second half primarily focus on cross-situational dilemmas and problems.

Chapter 2, an essay by Penman, argues that moral orders undergird all communicative practices. Penman identifies two that operate in courtrooms, and she suggests that the way to identify moral orders is through close analysis of the language games and "goals" displayed in a situation. Drawing on multiple instances of courtroom interaction, she posits the operation of a "fact" game and a "face" game, which relate in complicated ways to a justice and an honor morality. These moralities do not mesh well with each other. As a result, Penman argues, the courtroom's discourse rules unfairly disadvantage witnesses.

The third chapter, written by Jacobs, Jackson, Stearns, and Hall, focuses on divorce mediation. After demonstrating that the argumentative discourse that occurs in mediation is notably digressive, they consider why that is the case. The interchanges are digressive, they argue, because the talk is not directed to the "obvious" situational goal—that is, to resolve problems around child custody and visitation. When viewed from another vantage point, they show, the discourse is not at all digressive. The conversations between ex-husbands and -wives can be seen as centrally directed at demonstrating each spouse's good moral character and the other's blameworthiness, a goal that, over the course of back-and-forth exchanges, becomes the "obvious" one motivating the ex-spouses' communicative choices.

In chapter 4, Buttny and Cohen examine the way conversational goal attributions function in a therapy session between a married couple and a therapist. They consider how people account for what leads them to act, arguing that we cannot have direct access to people's goals but that goal-talk is an available resource that provides insight into what actors see as reasonable goals and reasonable procedures for attaining them. Buttny and Cohen analyze the opening segment of a couple's session in which each partner identifies the problems that brought them to therapy. Each partner's remarks, they show, specify not only the problem that brought the couple to therapy but also who is to blame and what the solution should be. These goal formulations, in turn, are taken up by the partner to be refuted, agreed with, modified, or whatever.

The next two chapters focus on interaction in particular relational contexts. In chapter 5, Coupland, Coupland, Giles, and Henwood examine the role of goals in intergenerational talk: in particular, initial conversations between middle-aged and elderly women. Drawing on extensive examples of middle-aged–elderly conversations, they show that at the level of conversational management, the goals of elderly and younger speakers are consonant; the two groups cooperatively create a smooth-functioning interaction by casting the young in facilitator roles and the elderly in the role of the center of attention. This smooth functioning, they illuminate, exists because of a broader goal incompatibility. Elderly people are stereotyped by younger speakers and seen as not possessing the same interactional wants and needs as the young themselves have.

In chapter 6, Rawlins considers what is involved when friends attempt to work back from each other's discourse to arrive at the meaning for the friendship. Working back to the meaning, Rawlins shows, rests on the answers that a friend gets to a complicated web of interconnected questions that concern identification of the action performed, assessment of its intentionality, and judgments about the act's consequences for the self, the friend, and society.

In the first chapter of Part II, Bavelas reviews the way psychology has used the intrapsychic concept "goal" to explain behavior. After describing several problems in using "goal" to explain discourse, she argues that the fundamental problem occurs because the two concepts are different reality levels: Discourse references behavior; goal references hypothetical constructs. Most psychological research involves heavy use of constructs and limited attention to behavior. The result is an "inverted pyramid," an approach, she argues, that is misguided. Drawing on 10 years of work with colleagues on "equivocation," she illustrates how they were able to "stabilize the pyramid" and develop a more data-sensitive, discourse-grounded approach to theorizing.

In chapter 8, O'Keefe considers the puzzling fact that certain communicative tasks reveal few individual differences, whereas others make visible major differences. Explanations of individual message differences typically appeal to differences among people's goal priorities. But this, O'Keefe argues, is insufficient to account for the kinds of message variety exhibited. To adequately account for differences, we need to take account of people's "message design logics." Using Brown and Levinson's (1978, 1987) politeness theory as a comparison point, a theory premised on a single design logic, O'Keefe demonstrates the need to have three distinct conceptions of how discourse and goals can be linked.

Chapter 9, written by conversational analysts Mandelbaum and Pomerantz, poses the question: What drives social action? The question is an interesting one, because conversation analysts and communication researchers have approached it so differently. Conversation analysts have largely ignored or been nonexplicit about participant intentions and concerns; communication researchers have regarded all social action as goal-driven. Drawing on a telephone conversation between two friends in which one asks a favor of another, Mandelbaum and Pomerantz show the usefulness of distinguishing five influences on social action, only a couple of which bear any resemblance to communicator notions of "goal."

Chapter 10, by Sanders, offers a model of how goals and talk mutually influence each other. Sanders sketches the typical way of conceiving of the relationship between talk and goals—a unidirectional one where preinteractional plans and goals are assumed to guide the expression of talk. Then, drawing on a telephone conversation between two nurses where one rejects the other's job offer, he illustrates the implausibility of the unidirectional model and shows the need for a model that posits a two-way relationship.

The final chapter, by Shepherd and Rothenbuhler, shows how the concepts "discourse" and "goal" draw on different intellectual traditions. The idea of "goal" is used most often in conjunction with individualistic, intentional psychological explanations of action. "Discourse" is more associated with collectivistic, sociological, social structure explanations. This creates problems for communicative theories that want to link them. Shepherd and Rothenbuhler present ways to solve this problem, including, for instance, taking account of the fact that goals are socially shaped as well as being expressions of individual desires.

Theorists have recently made convincing arguments about how science and society are interconnected and why social science should be concerned about practical action (Craig, 1989; Hall, 1989; Krippendorf, 1889). This volume illustrates one attempt to take the interconnectedness seriously. By providing conceptions of communicative situations that capture much of their usual complexity; by giving descriptors of a whole range of social and judgmental consequences associated with different communicative moves; by making explicit the ways communicative moves can shape or reframe the nature of the situation being faced; by building situational models of actor goal priorities that are both realistic and morally defensible; and by making explicit how goals are manifested in discourse, it is hoped that this volume can be useful in shaping communicative practice.

REFERENCES

Baxter, L. A. (1982). Strategies for ending relationships: Two studies. *Western Journal of Speech Communication, 46*, 223–241.

Bell, R. A., & Daly, J. A. (1984). The affinity-seeking function of communication. *Communication Monographs, 51*, 91–115.

Berger, C. R., & Bell, R. A. (1988). Plans and the initiation of social relationships. *Human Communication Research, 15*, 217–235.

Bilmes, J. (1986). *Discourse and behavior.* New York: Plenum Press.

Bingham, S. G., & Burleson, B. R. (1989). Multiple effects of messages with multiple goals: Some perceived outcomes of responses to sexual harassment. *Human Communication Research, 16,*

184–216.

Bisanz, G. L., & Rule, B. G. (1990). Children's and adults' comprehension of narratives about persuasion. In M. J. Cody & M. L. McLaughlin (Eds.), *The psychology of tactical communication* (pp. 48–69). Clevedon: Multilingual Matters.

Brown, P., & Levinson, S.C. (1978). Universals in language usage: Politeness phenomena. In E. N. Goody (Ed.), *Questions and politeness: Strategies in social interaction* (pp. 56–310). Cambridge, England: Cambridge University Press.

Brown, P., & Levinson, S. C. (1987). *Universals in language usage: Politeness phenomena.* Cambridge, England: Cambridge University Press.

Burleson, B. R. (1983). Social cognition, empathic motivation, and adults' comforting strategies. *Human Communication Research, 10,* 295–304.

Burleson, B. R. (1984). Comforting communication. In H. E. Sypher & J. L. Applegate (Eds.), *Communication by children and adults: Social cognitive and strategic processes* (pp. 63–104). Beverly Hills, CA: Sage.

Clark, R. A., & Delia, J. G. (1979). Topoi and rhetorical competence. *The Quarterly Journal of Speech, 65,* 187–206.

Cody, M. J., Canary, D. J., & Smith, S. (in press). Compliance-gaining goals: An inductive analysis of actor's goal-types, strategies, and successes. In J. Daly & J. Wiemann (Eds.), *Communicating Strategically.* Hillsdale, NJ: Lawrence Erlbaum Associates.

Cody, M. J., & McLaughlin, M. L. (1990). *The psychology of tactical communication.* London: Multilingual Matters.

Craig, R. T. (1986). Goals in discourse. In D. G. Ellis & W. A. Donohue (Eds.), *Contemporary issues in language and discourse processes* (pp. 257–274). Hillsdale, NJ: Lawrence Erlbaum Associates.

Craig, R. T. (1989). Communication as a practical discipline. In B. Dervin, L. Grossberg, B. J. O'Keefe, & E. Wartella (Eds.), *Rethinking communication: Vol. 1. Paradigm issues* (pp. 97–122). Newbury Park, CA: Sage.

Craig, R. T. (1990). Multiple goals in discourse: An epilogue. *Journal of Language and Social Psychology, 9,* 157–164.

Cupach, W. R., Metts, S., & Hazelton, V. Jr., (1986). Coping with embarrassing predicaments: Remedial strategies and their perceived utility. *Journal of Language and Social Psychology, 5,* 181–200.

Daly, J., & Wiemann, J. (Eds.). (in press). *Communicating strategically.* Hillsdale NJ: Lawrence Erlbaum Associates.

Dillard, J. P. (1989). Types of influence goals in personal relationships. *Journal of Social and Personal Relationships, 6,* 293–308.

Dillard, J. P. (1990). The nature and substance of goals in tactical communication. In M. J. Cody & M. L. McLaughlin (Eds.), *The psychology of tactical communication* (pp. 70–90). Clevedon, England: Multilingual Matters.

Forgas, J. P. (1983). Language, goals and situations. *Journal of Language and Social Psychology, 2,* 267–293.

Frese, M., & Sabini, J. (Eds.). (1985). *Goal-directed behavior: On the concept of action in psychology.* Hillsdale, NJ: Lawrence Erlbaum Associates.

Giacalone, R., & Rosenfeld, P. (Eds.). (1989). *Impression management in the organization.* Hillsdale, NJ: Lawrence Erlbaum Associates.

Graham, J., Argyle, M., & Furnham, A. (1980). The goal structure of situations. *European Journal of Social Psychology, 10,* 345–366.

Grimshaw, A. D. (1989). *Collegial discourse: Professional conversation among peers.* Norwood, NJ: Ablex.

Gumperz, J. J. (Ed.). (1982a). *Language and social identity.* Cambridge, England: Cambridge University Press.

Gumperz, J. J. (1982b). *Discourse strategies.* Cambridge, England: Cambridge University Press.

Hall, S. (1989). Ideology and communication theory. In B. Dervin, L. Grossberg, B. J. O'Keefe, & E. Wartella (Eds.), *Rethinking communication: Vol. 1. Paradigm issues* (pp. 40–52). Newbury Park, CA: Sage.

Hopper, R., & Drummond, K. (1990). Goals and their emergence in a relationship turning point: The case of "Gordon and Denise." *Journal of Language and Social Psychology, 9,* 39–66.

Jones, E. E., & Pittman, T. (1982). Toward a general theory of strategic self-presentation. In J. Suls (Ed.), *Psychological perspectives on the self* (pp. 231–263). Hillsdale, NJ: Lawrence Erlbaum Associates.

Krippendorf, K. (1989). On the ethics of constructing communication. In B. Dervin, L. Grossberg, B. J. O'Keefe, & E. Wartella (Eds.), *Rethinking communication: Vol. 1. Paradigm issues* (pp. 66–96). Newbury Park, CA: Sage.

Marwell, G., & Schmitt, D. R. (1967). Dimensions of compliance-gaining behavior: An empirical analysis. *Sociometry, 30,* 350–364.

McCann, C. D., & Higgins, E. T. (1984). Individual differences in communication: Social cognitive determinants and consequences. In H. E. Sypher & J. L. Applegate (Eds.), *Communication by children and adults* (pp. 172–210). Beverly Hills, CA: Sage.

Miller, G. R., Boster, F. J., Roloff, M. E., & Seibold, D. R. (1977). Compliance-gaining message strategies: A typology and some findings concerning effects of situational differences. *Communication Monographs, 44,* 37–51.

O'Keefe, B. J., & Delia, J. G. (1982). Impression formation and message production. In M. E. Roloff & C. R. Berger (Eds.), *Social cognition and communication* (pp. 33–72). Beverly Hills, CA: Sage.

Potter, J., & Wetherell, M. (1987). *Discourse and social psychology.* Newbury Park, CA: Sage.

Robinson, W. P. (1985). Social psychology and discourse. In T. A. Van Dijk (Ed.), *Handbook of discourse analysis: Vol. a. Disciplines of discourse* (pp. 107–144). London: Academic Press.

Rule, B. G., & Bisanz, G. L. (1987). Goals and strategies of persuasion: A cognitive schema for understanding social events. In M. P. Zanna, J. M. Olson, & C. P. Herman (Eds.), *Social influence: The Ontario symposium* (Vol. 5, pp. 185–206). NJ: Lawrence Erlbaum Associates.

Schank, R. C., & Abelson, R. P. (1977). *Scripts, plans, goals, and understanding.* Hillsdale, NJ: Lawrence Erlbaum Associates.

Schank, R. C., Collins, G. C., Davis, E., Johnson, P. N., Lytinen, S., & Reiser, B. J. (1982). What's the point? *Cognitive Science, 6,* 255–276.

Seibold, D. R., Cantrill, J. G., & Meyers, R. A. (1985). Communication and interpersonal influence. In M. L. Knapp & G. R. Miller (Eds.), *Handbook of interpersonal communication* (pp. 551–611). Beverly Hills, CA: Sage.

Smith, S. W., Cody, M. J., LoVette, S., & Canary, D. J. (1990). Self-monitoring, gender and compliance-gaining goals. In M. J. Cody & M. L. McLaughlin (Eds.), *The psychology of tactical communication* (pp. 91–135). Clevedon, England: Multilingual Matters.

Tannen, D. (1981). Indirectness in discourse: Ethnicity in conversational style. *Discourse Processes, 4,* 221–228.

Tannen, D. (1984). *Conversational style: Analyzing talk among friends.* Norwood, NJ: Ablex.

Tracy, K. (1990). The many faces of facework. In H. Giles & P. Robinson (Eds.), *Handbook of language and social psychology* (pp. 209–223). London: John Wiley and Sons.

Tracy, K., & Baratz, S. (1989, November). *Participating in intellectual discussion: A situation of paradoxical requirements.* Paper presented at the meeting of the Speech Communication Association, San Francisco, CA.

Tracy, K., & Coupland, N. (1990). Multiple goals in discourse: An overview of issues. *Journal of Language and Social Psychology, 9,* 1-13.

I

Discourse–Goal Linkages in Specific Face-to-Face Encounters

CHAPTER 2

Goals, Games, and Moral Orders: A Paradoxical Case in Court?

Robyn Penman
Communication Research Institute of Australia

All discourse analysis is concerned with making sense of a fundamental human phenomenon: communication. At the heart of discourse analysis is the assignment of meaning to communicative practices. This chapter is concerned with how we can assign meaning to communication occurring in a particular context: courts of law. This chapter is also concerned with doing so from a particular point of view, based on new developments in ways of thinking about social practices. These new developments have been taken to reflect a paradigm shift from modern to postmodern science (e.g., Bernstein, 1983; Toulmin, 1982).

Central to this new point of view is the recognition that the meaning of something does not reside in any outside, objective, or independent reality; rather, meanings are created out of our communicative practices (e.g., Gergen, 1982; Penman, 1988). Any account or explanation we give of communicative practice cannot be taken as a discovery in the real world but as the creation of a story to make sense of our world (Shotter, 1987). The issue here is what sort of story? In particular, what sort of story can we generate to make sense of the communication process in courts of law?

As a starting point, I propose that it needs to be a moral story. I have argued elsewhere (Penman, 1988, 1989) that the new metatheoretical framework being used here inexorably leads us to ask moral questions. These questions have been neglected in past research because of the old paradigm belief in scientific neutrality and distance from the object of study. Within that conventional framework, the researcher and writer was expected to act as a dispassionate chronicler and analyst of observed events, not as a proponent of, or commentator on, a moral position. Within this new framework, all communicative practices are taken to have a moral dimension, and researchers have the moral task of exploring it.

How we can explore this moral dimension is the subject of this chapter. A particular conceptual framework is developed, using three key concepts: goals, games, and moral orders. As is shown herein, understanding the goals and games being enacted in discourse provides the basis for inferring moral orders. Empirical data and case-study analyses of discourse in courtrooms are used to illustrate and further develop the conceptual framework.

A CONCEPTUAL FRAMEWORK

The notion that morality is connected to communication is not new. For example, in 1922, Dewey wrote an essay that was critical of the then-current moral philosophy. For Dewey (cited in McDermott, 1981), "the facts upon which it [morality] depends are those which arise out of active connections of human beings with one another, the consequences of their mutually entwined activities" (p. 722). Habermas, writing in contemporary times, made an analogous argument (e.g., see McCarthy, 1984). For Habermas, interaction is the dialectic of the moral life, claims to right and wrong being implicit in all modes of communication. Similarly, Cronen (1986) has put it: "There is no society we know of that does not operate by some set of obligations, prohibitions and legitimations" (p. 6).

The sets of rules for guiding and constraining action reflect general social orders; and within these general social orders are moral orders. What is allowed and not allowed and what is claimed to be right and wrong are indicative of a moral order. This observation is particularly pertinent to the courtroom situation: There we have a context that was explicitly established for the sanctioning and prohibiting of various actions. The law is a major moral institution in society; but there is more to the court's moral order than the body of law it upholds. In the very discourse between judge, barrister, and witnesses, moral orders are also being enacted. This is the critical point made by both Dewey and Habermas: that the moral order is not just connected in some way to communication; rather, it emerges from, and is expressed and negotiated in, that action.

I am proposing, then, that moral orders are indicated by sets of rules that guide communicative practice in different contexts. This suggestion, however, cannot be taken in a simple form. As Larmore (1987) has pointed out, although rules are undeniably a feature of morality, morality does not merely consist in adherence to rules. Indeed, it could well be the case that adherence to a particular morality leads a person to the conscious breaking of rules that are incommensurate with that person's morality. It could also be the case that there is more than one moral order being enacted in any given communicative context and that the joint "order" that emerges is not identical to that held by any participant. These possibilities point out that the patterns of communication brought about in our descriptions of joint action are not necessarily the product of adherence to a single set of rules nor the product of conscious control by either participant. Indeed, as the general system theorists argued long ago, the communicative system that participants jointly bring about is more than the sum of their actions.

These complexities are well captured in Wittgenstein's (1958) notion of a "language game"; he proposed this concept in order "to bring into prominence the fact that the *speaking* of language is part of an activity or a form of life" (p. 11). This is analogous to the proposition that started the chapter: meanings being created out of communicative practice. Wittgenstein gave no precise definition of a language game. In fact, a precise definition would be contrary to his argument that the concept of a "game" cannot be neatly categorized as having certain features and not others. On the other hand, a language game does have at least one particular characteristic: It consists of a set of "moves" that appear to be employed according to a set of rules or conventions.

Wittgenstein and this chapter use the notion of *rule* in a loose sense. For Wittgenstein, a rule is like an order; it tells us to do something, but we can still choose to follow the order or not. Thus, people are not seen as rule-governed but as rule-following or rule-using: They are seen as being agents in the ethnogenic sense (e.g., Harré, 1979). Moreover, it is not necessary that participants in any language game know the rule, in the sense that they can articulate it. It is sufficient, as Wittgenstein argued with other games, that rules *appear* to be guiding the sequence of moves in the game.

The assumptions of a language game are pertinent to discourse in courts. It is highly likely that witnesses will not know (in the sense of being able to articulate) the rules in court, and yet they will have to follow them. The force of law, if nothing else, will make them appear to be following rules. They will appear to be following rules when recurrent patterns in a conversation occur, and these patterns can be taken as indicative of some adherence—or deviation—from a given game. This, according to Wittgenstein, is no more nor no less than how we identify a game of tennis or poker and how we distinguish one type of game from another.

To be able to identify the nature of the game, it is useful to make a distinction between two different types of rules: constitutive and regulative. This is a common distinction employed by rule theorists (e.g., Pearce & Cronen, 1980), as well as one that is used in this chapter. But it is the concept of constitutive rules, in particular, that brings us back to our original question: the assignment of meaning. Constitutive rules are just that—rules that say what actions count as, or what they mean.

The concept of *goal* is usually assumed in constitutive rules. When we say that that action counts as asking a question, we are, in fact, describing the action in terms of its effect or goal achieved (the asking of a question). It is in this sense that *goal* is used here; not the conventional behaviorist sense of a preconceived purpose. Rather, goals are taken as being emergent in the interaction between people. Our description of action in terms of goals emerges from the discourse as it proceeds. But this description is by no means a simple one.

In the first instance, there can be multiple descriptions of any given action. This multiplicity occurs for two reasons. First, actors, in their labelling of actions, can assign multiple goals. In other words, we may act with the intent of achieving more than one goal at once, and/or we can construe another's actions as being multiply goal-oriented. Recognizing the possibility of multiple goals is not new. In fact, for some, it is taken as a "commonplace" (e.g., Farrell, 1983, p. 263). However, the second reason for multiplicity is less frequently accepted: that different people can apply different goal descriptions to the same action. These two "sources" of multiplicity create problems for actors and researchers alike.

Second, the description of any given action must be seen as subject to infinite revision (Gergen, 1982). This assertion arises initially from the understanding that any action, communicative or otherwise, takes place within broader temporal and structural contexts. Thus, the labeling of a given communicative action at a particular point in time and in a given structural context is subject to constant revision as the retrospective and emergent contexts change with the process. In other words, the labeling of a given communicative act as meeting a particular goal is a function of context, and this context is continually changing. As the context changes, new goal descriptions emerge.

The important point is that the basis for any particular description of communicative acts is not fundamentally empirical; it relies instead on a weaving of interdependent and continuously modifiable interpretations. Given that the action itself has no independent ontic status (e.g., Anscombe, 1957; Winch, 1958), our concern needs to be with the manner of description per se; that is, with the manner of the story we develop. Taking the propositions given before, we need to develop a manner of description that allows for the possibility of multiple goals and multiple interpretations occurring within a constraining and changing context.

As is shown hereafter, this description is aided by a rule inference process. Our assignment of meanings to acts in terms of goals employs a set of constitutive rules, and our descriptions of the ensuing games rely both on those constitutive rules and on the further identification of regulative rules. In other words, it is via the rule identification process that both goals and games are identified and moral orders are inferred.

GOALS AND GAMES IN COURTROOM DISCOURSE[1]

In this and the ensuing sections of the chapter, the conceptual framework is developed further as it is applied to communication in courts of law—with the aim of describing the moral orders in court. The data for this application come from audiotapes and transcripts of 18 complete court hearings in two types of Australian courts: upper (Supreme Court) and lower (Petty Sessions). The cases cover both criminal and civil trials and come from the courts of eight different judges. The focus for analysis is the communication process between judge, barrister, and citizen in the witness box (defendant, plaintiff, accused, expert witness, etc.) during the major episodes of examination-in-chief and cross-examination.

Informational Goals: The Official Game

All courts have a formal code of conduct that defines the nature of the roles and the terms of engagement of conduct. For the purposes of this analysis of courts that use the adversary system of justice, the three major roles of judge, barrister, and witness are used; the "witness" role is filled by all who stand in the witness box. The basic rules that govern the engagement of the people in these three roles differ markedly from more everyday conversations (e.g., Atkinson & Drew, 1979). While the question–answer adjacency pair forms the foundation for the organization of talk in courts, speaking turns and roles are fixed. There can only be questions and answers. And it is only the barrister or judge who has the right to ask questions, and the witness is under strong obligatory pressure to answer what is asked. Moreover, because the sole right to ask questions belongs to the barrister and judge, they also regulate when and for how long the witness answers.

Although this formal code of conduct in courts defines the nature of the roles and the terms of the engagement of conduct, there is not an elaborated written code on how the engagement is to proceed. The laws of evidence provide some clues, but not all. Thus, in order to identify the rules of discourse in courts, an empirical analysis was undertaken. Inasmuch as a full description of the methodology for this study has been reported elsewhere (Penman, 1987), methodological details are omitted here.

At least four different criteria have been used to identify rules of discourse: rule articulation, infringement recognition, sanction application, and behavioral

[1]The extended courtroom study described in this chapter was generously supported by an Australian Research Grants Scheme award, 1986–1988.

regularity (e.g., Shimanoff, 1980). All four criteria were employed in this study, with the emphasis on infringement recognition and sanction application. From over 100 hours of courtroom interaction, 27 discourse rules were identified. Some of these rules were of a form commonly found in other contexts, for example: "Do not start to speak until the other has stopped" or "Make your responses answer the question clearly and unambiguously." Other rules were peculiar to the legal setting, such as "Do not ask leading questions on examination" or "Witnesses are not permitted to give unrequested information."[2]

What is important about the set of rules as a whole is the assumptions about communication that can be inferred from them. The rules as a whole rely on assumptions that are analogous, if not identical, to those proposed by Grice (1975) in his cooperative principle, which is based on the following prescription: "Make your conversational contribution such as is required, at the stage at which it occurs, by the accepted purpose or direction of the talk exchange in which you are engaged" (p. 45). He further distinguished four general maxims or rules that must be observed in order to preserve coherence and cooperation: (a) quality (be truthful), (b) relation (be relevant), (c) quantity (say no more and no less than is needed), and (d) manner (be clear and orderly). All of the rules identified in courts could be construed under these four maxims.

The findings from this study allow us to draw some conclusions about the goals and games of the official courtroom discourse. In the first instance, we can identify two major sets of constitutive rules and two major sets of regulative rules: the maxims of quality and relation and of quantity and manner, respectively. The constitutive rules of quality define what counts as truth and what does not. Four specific rules fall into this category: do not ask speculative questions, do not ask leading questions, do not give generalities or draw conclusions, and give personal knowledge/experience only. What is assumed by these rules is that truth can only be specific, literal information that the person has directly acquired. Moreover, it can only be about events that are directly observable or experienceable. The constitutive rules of relation are concerned with relevance, and all rules specify that the only information that counts is that which is relevant to the legal issue at hand. The two sets of regulative rules order the temporal progress of the discourse such that witnesses are only allowed to directly and precisely answer the question by giving no more and no less than the information requested, and it must be given in a precise, legally logical way. This legal logic requires that information be given in terms of discrete and concrete events and must be located precisely in time along a presumed causal pathway—elements of a primitive Cartesian logic.

The overall goal of these rules of discourse in courts can to be taken to be

---

[2]The rules identified are not unique to the Australian setting. Reference to Danet (1980) and Woodbury (1984) show the same general set in US courts. Further reference to legal books on laws of evidence in the US and the UK provide further support.

analogous to that described by Grice—that of the maximally efficient gathering of information. In other words, the rules of courtroom discourse are aimed at the general goal of obtaining factual information in the most efficient manner. For both Grice and the courts, this informational goal is premised on the assumption that we engage in communication for purposive, rational reasons. Although this has been a fundamental premise of traditional frameworks employing the goal construct, it is not a premise that is always demonstrable in communicative practice. As various discourse studies have demonstrated, people do not always behave in a cooperative, rational and/or purposive manner (e.g., Keenan, 1976; Penman, 1987).

Given the nature of the overriding goal and the rules used to attain it, I propose to call the official game enacted in courts the "fact game." The analysis cannot rest here, however; there can be more than one goal and more than one game. Nofsinger (1983), in his strategic analysis of courtroom conservation, also recognized that the informational goal was not the only one possible: "Other witnesses appear oriented toward personal goals: to avoid self-embarrassment or self-incrimination, . . . , and so on" (p. 247). My research suggests that it is not just some witnesses, some of the time, that are dealing with other goals. There were a number of indicators in the analysis just summarized to suggest that far more than the official game was being enacted and far more than the official goal was being achieved in all the court cases.

The most obvious indicator that there was more going on than just the fact game was the number of conversational difficulties identified in the rules analysis. Difficulties were identified as occurring whenever the judge or barrister interrupted the process to evoke or imply a rule and whenever any participant requested resaying in various forms. Approximately 600 difficulties were identified, some lasting for only one exchange but others for a number of minutes.[3] Of import to the present argument, there was no particular role (barrister or witness) or episode (examination and cross-examination) that led to more difficulties than others. Almost as many difficulties had their beginnings in question-asking by the barrister as they did in response-giving by the witness, and a roughly equal number of difficulties occurred in examination and cross-examination.

It was also observed that, although the discourse rules and formal game in courts parallels Gricean assumptions, the conversations were far from cooperative efforts by both parties. A contradiction, in fact, appears to exist: courts need to coerce participants to be cooperative. The study identified a number of coercive devices employed to make witnesses act "properly." The most obvious ones included instructions and orders from the judges to answer in the proper way and the refusal to accept any information that had not been solicited or was

---

[3]Because of the variable length of these difficulties, it is not possible to give a precise comparative figure of "no difficulty."

not relevant. Less obvious, but equally powerful, devices are contained in the frequent use of closed questions in cross-examination—such questions forcing witnesses to answer in ways the barrister wants. Moreover, failure to comply in manner and/or content to the requests and directions of the court can bring about the threat—or actuality—of finding the witness in contempt of court.

What is neglected both in Grice's model and in the official discourse rules in courts is a critical feature of all communication—that information is a function of the nature of the relationship and the broader context in which it is given. Within the court's official model of discourse, words are not seen as doing things, as having illocutionary or perlocutionary force, or as being a function of their context. Instead, words are seen only as the means for establishing facts, and the rules evoked for regulating this procedure are aimed at maximum efficiency in the gathering of facts. Communication is taken only as something instrumental in the legal process. As a consequence, witnesses are also seen as something that is simply instrumental to the process. That they are seen as no more than this is further evidenced by the observation that there are no formal rules to regulate the relational aspects of discourse.

Facework Goals: The Unofficial Game

The absence of any formal rules that could readily be identified using the procedure of the preceding study led to the need to adopt another method of analysis to explore what other games were being played. As a way of illustrating the problem and the methodological complexities raised, I use the following extract, which is typical of many of the cases studied. This is from a case of theft, and the homeowner whose house had been robbed is being cross-examined about his insurance. The extract opens with the barrister asking the witness (a non-native English speaker) for the *fourth* time whether or not he was insured against theft:

Example 1

B1:   *So* you were not insured?

W1:   I never thought robbers were going to come to rob the place.

B2:   I am asking you whether you were insured against the house?

W2:   I just give you the right answer.

B3:   You were not insured against theft?

W3:   I just give you the right answer. My house is worth $120,000. I do not believe insurance and I have put $60,000 on it and I have $30,000 to $50,000 jewelry and clothes and everything and I do it for $15,000 because we do not expect to come robbers into my house.

B4: You do not expect robbers to come into your house?

W4: No for burn or anything. We just give them for cover something.

B5: But you kept the pistol there in case robbers came into the house, you were saying?

W5: When they come, that is the reason we keep them.

B6: Did you expect people to come in and rob your house or not?

W6: No.

B7: Nothing further, your honor.

This extract illustrates part of a conversational difficulty identified from the preceding rules analysis. It also illustrates a segment of courtroom conversation in which the witness is not adhering to the official fact game. But that is not to suggest that he is not enacting some other game with some other goal. One reading of this extract would suggest that, to every closed question of the barrister, the witness gives a rationale or justification but does not directly answer the question. Instead, he appears to be trying to establish the reasonableness of his actions. Yet, by the close of the episode, the barrister, without getting the answer he originally wanted, also seems to have established, in contrast, the unreasonableness of the witness' actions.

These dynamics can be captured by proposing that another game is being played: a very serious game centered on facework goals. In Goffman's (e.g., 1959, 1972) pioneering work on social interaction, the notion of "face" acted as an important explanatory construct. He took *face* to mean "the positive social value a person effectively claims for himself . . . , in terms of approved social attributes" and *facework* as "the actions taken by a person to make whatever he is doing consistent with face" (1972, p. 5). Others who have used this notion (e.g., Brown & Levinson, 1978, 1987) have extended the usage of the term. It need not be the case that facework is simply about maintaining face consistency or repairing damage done; it could also be about the presentation and development of a particular face or even the deprecation of one. This broader concept is used here.

Brown and Levinson's (1978, 1987) theory of politeness, premised on this notion of face, has provided an important basis for a broad range of studies and has had a substantial impact on the area of conversational analysis. From this theory and the studies using it (e.g., see Brown & Levinson's review, 1987), a complex picture of facework can be developed. Further complexities for analysis are suggested by critical reviews of the theory (e.g., Coupland, Grainger, & Coupland, 1988; Craig, Tracy, & Spisak, 1986; Tracy, 1990) showing that it is not without its problems. On the basis of these studies, there are at least six characteristics that contribute to the complex dynamics of facework. These six characteristics are described hereafter and illustrated with examples from the court cases under study here.

In the first instance, we need to differentiate between two types of face: (a) that concerned with a positive self-image (positive face) and (b) that concerned with freedom of action and freedom from imposition by others (negative face). As Brown and Levinson (1978, 1987) have shown, this is an important conceptual distinction. Moreover, Craig et al. (1986) have shown that actors also make similar distinctions between positive and negative face. A clear example of negative facework can be seen in the first line of the extract given earlier. Although all questions can be seen as threats to the negative face of the other, B1 is an extreme version of it. By posing the question as an assertion, the barrister is attempting to restrict the witness to answering only "no," thus constraining his freedom of action and impinging on negative face.

Second, it is important to recognize that facework can be directed towards the self as well as the other. Most workers employing the notion of facework have concentrated on the facework directed toward another: We either honor or threaten the other's face (Shimanoff, 1987) or cooperate or antagonize the other (McLaughlin, Cody, & O'Hair, 1983). Yet, in Goffman's original conception (e.g., 1972), there was a strong emphasis on the work done by an actor on his or her *own* face. And again, Craig et al. (1986) have shown that actors are aware of both self and other facework. Utterance B1 in Example 1 illustrates facework directed at the other. In contrast, W4 illustrates self-directed facework. In the context of the question asked at B4, the extended answer at W4 can be seen as a justification for the witness' action that acts to make him appear to be a reasonable person. This utterance, then, can be seen to support the witness' positive face (self-image).

Third, we must allow for the possibility that utterances can be multifunctional. This possibility was argued for in the introduction and has been demonstrated in the work of Craig et al. (1986) and Baxter (1984). Thus, different facework strategies can not only be inferred from the same utterance but can be identified simultaneously with the very same language use. If we return to the first lines of the exchange in the extract and take into account the preceding and consequent contexts of the utterance, it is possible to identify three potential goals. In the first instance, we can infer that the witness' "failure" in W1 to answer the barrister's questions threatens the barrister's own freedom of action in his next move: He is constrained to repeat the question if he wishes to pursue his informational goal. Second, the witness' answer can be seen as a justification for his action, and, thus, it protects his positive face. Simultaneously, his refusal to answer the question directly can be interpreted as also protecting his negative face, in that he has demonstrated more freedom of action that the preceding question "allowed."

Many facework strategies, however, are not as clear as the examples just given. This is the fourth important characteristic of facework: Strategies can be expressed in either a direct or an indirect way (Haverkate, 1986; Brown & Levinson, 1978). Kearsley (1976), in his review of taxonomies of questions, identified the direct–indirect dimension as the major distinguishing feature of all questions. And the works of Robinson and Rackstraw (1972) and Goffman (1976) provide an equivalent basis for responses. It is the indirect expressions that give rise to many problems of interpretation on the part of both listeners and observers. However, it is also this indirectness that allows actors in conversations some flexibility. Indirectness can be used in such a way that face is not "lost" if alternative interpretations are made by the other. Indirectness can also be used so that the actor is unlikely to be directly threatened for a certain implication. Again, W1 is a good example of an indirect reply from which a multifunctional facework maneuver can be inferred; seeming to deal with positive and negative face at the same time.

The fifth characteristic that needs consideration is the temporal characteristics of strategies. The very notion of strategy implies that a goal is desired. However, it is not necessarily the case that the goal is an immediate one or that the effect of the strategy can be discerned immediately. In these circumstances, it is not necessarily possible to even determine if a strategy has been employed. The very nature of conversations makes it possible for, say, a superficially simple and nonthreatening sequence of utterances to occur which, over time, has a cumulative face-threatening or enhancing effect. This is illustrated at the end of Example 1. At B4, a seemingly simple and minimally face-threatening question is being asked, but after B5, the initial question at B4 now seems to be part of a longer strategy to discredit the witness. The importance of temporal context is well recognized by conversational analysts, as is the importance of context in general. The context-dependent nature of facework, in particular, has been documented by Craig et al. (1986) and by Shimanoff (1977).

Finally, we need to consider the underlying dimensions of facework. Various continua have been suggested: (a) cooperation–antagonism (Craig et al., 1986), (b) aggravation–mitigation (McLaughlin et al., 1983), and (c) honor–threat (Shimanoff, 1987). All of these proposals are concerned with a dimension that incorporates the extent to which one person helps or hinders the facework of the other. They do not, however, conceptually allow for helping or hindering one's own facework. A more encompassing definition is needed. Just such a dimension has been proposed by Harré (1979)—that of respect and contempt. It is possible to conceive of actors being respectful or contemptuous to *their* own self-images and desires for freedom of action as much as *they* can be respectful or contemptuous of the other's faces. Given the conceptual arguments earlier and the concerns of this chapter with moral orders, the respect–contempt dimension provides one obvious means of organizing descriptions of facework strategies that can be self- and/or other-directed. It also seems a particularly pertinent one for courts, especially given their overt concern with issues of contempt (of court).

Following the arguments of Harré (1979), it is assumed that the major goal of all facework is the generation of respect for self and the avoidance of contempt. In addition, contempt can be given as part of the other's facework strategies and incurred by the self in certain circumstances. These goals can be achieved directly or indirectly. Direct facework strategies orientated towards contempt are the equivalent of Brown and Levinson's (1978) "bald, on-record" face-threatening acts. Direct facework strategies orientated towards respect include some of Brown and Levinson's politeness strategies. Less direct approaches to facework include Brown and Levinson's "off-the-record" strategies as well as other of their politeness strategies. Strategies may co-occur or consecutively occur in any one utterance such that a number of strategic pathways may be woven at any one time.

Given the complexity of facework dynamics, it seems obvious that interpreting facework strategies in conversations is difficult. Nevertheless, it is still possible to apply an interpretative schema that allows us to make some sense of the dynamics of facework in courts. The detailed rationale for, and description of, this schema is given in Penman (in press). The approach is illustrated with the following examples from a criminal case of alleged assault. In the first example, a presumed victim to an alleged assault charge is being examined by the prosecuting lawyer.

Example 2

B1: What happened after you were struck? Did the man stop striking you, or did something happen?

W1: I commenced to get up, and then he came from behind me and put his arms around me and commenced squeezing my chest.

B2: When you say he put his arms around you, did he put his arms right around you?

W2: Yes.

This extract is a very simple one in which facework seems at a minimum, although the cumulative potential is there with the emergent context. The extract is given because it illustrates two different question styles and two different answer styles that can be interpreted as having different, although minimal, facework effects. In B1, the barrister employs an open, direct question, then moves to start a closed question but opens it up again with the "or did something happen" hedge. The overall utterance seems to have the effect of compensating for, or softening, the impingement on negative face that occurs with questions and is thus described as having a possible cumulative effect on protecting the negative face of the other. In responding to the open question, the witness complies with an extended answer, thus having the possible cumulative effect of being in some control of the information given and therefore of protecting the negative self. After the opening question and extended response of the witness, the barrister contains the direction of information by focusing on specific details of the event. This is shown in B2, where the closed question acts as a threat to the negative face of the other. The response to this closed question is a simple compliance that can be taken as a threat to the negative face of self.

It is of value to contrast the preceding example with one of the same witness being cross-examined about the same event. Here, the facework is again relatively simple but does include some utterances that can be interpreted as multifunctional.

Example 3

B1:   And then you say he grabbed hold of you again?

W1:   Yes.

B2:   Were you doing anything when he grabbed hold of you?

W2:   I was trying to get free.

B3:   No, before he grabbed hold of you?

W3:   No.

B4:   You were *just* standing there, were you?

W4:   Yes.

B5:   You were not shouting or screaming or threatening to hit him or trying to hit him?

W5:   I was just holding my chest.

B6:   And then he grabbed hold of you?

W6:   Yes.

B1 illustrates a common facework strategy in courts. In asking the question as a statement, it can be taken as a direct threat to the witness' negative face. At the same time, the inclusion of the phrase "you say" seems to put the witness on notice that the barrister is skeptical about what the witness has said, thus acting to threaten the witness' positive face at the same time. This same pattern is repeated in B4 and B5. And the witness, seeming to realize the threat to positive face, appears to protect himself in his fifth utterance by explaining why he was just standing there; that is, he seems to be trying to make his act reasonable.

In employing the facework interpretative schema in the preceding manner on a number of court cases, it became obvious that facework maneuvers could account for a wide range of the previously identified conversational difficulties. In other words, difficulties were arising because both the witnesses and barristers were dealing with goals other than purely informational ones. It also became obvious that the official game, and the rules of discourse employed to maintain it, places the witness at a disadvantage in the face game. Witnesses' facework was almost always directed towards their own face—and usually towards protecting it—whereas barristers' facework was most commonly directed towards the witness, and usually threatening it. Moreover, it was also observed that witnesses appeared to have many more multifunctional utterances than barristers, especially when being cross-examined. In all, it appeared as if witnesses' facework was, on the whole, far more complex than that of barristers. This makes sense when we consider the nature of the adversary process in courts: It is a process in which the barrister holds the power position and the witness is relatively powerless, and it is a processes that includes episodes of cross-examination with the aim of discrediting witnesses' accounts (and often the witnesses themselves).

MORAL ORDERS IN COURT

The preceding analyses have suggested that there are two major games being played in courts: an official fact game and an unofficial face game. But these games are not played independently of each other. In order to explore the nature of their relationship with each other and to proceed to infer the moral orders, we need to introduce the concept of hierarchical levels of meaning: a common approach (at least within logic) to the issue of multiple meanings.

The most well known hierarchical relationship of meaning is the concept of report (informational) and command (relational) elaborated by the Palo Alto group (e.g., Watzlawick, Beavin, & Jackson, 1967). But this conception is limited to two levels of meaning and assumes a fixed relationship between the levels such that the relational is always superordinate to the informational. In contrast, Pearce and Cronen (1980) have proposed a hierarchical model of meaning that identifies at least six levels of meanings for communicative acts: (a) content (informational), (b) speech act (relational), (c) episodes, (d) relationship, (e) life scripts, and (f) cultural patterns. A similar proposal can also be found in the work of Frentz and Farrell (1976). The model of Pearce and Cronen is used here because of the supportive empirical studies and the compatibility of their metatheoretical position.

The six levels of meaning in the Pearce and Cronen model are hierarchically arranged in that each level is seen as superordinate to the one below it in terms of temporal features. In other words, meanings at each level in the hierarchy are generated over longer spans of time. A number of empirical studies (e.g., Harris, 1980; Pearce & Conklin, 1976) have indicated that actors themselves employ these different levels of abstraction in their own interpretations of actions, thus lending support to the model. These levels, however, are not meant to be taken as fixed in number or as inviolate in the hierarchy. The work of Cronen, Johnson and Lannaman (1982) clearly demonstrates that not all levels are necessarily relevant to a given situation and, most importantly, that there is some degree of reflexivity inherent between levels. Relationships between meanings at two different levels of organization involves two forces: the *upward implicative force* and the *downward contextual force* (Cronen et al., 1982). In most situations, it appears as if the downward force is the stronger in that meaning at, say, the speech act level is affected more by the episode definition than the episode definition is affected by the speech act. It also is possible, however, that the two forces are equal. When both forces are equal, a reflexive loop is formed—the prime criterion for a paradoxical situation.

I have already demonstrated that the fact game has the overriding goal of information and that the face game is a relational one played at the speech act level of meaning. These goals are at the two lowest levels in the hierarchical model of meaning. Superordinate to these levels is that of relationship. This is the level that is concerned with how and on what terms people engage. It is also the level that, in usual circumstances, provides the context, along with episode, for interpretation of both the speech act and content levels of meaning. In other words, the relationship level in courts acts as the contextual frame for interpreting both the face and fact game. What, then, are the features of this relationship level in courts?

Perhaps one of the most obvious features of judicial communication is the extent to which it is formalized and ritualistic and in which every actor has a well-defined role to play. The main roles, and the ones of concern here, are those of judge, barrister, and witness. The roles assigned to each actor are reinforced not only by title but by a number of nonverbal indicators including dress, place in the courtroom, and the arrangement of furniture. The sum total of these indicators act to place the role of judge and barrister—the representatives of the court—in a superordinate position and to place the witness in a subordinate one (see, e.g., Carlen's 1976 analysis). It is, in fact, a formal asymmetrical power relationship that is further reinforced by the terms on which the barrister/judge and witness can engage. Thus, both the fact and face games are played out in the context of this formal, asymmetrical power relationship.

This asymmetrical relationship, and the games it contextualizes, is itself contextualized by higher order levels of meaning. It is these higher levels of meaning and the games they give rise to that indicate the moral orders of courtroom discourse. In order to explain this assertion, we need to consider Fig. 2.1, which depicts the goals, games, and moral orders in courts.

As is indicated in Fig. 2.1, the superordinate meaning frame for all courtroom discourse is the institutional frame. This is equivalent to Pearce and Cronen's (1980) level of cultural pattern; the institution of law being a major element in any cultural "pattern." The official fact game and the fundamental premises of

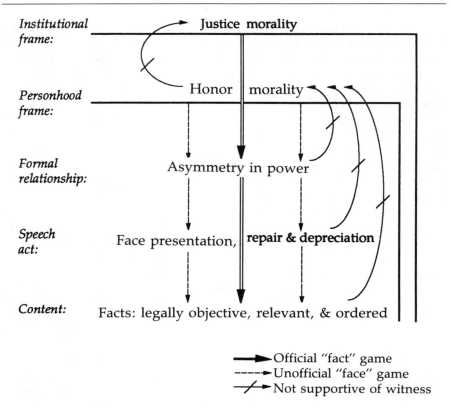

Institutional frame: Justice morality

Personhood frame: Honor ‖ morality

Formal relationship: Asymmetry in power

Speech act: Face presentation, **repair & depreciation**

Content: Facts: legally objective, relevant, & ordered

➤ Official "fact" game
----➤ Unofficial "face" game
⟶ Not supportive of witness

FIG. 2.1.   A model of the goals, games, and moral orders in courts.

the legal institution lead to the claim that the moral order contained at the institutional frame is a justice morality. This justice morality condones the use of impartiality and clear reason in making a just determination from the legally defined facts of the case. Within this justice morality, only the official fact game can be explicitly acknowledged. This game requires the formal set of relationships between barrister/judge and witness—that relationship in which the court and its representatives are formally empowered to use the witness to arrive at the facts of the matter in the most efficient and expeditious manner.

However, in playing this official game, a number of meaning contexts are denied—most importantly, that at the speech act level. It is via this context that another equally important but unofficial game is played: the face game. Examples of the face game were described in the previous section. The moves that appear in this game strongly suggest that it stems from another moral order—an honor morality. Harré (1983) has identified certain features of honor moralities that well fit the situation in court. In the first instance, honor moralities are typified by asymmetrical relations of respect and condescension—as is clearly the case in court, not only at the formal relationship level but in the very playing of the face game itself. Dueling and the use of champions are also characteristic of honor moralities and, again, this seems to apply directly to courts. In this situation, we have the barrister acting as champion for one party, engaging in a verbal duel against the other. Unfortunately, in the court situation, they do not move the people needing champions from the center of the dueling circle. The duel is enacted both through the people involved and with them involved.

I suggest, then, that both the witness and the barrister are unofficially operating within an honor morality. And, despite the lack of formal rules, the unofficial game and its honor morality is still seen to count (in important ways) for both the judge and the jury. Work by Backman (1976) suggests that juries use an honor morality to make decisions regarding guilt and innocence. And my own analyses of judges' instructions to juries show the frequent use of the instruction to "consider the witness' demeanour," that is, how they presented as a person. The importance of this and its bearings on the facts is clearly demonstrated in the summing up to the jury by a Chief Justice in the Supreme Court at the end of one of the cases used in the study reported here:

> You, ladies and gentlemen, are obviously the judges of the facts in this case . . . I proceed to tell you immediately what a question of fact is. A question of fact is something which answers the question "What did happen?". . . . I shall tell you what evidence is . . . Every word that they [witnesses] utter is evidence in the case. You have to make up your mind what you thought of those witnesses. You do not leave your knowledge of mankind and your commonsense, as I say, outside the jury room or, indeed outside the courtroom when you sit and listen to the evidence. You come because you have experience of mankind. That is why you are chosen and it would be quite inimical to the interests of justice if you forgot about that when you went into the jury room. You must make an assessment of each of the witnesses.

This extract is quite a succinct account of what does happen: The facts of the case are considered in the light of what is thought of the witnesses presenting the evidence for the facts. But what it fails to recognize is that, in arriving at the facts, the witnesses are not in control of their self-presentation. Indeed, the rules of the official game appear to mitigate against a presentation of their selves in the best light possible. The witness, in trying to maintain his or her honor, still has to play the unofficial game within the context of the formal court relationship—one in which he or she has no formal power. From this relatively powerless position the face game is played, or attempted to be played, at the speech act level. But this still feeds into the content level and the fact game.

In fact, it seems that the face game played out by the witness is actually incompatible with the official fact game. The lack of formal power, the unofficial nature of the game, and the necessity to provide objective, legally relevant facts all act against the witness appearing to be an honorable, reasonable person. How can a witness appear to be reasonable when a barrister asks him what he did after being hit the first time and before being hit the second time? How can one reasonably answer an unreasonable question? How can a witness appear to be honorable when the fact game played by the barrister forces her to give a yes or no answer with no rationale for her behavior? This also applies to the barrister using his or her witness to present the evidence-in-chief. The very rules of the fact game and the use of the barrister to develop the facts provides ideal grounds for lack of coherence. Contrarily, the very same situation maximizes the potential for discrediting the witness on cross-examination; lack of coherence being a common indicator of unreasonableness.

If we take the dynamics as a whole, as illustrated in Fig. 2.1, it can be shown that there is a rather strange set of loops in the hierarchy of meanings that can readily catch both witnesses and barristers in a paradoxical loop. Within the official game emanating from the institutional context, there are no strong reflexive loops. Using the model of Cronen et al. (1982), the downward contextual force appears much stronger than any upward implicative force: that is, the justice morality sets the meaning context for the relationship and content levels without being strongly affected by any upward implicative force from those lower levels. However, when we introduce the unofficial game, it can be seen that this produces a strong upward implicative force. The content level does affect the speech act level; the speech act level does affect meanings at the honor morality level, and this honor morality does feed into the justice morality level; albeit, it is all done implicitly. And thus a reflexive loop is brought about.

The reflexive loops between levels of meaning indicate the potential for a paradoxical situation. This need not be problematic in all instances; however, as Cronen et al. (1982) have demonstrated, greater confusion and psychological harm is generated from such reflexive loops when higher levels of meaning become entangled and when there are no strategies available for resolving the strange loop. This seems to be the case in court with the outcome of witness confusion and distress when caught in the paradox. Other studies (e.g., see Danet, 1980) have clearly documented that distress *is* experienced by all manner of witnesses, whether they win or lose a case and whether they are the main actors or only minor supporting witnesses. The present analysis provides a means of accounting for this distress. It is the contention of this chapter, then, that the moral orders enacted in courts and their associated games are incommensurate with each other and potentially incommensurate with any reasonable notion of justice.

CONCLUSIONS

The general aim of this chapter has been to consider the nature of communication in courtrooms from a particular point of view: a point of view based on new developments in ways of thinking about social practices. This new point of view called for the development of a moral story—a story about the moral orders in courts. The concepts of goals and games were used to develop this story. Here, I showed how goals and games could be inferred from the discourse dynamics and how these pointed to particular moral orders. The usefulness of this approach can perhaps be best assessed by what it created and what purpose it could serve.

What was created was an extraordinarily complex picture of the conversational dynamics in court, centered around two very different games. Moreover, it was a picture that brought to the fore a set of dynamics that it is not recognized within the legal institutional frame. Within that frame, communication is seen simply as a tool for legal ends, and so are the people in the process. Yet, despite the court forcing communication into a simple, instrumental role, it is unable to contain it as such. The end product is a potentially paradoxical situation in which two games—the fact game and the face game—and two moral orders—those of justice and honor—are incommensurate.

Recognition of this situation provides the basis for a critical reconsideration of the judicial process based on an adversary system. In general, the analyses and arguments lead to the conclusion that the process of justice as enacted in the adversary system neither facilitates the establishment of the facts of the case nor ensures a just hearing in the best possible manner. The facts that are established are severely distorted, because the court ignores or denies the critical role of context and the process whereby the so-called facts are established. Moreover, the court's formal rules of discourse and the adversary process, combined, act to treat all witnesses as worthy of contempt while at the same time demanding that the court and its representatives are treated with respect. The court treats all witnesses as worthy of contempt by not explicitly recognizing the importance of the face game in the witness examination and cross-examination procedures.

The failure to provide a context in which the face game can be played fairly raises serious questions about the value that is often placed on judgments of "demeanour." Persons can display a negative demeanour for all sorts of reasons other than being in the wrong or being the guilty party. For many people, the most obvious reason is likely to be the subtly—and sometimes not so subtly—contemptuous way in which they are treated as witnesses. This contemptuous treatment is evidence not only in the restrictions on witnesses playing the face game properly but also in the general limitations placed on freedom of expression. The International Covenant on Civil and Political Rights states that "everyone shall have the right to freedom of expression [and] this right shall include the freedom to seek, receive and impart information and ideas of all kinds" (Australian Law Reform Commission, 1984). It is difficult to see how the rules of discourse used in the adversary system ensure this right to freedom of expression. In fact, it seems that certain of the discourse rules, such as those concerned with the Quantity Maxim, actively go against the maintenance of the right to freedom of expression. Witnesses are not able to answer more than is asked. They are not able to say anything that the court considers irrelevant. Witnesses in courts simply are not free to impart information and ideas of all kinds.

A further aspect of the contemptuous treatment of witness is the imposition of an atypical set of discourse rules. As was argued earlier, the formal rules employed in courts are quite different from those typically employed in other contexts with which the witnesses are more familiar. Thus, the witnesses are at a great disadvantage when forced into the court's model, and this disadvantage is exacerbated by their inability to negotiate the situation and, most importantly, to play the face game fairly.

In all, it seems that full access to justice is not ensured in the adversary system. To the contrary, the procedure seems distinctly unfair to the citizen participating in the process, whether that citizen be a defendant, plaintiff, accused, or ordinary witness. As Lord Devlin (1979) more cautiously suggested, the process inherent in the adversary system of justice leaves much to be desired. And that which is left to be desired is precisely what should be ensured: access to justice.

REFERENCES

Anscombe, G. (1957). *Intention:* Oxford: Blackwell.
Atkinson, J. M., & Drew, P. (1979). *Order in court.* London: Macmillan.
Australian Law Reform Commission (1984). *Issues Paper No. 4.* Canberra: Australian Government Publishing Service.
Baxter, L. (1984). An investigation of compliance-gaining as politeness. *Human Communication Research, 10,* 427–456.
Bernstein, R. (1983). *Beyond objectivism and relativism.* Oxford: Blackwell.
Backman, C. (1976). Explorations in psycho-ethics: The warranting of judgments. In R. Harré (Ed.), *Life sentences* (pp. 98–108). New York: Wiley.
Brown, P., & Levinson, S. (1978). Universals in language usage: Politeness phenomena. In E. Goody (Ed.), *Questions and politeness: strategies in social interaction* (pp. 56–350). Cambridge, England: Cambridge University Press.
Brown, P., & Levinson, S. (1987). *Politeness: Some universals in language usage.* Cambridge, Cambridge University Press.
Carlen, P. (1976). *Magistrates' justice.* London: Martin Robertson.
Coupland, N., Grainger, K., & Coupland, J. (1988). Politeness in context: Intergenerational issues. *Language in Society, 17,* 253–262.
Craig, R. T., Tracy, K., & Spisak, F. (1986). The discourse of requests: Assessment of a politeness approach. *Human Communication Research, 12,* 437–468.
Cronen, V. (1986, May). *The Individual in a systemic perspective.* Paper presented at the 15th anniversary meeting of Interaktie Akademie, Antwerp, Belgium.
Cronen, V., Johnson, K., & Lannaman, J. (1982). Paradoxes, double-binds and reflexive loops: An alternative theoretical perspective. *Family Process, 20,* 91–112.
Danet, B. (1980). Language in the legal process. *Law and Society Review, 14,* 445–564.
Devlin, P. (1979). *The Judge.* Oxford: Oxford University Press.
Farrell, T. (1983). Aspects of coherence in conversation and rhetoric. In R. T. Craig & K. Tracy (Eds.), *Conversational coherence* (pp. 259–284). Beverly Hills CA: Sage.

Frentz, T., & Farrell, T. (1976). Language-action: A paradigm for communication. *Quarterly Journal of Speech, 62,* 333–349.

Gergen, K. (1982). *Towards transformation in social knowledge.* New York: Springer-Verlag.

Goffman, E. (1959). *The presentation of self in everyday life.* Garden City, NY: Doubleday Anchor Books.

Goffman, E. (1972). *Interaction ritual: Essays on face-to-face behavior.* Harmondsworth, UK: Penguin.

Goffman, E. (1976). Replies and responses. *Language and Society, 5,* 273–313.

Grice, J. (1975). Logic and conversations. In P. Cole & J. Morgan (Eds.), *Syntax and semantics: Vol 3. speech acts* (pp. 41–58). New York: Academic Press.

Harré, R. (1979). *Social Being.* Oxford: Blackwell.

Harré, R. (1983). *Personal Being.* Oxford: Blackwell.

Harris, L. (1980). Analysis of a paradoxical logic: A case study. *Family Process, 19,* 19–34.

Haverkate, H. (1986). *A model for analysing politeness strategies in verbal interaction.* Paper presented at the 11th annual meeting of the World Congress of Sociology, New Delhi.

Kearsley, G. (1976). Questions and question asking in verbal discourse: A cross-disciplinary review. *Journal of Psycholinguistic Research, 5,* 355–375.

Keenan, E. (1976). The universality of conversational postulates. *Language in Society, 5,* 67–80.

Larmore, C. (1987). *Patterns of moral complexity.* Cambridge, U.K.: Cambridge University Press.

McCarthy, T. (1984). *The critical theory of Jürgen Habermas.* Cambridge, U.K.: Polity Press.

McDermott, J. (Ed.). (1981). *The philosophy of John Dewey.* Chicago: University of Chicago Press.

McLaughlin, M., Cody, M. & O'Hair, H. (1983). The management of failure-events: Some contextual determinants of accounting behavior. *Human Communication Research, 9,* 208–224.

Nofsinger, R. (1983). Tactical coherence in courtroom conversation. In R. Craig & K. Tracy (Eds.), *Conversational coherence* (pp. 243–258). Beverly Hills, CA: Sage.

Pearce, W. B., & Cronen, V. (1980). *Communication, action and meaning.* New York: Praeger.

Pearce, W. B., & Conklin, F. (1976). A model of hierarchical meanings in coherent conversation and a study of indirect responses. *Communication Monographs, 46,* 75–87.

Penman, R. (1987). Discourse in courts: Cooperation, coercion & coherence. *Discourse Processes, 10,* 210–218.

Penman, R. (1988). Communication reconstructed. *Journal for the Theory of Social Behaviour, 18,* 391–410.

Penman, R. (1989, March). *Good theory & good practice: An argument in progress.* Paper presented at the 10th annual Discourse Analysis Conference, Philadelphia.

Penman, R. (in press). Facework & politeness: Multiple goals in courtroom discourse. *Journal of Language and Social Psychology.*

Robinson, W. P., & Rackstraw, S. (1972). *A question of answers: Vol 1.* London: Routledge & Kegan Paul.

Shimanoff, S. (1977). Investigating politeness. In E. Keenan & T. Bennett (Eds.), *Discourses across time and space.* (pp. 213–241). Los Angeles: University of Southern California Press.

Shimanoff, S. (1980). *Communication rules.* Beverly Hills, CA: Sage.

Shimanoff, S. (1987). Types of emotional disclosures and request compliance between spouses. *Communication Monographs, 54,* 85–100.

Shotter, J. (1987). The social construction of an "us": Problems in accountability and narratology. In R. Burrett, P. McGhee, & D. Clarke (Eds.), *Accounting for personal relationships: Social representations of interpersonal links* (pp. 1–37). London: Methuen.

Tracy, K. (1990). The many faces of facework. In H. Giles & P. Robinson (Eds.), *The handbook of language and social psychology.* (pp. 209–226). Chichester, England: John Wiley.

Toulmin, S. (1982). The construal of reality: Criticism in modern and postmodern science. *Critical Inquiry, 9,* 93–111.

Watzlawick, P., Beavin, J., & Jackson, D. (1967). *Pragmatics of human communication.* New York: Norton.

Winch, P. (1958). *The idea of a social science*. London: Routledge & Kegan Paul.

Wittgenstein, L. (1958). *Philosophical investigations* (G. Anscombe, Trans.). Oxford: Blackwell. (Original work published 1953)

Woodbury, H. (1984). The strategic use of questions in court. *Semiotica, 48,* 197–228.

CHAPTER 3

Digressions in Argumentative Discourse: Multiple Goals, Standing Concerns, and Implicatures

Scott Jacobs
Sally Jackson
Susan Stearns
University of Oklahoma

Barbara Hall
University of Illinois

A recurrent problem in argumentative discussion is that arguments get extended in ways that seem to lose the original point of contention, or they go off in directions that otherwise sidetrack the discussion. This can happen interactionally, in the back and forth of denials, objections, refutations, counters, rejoinders, and so on; or it can happen monologically, as a single arguer piles on elaboration and supplementation in a way that drifts from the point that he or she was ostensibly making in the first place. This is the stuff that squabbles, nitpicking, tirades, and ramblings are made of.

Digressive and superfluous arguments are slippery phenomena. They have no clear-cut starting point. Their appearance is cumulative and retrospective; they become fully evident only after they are already well under way. They stand somewhere between a seamlessly smooth flow of coherent discourse and a jarring, off-the-wall comment or an abrupt break from the current topic. They often leave the observer feeling bewildered or befuddled, wondering just what the point has been. But this is not always so; we have located a set of cases where this confusion resolves itself. These cases unfold in ways that invite inferences that make the discourse more or less intelligible.

In this chapter, we analyze what is going on when such cases occur and what they can tell us about principles of coherence in discourse. First, we analyze a series of cases to see *how* they are constructed and understood, and just what it is that happens to make them *appear* digressive or superfluous. Then, we consider *why* such events might *occur*. We locate our explanation in the process of managing competing conversational goals.

43

SOME CASE STUDIES

The characteristic features and special construction of the kind of phenomena we have in mind are illustrated in Cases 1 through 4, following. These four cases are part of a broader pool, all drawn from transcripts of disputes between divorcing couples brought together by a court-appointed mediator to settle on visitation and custody arrangements for their children.[1]

Case 1 illustrates both superfluous elaboration and interactional digression. The episode begins in a typical fashion: the wife raises a problem in the current visitation arrangement that calls for some sort of resolution.

Case 1

129 W: Alright there's something else that I don't know what to do about.
        David calls me up a week ago he's supposed to have Susan this coming
        weekend. I made plans about a month ago to go away this next weekend
        because I wouldn't have Susan. Plans with two other couples he calls me up
        a week ago, well he has something he has to do so he's not taking her. What
        am I supposed to do? Who is I I mean I do I was in the middle of moving I
        couldn't even concentrate on it at the time you know trying to figure out what
        to do I do have these plans. I guess I can take her with me but I thought the
        whole point is that when he has custody he has custody and I'm not allowed
        to be involved in what arrangements he makes for her and vice versa.
                                                [   ]
130 M: Okay and
        Ordinarily what most parents do in a situation like that is that if something

---

[1]All data for this study come from verbatim transcripts of 20 mediation sessions conducted for the Los Angeles County Family Mediation and Conciliation Court. Sessions were taped with the consent of disputants and mediators. Names, dates, and locations have been changed. The transcripts were provided by William A. Donohue of the Department of Communication, Michigan State University. The audiotapes were part of approximately 80 collected by Jessica Pearson, Director of the Research Unit of the Association of Family and Conciliation Courts, Denver, Colorado, through a project funded by the Children's Bureau of the United States Department of Health and Human Services (90-CW-634).

Transcriptions approximate the rules presented in the appendix to Schenkein (1978). Empty parentheses indicate an inaudible or unintelligible utterance. Brackets indicate points of interruption and overlap. Equal signs mark a continuous stream of talk between two speakers or by the same speaker. Underlining indicates vocal stress.

The court required all disputants to attempt mediation prior to litigation. Mediators had the job of guiding discussion toward a written settlement. They generally followed a format of identifying sources of conflict and exploring proposals for settlement. Appropriate issues for discussion were limited by this officially authorized agenda. The mediation service is described in more detail by Pearson and Thoennes (1984).

comes up for you you're not able to have Susan with you that you make the plans for her care during that time she was to have been with him, before you do so however you could call as a courtesy to Lisa and to the mother and say hey I won't be there would you like to have her with you that weekend and it who knows maybe it's something that you would have wanted to include her in. So then you would have said sure I'll be happy to take care of her. We'll switch weekends.

131 W: It's not normally a problem like that except in this particular case we made plans to go away
        [ ]

132 M: Okay Okay so ordinarily after having been giving Lisa a chance to do that, uhm, most people feel that it's the responsibility of the parent that is to have had the child that weekend to take care of the child. Is that how you'd like to do that from now on?

133 W: That's fine with me and I am normally not like even the one day a week I could see (dumping that one day and doing something different). My schedule is fairly flexible you know with some notice. This particular thing I I just felt <u>really</u> put out because he was coming on you know I can't take her this weekend so I want another weekend and I you know my plans were not important what about me? You know of course if it came down to that that he's gonna go on not taking her I guess I got her, she's my daughter I mean what am I gonna do I just feel that you know there's some responsibility involved in this thing =

134 H: = I didn't give you an <u>ultimatum</u> like
 you're making it sound. I asked if we could switch =
 [   ]   [   ]

135 W: not ultimatum   Okay but

136 H: = weekends Okay you didn't even give me an answer
                [

137 W: you did it because

138 H: you didn't give me an answer you just said I I'll think about it I'll think about it you didn't <u>even</u> give me an answer if you had given me an answer I would have known what I what I could do or what I couldn't do, <u>Okay?</u>
 But I tried (I just wanna make that clear)
 [   ]

139 W: I guess I just didn't okay first of all I knew this was coming up and I guess I didn't believe that if I said to you so you have her this weekend and that's your weekend that that would be the end of it
 ((PAUSE))

140 H: You know I've always maintained that if we could talk we could work things

out you know, <u>we can't talk</u> so (we can't go) through with this, you don't trust me <u>you don't believe a word I say</u> so <u>we can't talk</u> =

141 W: = How much do you trust me? You had to put into the property settlement agreement that I shouldn't take the microwave oven that's built into the wall, the dishwasher that's built in

142 H: (   )

143 W: You put that in that I shouldn't take that out of the house, trust?

144 H: You took the little spigot to turn the uh sprinklers on
          ((laughs in the background))

145 W: I got it

146 M: You guys arguing about that?

147 H: You took the fireplace screen ((laughs))

148 W: (Same reason   )
                           [   ]

149 M: Come on

150 H: I can't believe you took the fireplace screen

151 W: David we feel that you totally screwed us =

152 H: = Fine, you feel like I <u>totally screwed</u> you you had a you had a you had a top lawyer and I had a <u>top</u> lawyer and I <u>totally screwed you</u> =

153 W: = That's right =

154 H: Okay, how much did we spend? twenty thousand dollars on attorneys fees, between the two of us (and that's just before it started)

155 M: Okay at some point now you you've gotta work some things out in a different way perhaps. What do you wanna do at this point? Uhm think about this and come back in a couple of weeks?

Pretty clearly, things have gotten off track or have otherwise gone awry. Let us consider in detail what happened.

Turn 129 opens with the projection of a conventional activity sequence (Jacobs & Jackson, 1981). The wife (W) raises a problem "that I don't know what to do about" that ostensibly calls for advice from the mediator (M). So, W has, in effect, opened a conversational project that would center on explaining and/or justifying the nature of the problem, proposing solutions to the problem, discussing the possibilities, and settling on some mutually acceptable resolution. And, in 130/132, this seems to be the direction that the discussion moves in as M offers a conventional solution to the category of problem that W describes. But the way that W describes the problem and follows up on M's suggestion do not cleanly fit the format.

In 131, W may simply be mitigating the imposition created by the problem she raised; but W's statement also literally denies the need for a categorical solution—she is concerned with "this particular case." In 133, even though she immediately accepts M's proposed solution, W rephrases the theme of 131 that this is not "normally" a problem. Then she recounts more details of "this particular thing." It is not clear how these elaborations contribute to the activity sequence that she herself initiated.

Likewise, the details recounted and their phrasing have an off flavor. Their design seems to reflect more than the need to clarify the nature of the problem or to justify the importance of finding a solution. Why, for example, would she choose to baldly describe the husband's (H) calls as saying "so he's not taking her" (129) and "he was coming on you know I can't take her this weekend so I want another weekend" (133) and as otherwise forcing W to take the daughter ("if it came down to that he's gonna go on not taking her I guess I got her")? By the end of turn 133, the primary point seems to have developed into dramatizing W's victimage and emphasizing H's moral accountability. Even the details recounting W's frustration and inconvenience (e.g., "I just felt <u>really</u> put out" "you know my plans were not important what about me?") fit this emergent design. Censure, not a solution, seems to be the point now.

In turns 134, 136, and 138, rather than the acceptability of the mediator's proposed solution, H takes up the implications of the way W has characterized his conduct. His final comment ("But I tried I just wanna make that clear") bids to close discussion, treating his account as a temporary suspension of the main point, that is, as an aside. But return to M's proposal requires that W let pass H's characterization of her conduct, which excuses H by shifting blame to W. This potential is lost when W defends herself in 139 and ruptures the bracketing. And this defense returns blame back to H: He would not have taken Susan even if she had asked. This progressive sliding of focus through blame and counterblame continues in 140, when H turns W's account against her. He formulates her lack of trust in him as *her* problem and implies that this is the source of blame for their continued conflict.

Notice that, in 139 and 140, neither H nor W make any reference back to M's proposed solution as a possible closure point. By this time, the point of the dispute has clearly shifted from concern with a problem in their custody arrangement to concern with establishing blame for the conflicts in their relationship. In 141, W returns H's charge in kind, and the two begin exchanging illustrative accusations through turn 150. Then, in 151, W shifts to a broad justification for her actions, and H begins to take up the question of who screwed whom in their divorce settlement. By this time it has become clear that H and W are not inclined to return to the initial problem, and M finally intervenes to terminate the whole session, suggesting that this is not a productive way to "work some things out."

So, in Case 1 we find an episode in which disputants fail to follow through on the activity that was opened by W's first utterance. That conversational project is abandoned both monologically and dialogically. A striking feature of the interactional digression is the chaining out of the argument. The moves that form the links in the chain exhibit a local relevance to immediately preceding turns with a loss of attention to the broader issues that would give continuity to the episode as a whole. Successive moves in such a chain exhibit a failure to respond to prior moves as raising *sub*issues that must be addressed with respect to the problems and proposals that initiated the episode in the first place.

Case 2 further illustrates this chaining out. The episode begins in a standard way: offering a proposal for consideration. The mediator (M) has just summarized the husband's (H) custody proposal and now asks for the wife's (W) response.

Case 2

177 M: = could you consider working on such a plan

178 W: No.

179 M: And, could you say why.

180 W: Yes because I want the kids to live with me and have
        visitation rights and if he chooses to move out of state,
        if he wants to leave his kids behind, that's his
        business.

181 M: I see.
        [

182 W: Well. I I feel bad about it I feel sorry for my kids
        because I know that that they love him very much, and I
        think they love both of us equally and I don't think it's
        right to try and alienate the children from either
        parent, no matter but how you know, regardless of how I
        feel about him, I know that the kids love him, and, I
        just I feel do that to them or
                              [

183 H: See my reasoning for
                              [   ]

184 M: Okay I think that's a
        very good point
               [

185 H: Ok my reasoning =

186 M: then no matter, I'll let you say that, no matter what

your angers are at each other, it is not good for your
kids to alienate them from the other parent
[   ]

187 H: No, oh   I   know it. But, on
the same thing, I don't feel that it's right for her to
be carrying on the way she does, and with the children
see what's going on I don't think that's   good
[   ]

188 W: Carry on how. I've not
been seeing anybody
[

189 H: Oh, God, I forget. If you're going to end up in a mental hospital =

190 W: = Pete =

191 H: = and your mom has to watch the kids and (she) ask
[

192 W: I was emotionally
upset because you have the children, I didn't know where
you were living, I w- I have a phone number that I've
called (you on the) answering machine, you would not
recall return my call for weeks

193 H: Margaret you know why I wouldn't return your call?
[   ]

194 W: Who   wouldn't   be   upset,
Who wouldn't be upset
[

195 H: You know why I didn't return the call? I
listened to your phone call   I've   Okay
[   ]   [

196 W: Go ahead and   tell me, go ahead and tell me
Peter I've already heard it from my mother's =

197 H: = I've listened to all your phone calls
[

198 W: you-   you're not gonna embarrass me
(   )
[

199 H: I've listened to all her phone calls, and all her phone
calls are hi where's the kids how're they doing okay well
ah let me tell you about my boyfriend Claude well I just
took twelve hundred dollars worth of cocaine, uh

```
          I had anal sex with Claude I did this =
          [
200 W:    Pete, you can lie all you want =

201 H:     = oh I'm not lying
                                ]
202 W:    you (              ) this woman doesn't care.
                         [
203 M:                        Okay                okay

204 W:    Think of some more things Pete I was a prostitute I
          murder people
          [                          ]
205 H:    Well, I wouldn't doubt it the way you =
                                        [
206 M:                                              okay

207 H:     = carry on
          [
208 W:    go ahead say anything you want
                    [                    ]
209 M:              let's   just   let's   just   stop   for
          a moment I have a suggestion for the two of you
          [                                          ]
210 W:    you  know,  it  doesn't  embarrass  me  a  bit  you  can
          yell it to the world

211 M:    Okay. Let's just stop for a moment and and let's see
          what might be a solution to all of this 'cause this isn't
          going to help you to keep going back and forth like this.
```

Case 2 begins with the projection of a conventional activity sequence. In turn 177, M offers a proposed visitation agreement. In turn 178, W rejects the proposal, and she accounts for her rejection in turn 180. In 182, W appears to try to mitigate some of the harshness and indifference suggested by her first remarks ("if he chooses to move out of state, if he wants to leave his kids behind, that's his business"). In particular, by saying, "I don't think it's right to try and alienate the children from either parent," W can be heard to affirm an appropriate concern for her children and to deny possibly improper motives for her refusal. M then takes up this value in 184 and 186 and certifies it as an impersonal principle for deliberations. In 187, H quickly concedes this point and then returns to his proposal, denying that this point tips the balance in favor of W: "on the same thing" W's "carrying on" is not good for the children to see.

Something else, though, hovers over this discussion, as becomes apparent in the moves that follow. Notice that W has formulated her account in a way that is laden with potential implications for the blameworthiness of H. Her reference to alienating the children from their parents can also be heard as implicitly accusing H of doing just that. And M's decision to take up this point also has the whiff of reprimand.

In fact, H seems to shift the focus of his reply from simply explaining his reasoning for wanting to move the children with him out of state (see 183 and 185) to defending himself against an accusation. He interrupts M's speech and phrases his rationale in a way that has dual force: His account can provide a reason to give custody of the children to him; but it also pretty clearly serves to defend his character as a parent and to attack W's character. W's "carrying on" may excuse what H may be doing to alienate the children from their mother.

In 189 and 191, H sarcastically dismisses W's denial and plea of ignorance, and he suggests that she is the sort of person who might end up in a mental hospital (H has previously introduced the fact that W is currently an outpatient). Like 187, this charge might bolster H's case for custody of the children. But this relevance seems more potential than actual, not being indicated by any overt textual connection. By this time, the local, pairwise focus of the dispute seems to have overwhelmed any connections to the initial question of H's proposal to take the children out of state. Most obviously, H's move stands as a serious moral indictment in its own right.

In 192 and 194, W excuses her institutionalization, and she does so in a way that blames H. And although it might be inferred from her initial remarks that if W had the children she would not be emotionally upset (so she would be able to care for them), this connection is not explicitly drawn. In fact, although she could have elaborated her turn in a way that would develop the claim that she could properly care for the children, W has instead developed her excuse in a way that focuses on the blameworthiness of H.

H then excuses his failure to return calls (193, 195, 197, 199) in a way that graphically accuses W of moral failure and illustrates how W is "carrying on." Notice that, although this charge was originally introduced by H as, possibly, a reason for claiming custody of the children, it now simply serves to return blame for blame. His report of W's phone calls does not deny that W would be emotionally capable of handling the children. Nor is it formulated as a belated answer to W's denial in 188 (how she has been "carrying on"). Its immediate and primary force seems to be to excuse H's failure to answer W's calls and to establish W's moral inadequacy. In 209 and 211, the mediator finally intervenes and declares that this "going back and forth" is not helpful to finding "a solution."

Cases 1 and 2 suggest that it is a disengagement from purposes and projects initially opened in an episode and a shifting of point and purpose that create the appearance of digression. The appearance of superfluous elaboration results from a similar disengagement. Here, disputants add information that is not clearly helpful in developing the ostensive point of the initial utterances, or they phrase their subsequent contributions in ways that emphasize or focus on issues that are extraneous to the point initially being developed. Once again, subordinate structures of discourse become functionally disengaged and appear to pursue new issues or points without closing or returning to the issues or points that initiated their development in the first place.

Consider H's contributions in turns 306, 308, and 310 of Case 3. The segment begins with W answering why she has rejected H's proposal to return to a previous joint custody schedule.

Case 3

305 W: But that arrangement didn't work out. Even though uhm because sometimes he would say well uhm I didn't get to keep them on Sunday so let me make up for Sunday on Wednesday on one of your day and

                [   ]

306 H: Because she'd (come by) and she'd say well you gotta go to work in the morning so I'm gonna take the kids just like that

307 W: No I don't (I just said for)

        [   ]

308 H: That's why I'd just ask her for a change of days okay? Uh just before uh just before uh this this this been about a few weeks ago uh she had to uh go to work early on I forgot one day she had to go to work (and then I had them) so we alternated I took she took my Tuesday and I was to take hers Wednesday night she comes driving over to the house saying I'm gonna have to take the kids she calls her lawyer telling him that I'm keeping the kids keeping them from their appointments and keeping them from their medication, she had poured the medication down the drain the night okay I

                [   ]

309 M: Okay I (don't need to hear that)

310 H: But the point was is that even then it was my night we had agreed to change that night and she could have taken them to the appointment the next morning anyway

311 W: We didn't agree (There's no use) arguing about that

H's contribution in 306 is positioned as a refutation of W's claim that his proposed joint custody schedule could not work out because H would not keep it. His point is that he did not keep the schedule because W would not keep it (and so the schedule could work out if W would just keep it).

Notice, however, that his story increasingly focuses on details related to moral rather than to practical concerns. It functions not only to refute W's claim, but also to defend H's conduct by shifting blame to W. H assembles details in a way that shows W's conduct to be not just unnecessary but positively malevolent. In 306, H claims that W would take the kids "just like that," and this moral tinge continues in 308. He develops a variety of morally charged points that do not have clear relevance to practical concerns: W driving over—at night and apparently without warning, W calling a lawyer, W pouring her child's medication down the drain. The irrelevance of this information is indicated by M's refusal to hear it (309).

And, in 310, H formulates "the point" in a way that is quite equivocal. Not only might this formulation of the point be saying that H's actions were not the cause of the breakdown in the old arrangement and that W's conduct was unnecesary; but this formulation of the point might also be saying that W is capricious and is doing these things to harass H.

So, contributions in Cases 1 and 3 appear superfluous, because they offer information that goes beyond what is required to develop (justify, clarify, explain) the point that the speaker is ostensibly trying to make in the first place, or because they phrase utterances in a way that emphasizes information that is incidental to that point. Moreover, like the chaining out of digressions, the piling on of superfluous elaboration appears to have another point: avoiding blame oneself and/or blaming the other party.

The pragmatic and communicative quality of all these cases might be brought into sharper relief by considering a superfluous elaboration and digression that (perhaps) turns out not to be so. Part of what contributes to the appearance of digression or superfluousness is the absence of overt and unequivocal textual cues to confirm the presumption that the arguments relate back to the initial point. By seeming to *withhold* such cues and by failing to deny plausible alternative points, disputants make it difficult to sustain the impression that their contributions are related to the initiating point of discourse. If digressions and superfluous elaborations result from a failure to clearly anchor utterances to a given purpose, then conversely, contributions that might not at first appear to be pertinent can be made so by constructing such a connection; consider Case 4.

Case 4

023 M: Whatever ((PAUSE)) your situation, this child should be
seeing both of you frequently. And I mean, the the

                younger children are, the b- the more often the more
                frequent, the visits should be. Not necessarily long

024 H: Well I tried to make an effort to see her everyday but
                her mother kind of kept her away ((PAUSE)) or ((PAUSE))
                or I couldn't go see her or else she would say that she
                wasn't going to be home or she didn't want company, but
                I'd, I would go and see her at lunch, the same as before I would always go
                home for lunch and we both worked the
                same distance and I always, came home for lunch, took her
                downstairs and made lunch for her?

025 W: Oh I love to comment on some of those (   ) you would
                come down and see Abigail without telephoning that you
                were coming, you were coming in during Abigail's dinner
                time

026 H: I never stopped her from eating dinner (   )=

027 W: =Okay look it's very distracting for her, when her Dad's
                there, and she's gonna play, for her to sit down and eat
                her dinner. And that you're not only distracting her
                you're distracting the rest of the family.

028 H: But your mother used
                     [   ]

029 W: And it's very inappropriate for you, to show up
                without telephoning

030 H: But your mother used to tell her (   ) that if she didn't
                want to eat to get away from the table. And it was just
                like that.

031 W: It is just like that she's finished
                     [   ]

032 H: All right so what is what's the problem
            then
            [

033 W: When she's finished eating she's excused from the table.
                ((PAUSE)) But, let's stick with the issue which is, you
                were showing up (   ) telephoning.

034 H: If you said that=

035 W: =and also, if my mother had something to do in the evening
                you, according to the court's regulation you're
                there at her convenience. Not she there at your
                convenience.

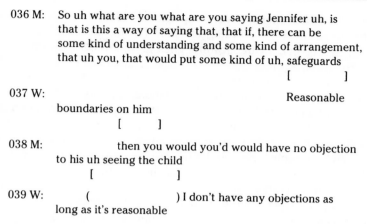

036 M: So uh what are you what are you saying Jennifer uh, is
that is this a way of saying that, that if, there can be
some kind of understanding and some kind of arrangement,
that uh you, that would put some kind of uh, safeguards
                                                [   ]
037 W: Reasonable
boundaries on him
           [   ]
038 M: then you would you'd would have no objection
to his uh seeing the child
           [   ]
039 W: (   ) I don't have any objections as
long as it's reasonable

The segment begins with M expounding on the conditions for a proper visitation/custody arrangement. The interaction then seems to shift into the typical defensive excuses and exchange of blame and accusations (024, 025) that we have seen elsewhere. H takes M's remarks personally and defends himself by shifting blame to W. Then W makes an extensive countercomplaint that has even less obvious bearing on the point M was trying to make. If anything, W's jumping from point to point is even more jangling than previous cases. But whether or not it at first appears to be digressive, the episode is overtly brought back into line when M and W, in turns 036 through 039, formulate W's complaint in a way that makes it appear relevant to the activity M opened: discussing the conditions for a proper settlement.[2]

A PRAGMATIC ANALYSIS

So, what is going on here? As we indicated earlier, there are really two questions to ask: First, how are these cases constructed and understood so that they appear digressive or superfluous? Second, why do they occur?

Regarding the first question, it is instructive to compare the inferences

---

[2]One might wonder whether the interpretations offered here are shared by disputants and mediators. Textual evidence throughout the cases we have collected suggests that participants themselves see the digressive and superfluous quality of the remarks, even though they may go along with them or even produce them. For the cases we have displayed: In Case 4, turn 36, M feels the need to formulate the point of what W is saying. And in turn 33, W herself says, "But, let's stick with the issue." Likewise, in Case 3, turn 310, H tries to formulate what "the point was" of his remarks—after M had ruled out his remarks as unnecessary. In Cases 1 and 2, the mediator finally shuts down the digression. And in Case 1, turn 138, H tries to bracket his remarks as a temporary aside. All of these contributions imply a recognition that things have gotten off track.

associated with digressive exchanges and superfluous elaborations with Gricean conversational implicatures. According to Grice (1975), the basic pattern of reasoning in working out an implicature goes as follows: A search for an implicature is triggered when the listener sees that, if taken literally and directly, what the speaker has said violates the *Cooperative Principle* (CP) or its attendant *conversational maxims*. Assuming that the speaker is, in fact, trying to be cooperative, the listener searches for an implicature that, if it were intended, would produce a message compatible with the CP. Once a candidate implicature is generated, the listener checks if the speaker could reasonably expect him to entertain such an implicature. If so, and if the speaker does nothing to stop the inference, the listener assumes that the speaker intends to convey the implicature. This pattern of inference closely resembles what is going on with the digressions and superfluous elaborations that we have examined.

First, like implicatures, these cases invite inferences that make the discourse appear pertinent, sensible, and otherwise intelligible (at least, to some degree). Accusation and blame come to be seen lurking behind the manner and content of superfluous elaborations. Digressive objections, refutations, and counterarguments chain out in ways that convey complaint, excuse, criticism, and so on. Like indirect speech acts, one discourse function comes to "piggyback" on the other. And the piggybacking function eventually comes to be seen as the intended point of the utterances while the initial argumentative function is reduced to a vestigial, pro forma vehicle for this piggybacker (see Clark, 1979).

So, for example, the wife's superfluous elaboration in turns 129, 131, and 133 of Case 1 began ostensibly as development of a problem calling for solution and emerged into a complaint calling for censure. Similarly, in Case 3, the husband's elaboration is initiated as a refutation but develops into a moral charge. The digressive chaining in both Case 1 and Case 2 apparently serve initially as refutations or other supporting argumentation; but they also serve to excuse, blame, and criticize. And these are the functions that get taken up in response, to the point that they dominate the sense of what is happening.[3]

Second, the inferences not only look similar to Gricean implicatures, but this attributional process is triggered by violations of a principle of discourse coherence captured by Grice's (1975) *Cooperative Principle:* "Make your contribution such as is required, at the stage at which it occurs, by the accepted purpose or

---

[3]Like Brown and Levinson's (1987) politeness strategies, there also appears to be a systematic motivational attribution behind these implicatures: remediational facework. For politeness strategies, knowing that someone may be saying something to be polite justifies and gives direction to the search for an implicature (i.e., what they are really saying or doing). Similarly, knowing what someone might be up to in a divorce battle creates a dual basis for deciding that what is going on is not just the development of an argumentative substructure to the initiating act or activity. On the one hand, there is a positive reason to suppose that the speaker is doing something else—something having to do with a concern for remediation. On the other hand, the speaker does nothing to prevent this attribution.

direction of the talk exchange in which you are engaged." And, more specifically, the violations appear to deviate from the *conversational maxims* that Grice posits to be very general strategies for communicating in a cooperative fashion. The cases we have examined violate the *Relation Maxim* (have a point relevant to the purpose of the exchange); the *Quantity Maxim* (provide whatever, but only information that is needed for the purpose of the exchange); and/or the *Manner Maxim* (use a style that is perspicuous, clear, orderly, unambiguous, not obscure, and so on).[4]

Following the CP and its maxims presupposes an orientation toward "an accepted purpose or direction" of the exchange. In the cases we have examined, there is an ongoing act or activity that has not yet reached closure and that establishes just this sort of orientation. The impression of there being a digression or superfluous elaboration is the impression of a deviation from this accepted purpose or direction.

Here, however, the parallel ends. The inferences associated with the digressions and superfluous elaborations that we have located are not proper Gricean implicatures. Conversational implicatures are *purpose-conserving* inferences. The inferences that make digressions or superfluous elaborations intelligible are *non*conserving. For Grice, an implicature is a message that fits the accepted purpose or direction of the exchange. That fitting is part of the test of its adequacy as a candidate interpretation. Digressions and superfluous elaborations are made intelligible and sensible only by abandoning the assumption that what the speaker intends to convey fits the accepted purpose or direction of the exchange. A *new* purpose or direction must be constructed, and it must be assumed that the still-open activity is no longer being pursued. The intelligibility of a communicative act (finding a point to the act) is preserved at the cost of the cooperativity of that act (seeing how the point fits the accepted purpose of the exchange).[5]

Our analysis of how digressions and superfluous elaborations are understood and conveyed also suggests an answer to the second question of interest: why such phenomena *occur*. The key to an explanation is to see why "piggybacking" is used and why it works in the way that it does. One general, systematic basis for

---

[4]Grice focuses on a single utterance or move taken in isolation as an immediate trigger for an implicature. In the cases of digressions and superfluous elaborations, the triggering may build over time from the cumulative force of small and/or potential anomalies taken as a whole. It is the *chaining out* of digressive moves or the *piling on* of superfluous elaboration (and failure to return to the original point) that triggers the inference process and makes the phenomena, as noted earlier, cumulative and retrospective in nature.

[5]One might think that what is going on is a variation of the kind of violation Grice discusses with deception—only here the listener catches it. But those violations *fail* if they are detected. These violations *succeed* in getting their point across only if they are detected. If these were simple digressions and superfluous elaborations, that is, ones that ended only in bewilderment and confusion, the comparison might be appropriate; but these cases communicate an implicature that resolves this bewilderment and confusion (e.g., the conveyance of blame).

the use of piggybacking can be found in the particular contextual features of mediation sessions. Mediation effectively presents many disputants with a double bind.

On the one hand, the officially authorized framework of mediation demands that disputants identify and solve problems and consider proposals for a mutually acceptable visitation/custody settlement. Mediators actively work to invoke this framework and to lead the discussion in this direction. It is for this reason that in the cases examined mediators often would help to initiate these projects or would intervene to stop departures from them. In each of the cases examined in this chapter, the dominant conversational project, initiated in the discourse, was compatible with those kinds of purposes and issues.

On the other hand, disputants often bring into these sessions a quite different understanding of what demands attention. These divorced or divorcing couples understand their situations in terms of an acute sensitivity to the implications that any issue holds for their moral identities. From this perspective, mediation sessions threaten (or promise) to become remedial interchanges (Goffman, 1971; Morris & Hopper, 1980; Owen, 1983). Here, the point of the activity is to restore a ritual equilibrium by means of moral censure. The problems, proposals, and arguments raised in the sessions take on the potential of becoming "priming moves" that call for accounts, denials, and other remedial action. The digressive chaining out of argument and counterargument and the dumping and piling on of morally tinged elaborations reflect disputants' preoccupation with defending themselves against the moral implications of the arguments made and with censuring the other party.

This orientation of disputants, however, reflects not so much explicit and planfully pursued goals as much as standing concerns. Terms like *purpose, goal,* and *plan* suggest a premeditation, a reflective awareness, and a narrowed, focused intention that need not be operative. Standing concerns may coalesce into actively pursued conversational projects, but they may also simply exist as virtual plans, goals, and demands that are continually in the offing and that emerge in locally relevant ways. They can work within the parameters of other projects rather than creating their own.

Concerns for face create a system of relevance that permeates the interpretive field of the disputants and colors the way in which they formulate their own contributions and the way in which they search for meaning in the contributions of others. These matters stand in the background as diffuse, nagging concerns that can make disputants seem touchy or hypersensitive to the way in which all things have a bearing on social identity. Matters of face, then, are concerns that *demand* attention in the sense that if a matter can be interpreted in this light, it should be, and if an opportunity to address these concerns arises, it will tend to call out those concerns.

The double bind faced by disputants comes about by the incompatibility of standing concerns for identity and face with institutionally sanctioned goals that are overtly initiated in the discourse. Because they are sensitive to potential identity-laden implications in what is said in the session, disputants often find implicatures piggybacking in the way discussed previously (even if they aren't really intended). If they respond to those implicatures, they risk sidetracking the discussion. But if they let those implicatures pass, they risk implicit admissions of guilt and acceptances of blame. Likewise, if they allow their own preoccupation with matters of moral identity to color the way they develop the kind of points that are officially sanctioned by mediation, they risk drifting from the main point themselves or opening themselves to responses that would sidetrack discussion. If they do not raise those matters, however, they cannot present what they see as relevant but morally laden information. Piggybacking moral concerns on argumentative functions is a natural consequence of the operation of these multiple demands on disputant contributions; but it also exacerbates the problems of managing these competing demands.

In the cases we have considered, disputants employ piggybacking in an attempt to reconcile the demands of both the official framework of mediation and their preoccupation with the moral implications of their divorce. At least at the start of the episodes, the phrasing and placement of their contributions are sensitive to the demands of the initiating conversational project. The chaining out of insults, threats, complaints, accusations, justifications, excuses, and other morally loaded acts rides on an argumentative exchange of objection and counter-objection. Complaints piggyback on the presentation of "problems" in visitation arrangements. Accusations are planted in rationales for custody. Character defects are used as excuses and as objections to proposals. The piggybacking of these functions reflects an effort to have one's cake and eat it too. It's just that in the cases we have located, the disputants eventually eat the cake.

As disputants continue to load their contributions and interpretations with these morally tinged, secondary aspects of force and meaning, those aspects slide into a dominant position of meaning. As we have seen, digressions begin as arguments over side and subissues. But the presence of a piggybacking complaint or accusation creates a dual response demand that tends to be answered in kind. And the back and forth of blame and counterblame eventually takes on a focus of concern in its own right. As the chain grows longer, so do the inferential connections necessary to find any relevance to the issues that initially gave rise to the episode.

Likewise, superfluous elaborations are a way of addressing one set of demands while loading them with the concerns of another. Their superfluous quality may not be apparent at first, but it inevitably arises from continued unnecessary information or unusual emphasis. As the bearing of these contributions on the initial point becomes increasingly difficult to sustain, face concerns come to dominate both interpretation and response space.

CONCLUSION

Digressions and superfluous elaborations of the type we have studied in this chapter are interesting, not just because they are practical troubles that cooperative disputants try to avoid but often do not, but also because they provide insight into the principles and processes that underlie the management of multiple goals in conversation. These phenomena suggest that the communication of purpose is central to discourse coherence (Jackson, Jacobs, & Rossi, 1987), but that purpose is not a fixed value in working out an implicature. Contrary to the interpretive process that Grice (1975) has described; these implicatures are not purpose-conserving. Here, new purposes are attributed as the meaning of an utterance is found. Consistency with a given purpose does not become the standard for generating an implicature—only for triggering it. The value of both purpose and implicature are assigned simultaneously. Purpose becomes a variable whose value is assigned on the basis of whatever creates the best fit with a range of possible values for implicatures.

These phenomena also contribute to our understanding of how conversationalists manage competing demands. The cases we have studied further demonstrate that seemingly incompatible communicative demands often result in evasion, equivocation, indirection, or otherwise paradoxical forms of discourse (Bavelas, 1983; Brown & Levinson, 1987; Jacobs, Jackson, Hallmark, Hall, & Stearns, 1987; Pomerantz, 1978). Communication *can* involve skillful management of multiple constraints: The resources enabling integration of competing goals are, in some sense, available within the communication system (O'Keefe, 1988). But the availability of these resources is no assurance of their deployment. As discourse analysts increasingly take seriously the multifunctional nature of communication, they are likely to find that what is ordinary, natural, and unremarkable is often clumsy, half-baked, and far short of ideal.

ACKNOWLEDGMENTS

Earlier versions of this chapter were presented at the 9th annual conference on discourse analysis, Temple University, Philadelphia, PA, March 24–26, 1988, and at the 74th annual meeting of the Speech Communication Association, New Orleans, November, 1988. Preparation of this manuscript was partially supported through research fellowships and grants to the first and second authors from the Netherlands Institute for Advanced Study in the Humanities and Social Sciences, the University of Oklahoma Associate's Fund, and the University of Oklahoma Office of the Provost.

REFERENCES

Bavelas, J. B. (1983). Situations that lead to disqualification. *Human Communication Research, 9,* 130–145.

Brown, P., & Levinson, S. C. (1987). *Politeness: Some universals in language usage.* Cambridge: Cambridge University Press.

Clark, H. H. (1979). Responding to indirect speech acts. *Cognitive Psychology, 11,* 430–477.

Goffman, E. (1971). *Relations in public.* New York: Harper & Row.

Grice, H. P. (1975). Logic and conversation: In P. Cole & J. L. Morgan (Eds.), *Syntax and semantics: Vol. 3. Speech acts* (pp. 41–58). New York: Academic Press.

Jackson, S., Jacobs, S., & Rossi, A. M. (1987). Conversational relevance: Three experiments in the pragmatic connectedness of conversation: In M. L. McLaughlin (Ed.), *Communication yearbook* (Vol. 10, pp. 323–347). Beverly Hills, CA: Sage.

Jacobs, S., & Jackson, S. (1981). Argument as a natural category: The routine grounds for arguing in everyday conversation. *Western Journal of Speech Communication, 45,* 118–132.

Jacobs, S., Jackson, S., Hallmark, J., Hall, B., & Stearns, S. (1987). Ideal argument in the real world: Making do in mediation. In J. W. Wenzel (Ed.), *Argument and critical practice: Proceedings of the fifth SCA/AFA conference on argumentation* (pp. 291–298). Annandale, VA: Speech Communication Association.

Morris, G. H., & Hopper, R. (1980). Remediation and legislation in everyday talk: How communicators achieve consensus. *Quarterly Journal of Speech, 66,* 266–275.

O'Keefe, B. J. (1988). The logic of message design: Individual differences in reasoning about communication. *Communication Monographs, 55,* 80–103.

Owen, M. (1983). *Apologies and remedial exchanges: A study of language use in social interaction.* Berlin: Mouton.

Pearson, J., & Thoennes, N. (1984). The preliminary portrait of client reactions to three court mediation programs. In J. A. Lemmon (Ed.), *Reaching effective agreements* (pp. 21–40). Mediation Quarterly, no. 3. San Francisco: Jossey-Bass.

Pomerantz, A. (1978). Compliment responses: Notes on the cooperation of multiple constraints: In J. Schenkein (Ed.), *Studies in the organization of conversational interaction* (pp. 79–112). New York: Academic Press.

Schenkein, J. (Ed.). (1978). *Studies in the organization of conversational interaction.* New York: Academic Press.

CHAPTER 4
The Uses of Goals in Therapy

Richard Buttny
Syracuse University

Jodi R. Cohen
Ithaca College

The notion of "goals" is typically conceived of cognitively as that which leads to the formation of plans or strategies to achieve desired ends. This formulation may be said to represent the commonsense view, as well as an oversimplified version of some social scientific accounts (Bilmes, 1986). Here, we examine goals in a somewhat different fashion. Instead of conceiving of goals cognitively, as that which drives action, we look at how goals are used as social objects in conversation. Given the fact that persons explicitly or implicitly communicate their goals to others, what interactional consequences does the presentation of goals have for participants? In particular, we examine the use of goals during a couple-therapy consultation. Goals are constitutive of the problem–blame–solution structure of therapy. In telling problems, ascribing responsibility, and proposing solutions, clients and therapists alike are implying goals and ways to achieve those goals.

THE PROBLEM OF DESCRIBING HUMAN ACTION

Our Western, commonsense beliefs about human action are grounded in the dualistic assumption that an actor's external behaviors are, for the most part, guided or directed by the actor's internal mental processes (Rorty, 1979). Such internal mental processes are not directly observable, with the exception, of course, of one's own. Such mental processes, which guide our actions, are identified by the familiar vocabulary of commonsense and social scientific terms, such as *motives, intentions, goals, plans, strategies, purposes, wants,* and *reasons.*[1] Notions such as goals, strategies, plans, and the like seem so central to our understandings of action as to be virtually indubitable. As the action–motion distinction illustrates, a person's arm does not merely move up; rather, a person raises an arm to perform an action in order to achieve some end or goal, for example, to cast a vote in an election, to ask a question in a class, or to signal a right turn (Melden, 1961). Human action is conceived to have some direction or point to it. So, in this sense, the notions of goals, purposes, and ends are constitutive or implicit in our very concept of human action.

In our present postpositivistic era in the social sciences, it is no longer considered radical or unscientific to use such cognitive concepts as goals, intentions, and the like in explanations of human behavior. There is a plethora of theories in communication studies, discourse analysis, social psychology, cognitive science, and action theory that take motives, intentions, and goals as central explanatory concepts. These mentalistic notions have provided a well-worn and useful vocabulary in the social sciences for our understandings and explanations of human action.

But, as Gergen (1989) has argued, claims using such mentalistic notions cannot be empirically supported in the same way as claims about observable phenomena. Commentators have pointed out that propositions about the mentalistic aspects of human action are based on analogies or metaphors (Geertz, 1982; Pepper, 1942; Sarbin, 1986). Once we adopt a root metaphor, such as *goals,* then we are prone to include auxiliary metaphors, such as *strategies, plans, games, actors,* and so forth in our theoretical vocabulary. We "look through" language to the world without realizing that the descriptive language we adopt will influence what we see. Description of empirical phenomena becomes "unpacking" the root metaphor and seeing related units in terms of this metaphor. Indeed, the languages of the human sciences may be ultimately metaphorical (Gergen, 1986).

In calling attention to the analogical status of goals in human action, we consider how persons interactionally use goals. Instead of conceiving of goals in the usual cognitive way, as that which leads to the formation of plans to achieve desired ends, we look at how goals are interactionally expressed and responded to; that is, how goals are explicitly or implicitly used.

This move of taking the notion of goals as social objects follows the lead by Mills (1940) in the classic paper on motives (also see Burke, 1936, and Peters,

---

[1]A problem in the literature is that the conceptual distinctions among these terms has not been worked out. The problem arises when the same term, such as *goals,* becomes used in different ways by different theorists (Craig, 1986). We cannot offer a remedy here for this linguistic and conceptual nonchalance, but Tedeschi and Reiss (1981) have provided a useful start to how to draw these distinctions.

1958). Mills argued that motives are not internal causes of action, but rather are ultimately a shorthand for the verbal resources that describe the actor's situated action. The question of the actor's motives usually only arises when an action seems unusual or deviant in some way and consequently needs to be explained, justified, or made understandable. Mills' argument can be readily extended to goals. Persons can verbally present their own actions as directed toward some goal or as part of a plan to achieve a goal. By presenting one's actions as goal directed, one can make intelligible or explain one's actions. In other words, goals are a way to "frame" one's actions, and the use of such frames can have interactional consequences. An individual's goals may be evaluated in a similar or dissimilar way by others. In on-going relationships, when important goals are not shared, this can create interpersonal tensions.

Therapeutic Discourse

A context that offers a rich body of material for the analysis of goals is a therapy session. Therapeutic interviews may be viewed as a particular kind of conversation, designed for intensive discussion and resolution of problems. Couple therapy, in particular, offers an interesting communication event, because wife and husband can present their respective accounts of the problems as well as respond to their partner's account. The telling of problems is not done for descriptive adequacy alone. Participants often tell problems in order to ascribe blame or responsibility to themselves or to others. In addition, problems are often presented along with solutions. The very way the problem is told can imply the teller's desired solution; so, therapy sessions may be seen as organized by a problem–blame–solution structure, and goals can be seen as implicit in a person's formulation of the problem, blame, and solution.

The therapist as recipient of the clients' problems attempts to work as a mediator by remaining neutral and not taking sides with either participant. The therapist may adopt an intervention strategy[2] that diverges from both the husband's and the wife's position. The therapist can be seen as attempting to reframe the couple's presentation of the "problem" into a more desirable formulation.

TELLING PROBLEMS AND IMPLYING GOALS

In the initial therapy session, the participants need to communicate to the therapist why they have come to therapy. This task is particularly interesting,

---

[2]The therapist has independently written a paper describing his perceptions and the intervention strategies he used in the session we analyzed (Sluzki, in press). The present chapter is not a duplication, because it is a more intensive, microanalysis focusing on how goals are used as an interactional resource, whereas the Sluzki paper (in press) gives an overview of the entire session from a therapeutic intervention perspective.

given the participation framework of couple therapy in which one's spouse is present to overhear and possibly respond to one's telling of problems to the therapist. In presenting problems, participants are simultaneously allocating responsibility and blame. Through such accounts, participants convey their goals and ways to achieve such goals. These tasks of telling problems, blaming, assigning responsibility, and indicating goals are accomplished through descriptions of one's own and one's spouse's actions. Such descriptions imply, rather than explicitly state, one's goals, because these goals may be face threatening to one's partner.

The following segment is the opening of a therapy consultation in which the the wife offers her initial formulation of "problems." We examine the structure of how problems are told through descriptions to see how blame and responsibility are implicated and the participant's goals are displayed. (See Appendix for the transcription conventions.)

(1) (T.03–T.15)

T.03   . . . what brought you to the consultation? (0.7) to start with?

W.04   To the couple therapy?

                       [

T.05   Yeah

W.06   (.hhh) well we were having (0.4) problems in our relationship
an::d the nature of the problems were .hh uhm revolved
around >ah sort of< the lack of communica:tion (.) ah inability
to interact with one another I I felt the need for more
interaction, and I was hoping that we would ah learn how to
interact better with one another (.) ah also I felt that uhm
we had been living sort of parallel life styles (0.4) in in
the sense that >we weren't really interacting< .hh and
communicating with one another (.hh) an:d I felt like we we
had become more or less roommates rather than partners or
friends or comrades or you know people who we could share
our emotions with you know that we could actually exchange
feelings and ideas with one another =

T.07   =Uh huh

W.08   = >and that's something< that I- I really (0.7) am hoping for =

T.09   =Uh huh >uh huh<

W.10   An:d I would say that's: probably the- the nuts and bolts of
the- of the real problem

T.11 Uh huh

W.12 An:d ah: we were hoping to see whether we could ↑ *improve
that*.
(0.6)

T.13 Um hmm >okay<

The wife answers the therapist's initial question by glossing their relationship as having "problems." She then proceeds to "unpack this gloss" and describe the problems (W.06). The problems are presented as due to, in part, a *deficiency*, that is, due to "the lack of" communication and an "inability" to interact with one another. Such a deficiency is heard as a problem based on the commonsense understanding that a married couple should communicate well. Quite simply, their "lack of communication" is inconsistent with the nature of their intimate relationship. (Interestingly, *whose* "lack" or "inability" it is [e.g., "ours," "mine," or "his"] is not mentioned at this point. As we see later, it becomes clear that the wife is ascribing the main difficulty to her husband.)

Her telling of the problem is structured by a series of *contrasts*. These contrasts serve to unpack the "communication problem." These descriptions present their current negative relational condition in the initial position, which is then contrasted to the desired, positive condition.

(2) (W.06)

W.06 . . . ah inability to interact with one another
I I felt the need for more interaction . . .

W.06 . . . we had been living sort of parallel life styles (0.4) in
in the sense that >we weren't really interacting< .hh and
communicating with one another (.hh) . . .

W.06 . . . I felt like we we had become more or less roommates rather
than partners or friends or comrades or you know people
who we could share our emotions with you know that we could
actually exchange feelings and ideas with one another . . .

Such contrasts allow for the the description of their present undesirable relational state (e.g., "inability to interact," "parallel lifestyles," and "roommates"). These are then *contrasted with her goals* (e.g., "more interaction," "really interacting," and "partners or friends" etc.).

In and through the telling of problems, the actor not only describes the problems but may also allocate responsibility for the problems, that is, ascribe blame. The wife's portrayal of troubles may be heard to ascribe blame to the husband at certain points. For instance, the wife reports that *she was the one* who "felt" the problems.

(3) (W.06)

I felt the need for more interaction . . .

I felt that uhm we had been living sort of parallel life styles . . .

I felt like we we had become more or less roommates . . .

Also, she indicates a "hope" for change from these problems.

(4) (W.06–W.08)

I was hoping that we would ah learn how to interact better . . .

. . . and that's something that I really (0.7) am hoping for

The wife's recognition of the problems and her expressed desire for change serves to *distinguish herself from her husband.* She is the one who "felt the need for more interaction" and recognized their interactional distance. Noticing the problems and professing the solution of "better communication" is a way for the wife to implicate that she ascribes blame to her husband.

Responses to the Telling of Problems

Couple therapy has another familiar structure, which we may gloss as "telling my side of the story." Therapists do not want to be seen as siding with or favoring one member of the couple over the other (Sluzki, in press). Consequently, the therapist will want to hear the husband's rationale for coming to therapy.

(5) (T.17–T.19)

T.17   What brought you to (0.7) couple therapy?

H.18   Well uhm (2.5) I agree that there are some thing (1.1) ah
        that could be impro:ved in our relationship (1.0) and ah
        (1.1) and one of the things was (1.2) why: (1.2) the interaction
        between us wasn't (.) (.hh) what W. thought it should be
        >a↑nd< (0.7) ah: what I thought it should be. (1.5) an:d ah
        al:so (0.6) how our long (.) history (.) together affected
        (.) the interaction now:. (1.0) ah and try and get (.) t- uh
        a grips on ah (1.0) on how we can improve our relationship
        (.) possibly by understanding what went on in the past and
        ah what's happening in the present (0.6) with some objective
        (.) help =

T.19   = Uh hum

The husband's opening statement to the therapist explicitly responds to the wife's version of problems. We can use the husband's uptake and response as his interpretation of the prior talk. Following the therapist's question (T.17), the husband responds in such a way as to reply to the wife's account. He begins with, "Well uhm (2.5) I agree" (H.18). The use of "I agree" displays a response, not directly to the therapist's question but to the wife's prior account of problems. However, immediately prior to uttering "I agree," he begins with the particle "Well," the vocalization "uhm," and a pause of 2.5 seconds. In other research, these features have been shown to display a delay such as in prefacing disagreements (Pomerantz, 1984), the non-granting of requests (Wootton, 1981), and face-threatening responses (Owen, 1981). This complicates the simple reading of "I agree" as a response to the wife's assessment. The husband's response appears to address the dual relevancies of agreeing with the wife that there are problems in their relationship while simultaneously minimizing the character or magnitude of those problems.

The husband's opening statement has a structural similarity to the wife's: he begins with a gloss of the problem, "there are some things (1.1) uhm that could be *improved* in our relationship" (H.18), and then proceeds to unpack that gloss with more specifics. Notice that his rendering of their problems is less severe than the wife's portrayal. He initially attributes the reason they are in therapy as due to the wife's dissatisfaction.

(6) (H.18)

H.18   one of the things was (1.2) why: (1.2) the interaction
        between us wasn't (.) (.hh) what W. thought it should be > and? <
        ah what I thought it should be.

His mentioning the wife's dissatisfaction before his own dissatisfaction suggests that she is the impetus for their coming to therapy. The one who is more dissatisfied in a relationship will likely possess more strongly held goals for change.

ASCRIBING GOALS TO OTHERS

An interesting feature of therapy as a communication event is the view of the therapist as "an expert of interpersonal relations." Therapists are commonly believed to have a specialized knowledge of marital problems and interpersonal communication. Social identities, such as "therapist as expert," can be accounted for, not only as a commonsense belief but, more fundamentally, in the interaction itself (Heritage, 1984). For instance, clients frequently defer to the therapist's questions, interruptions, and evaluations, and, at times, the clients attempt to align with the therapist in "opposition" to their partner. The therapist appears to exert considerable control over turn taking, for example, by directing questions, by cutting short critical descriptions, and by drawing out underlying assumptions, which results in a decrease in overlaps and marked silences (Buttny, 1990; Labov & Fanshel, 1977).

In our materials, we noticed that the therapist ascribed goals to the clients.

(7) (W.36–T.49)

W.36   Yeah I think- I mean in the past I've I've ah (0.9) been a
        lot (0.5) <u>less</u> open with my feelings and I've repressed a
        lot of my own feelings but I've been in therapy now for a
        while and ah::
                        [
T.37   For awhile? =

W.38   = Yeah

T.39   How long?

W.40   For about a year and a half

T.41   That's sweet of you! =

W.42   = Hhhh
                [
T.43   No it's (   )- it's great you know what frequently what
        happens with people in ther- individual therapy

W.44   Uh huh =

T.45   = They end up doing:: their own stuff and ah they leave ah their partners in
        another point in the planet

W.46   Uh huh ha ha (   )
                            [
T.47   And ah so you're trying to:: to- to bring him
        up to a point to ah: a mode (.) and a style that you have =
                            [ ]   [ ]
W.48   > Uh huh <   right

T.49   = developed through therapy that's very-very sweet of you.
        > *very nice* <.

A common structural feature of therapeutic discourse is the three-part sequence: therapist's question, client's answer, and therapist's assessment or comment on answer. Such sequences are characteristic of institutional discourse involving institutional representatives with some specialized knowledge (Coulthard, 1981; Mishler, 1984). The third part of the sequence, "assessment" or "comment on answer," provides a slot for the therapist to display expertise and also to maintain conversational control. T.37–T.41 is an instance of this sequence.

(8) (T.37–W.42)

T.37   For awhile? =

W.38   = Yeah

T.39   How long?

W.40   For about a year and a half

T.41   That's sweet of you! =

W.42   = Hhhh

Drawing on the conversational resource of the wife having been in therapy (W.36), the therapist asks her the length of her involvement in therapy (T.37; T.39), and then positively assesses her answer (T.41). The assessment here, "That's sweet of you!," seems odd coming from a therapist in that it may be taken in more than one way, for example, as ironic, sarcastic, or patronizing. In examining the therapist's assessment here (T.41), it should be pointed out that the therapist is not a native English speaker. The wife's muffled laughter at W.42 latched onto the therapist's remark may be seen as her recognition of the ambiguity of the therapist's assessment—as though the therapist is being ironic.

The therapist immediately responds with an overlapping "No," which appears directed to the wife's muffled laughter in order to deny his being ironic by his assessment. The therapist proceeds to explain his assessment (T.43–49). He *contrasts* "what frequently happens with people in individual therapy," that is, growing separate from their partner (T.43–45), to his formulation of the wife's actions of trying to help her husband (T.47–49). So, by labeling the wife's actions as designed to help her husband, the therapist is imputing the goal of working on their problems through therapy. This ascription of goals to the wife is also designed for the overhearing husband, because the wife's involvement in individual therapy is a point of contention between the couple. Quite simply, the therapist frames the wife's involvement in therapy not as something coming between the couple but as the wife's goal to help them as a couple.

The way goals are formulated or put into words is important for the therapist's intervention. His formulation of the wife's goals portrays her as trying to help her husband. This formulation seems to contrast with some of the wife's own descriptions in which she appeared to be disassociating herself from her husband through portraying his "deficiency" and her "need for communication" (see W.06). The therapist's positive formulation of her goals is consistent with his systemic perspective of the couple working together on relational issues (Sluzki, 1978, in press).

The therapist formulates the wife's goals again in addressing the husband.

(9) (T.49–T.55)

T.49   ((ADDRESSED TO WIFE)) . . . that's very-very sweet of you.
       > *very nice* <. ((ADDRESSED TO HUSBAND)) and if you do indeed
       to- to follow suit? you are in therapy yourself?

H.50   No:
         [

T.51   No of course

W.52   >I wish he were<
          ((laughter))

T.53   Uhm (.) so you are the one who needs to (   )
       >ahm< really (   ) apparently uhm (2.0) secretly
       couple therapy is for you (.hhh)
       (2.0)

H.54   Wha- what was the question? (*I'm sorry*)

T.55   I made- I made a statement (.) I have the impression that secretly family
       therapy-couple therapy is for you

As the therapist turns to the husband, we can see another question–answer–assessment sequence (T.49–51). The wife quickly adds her "wish" that the husband would go to therapy (W.52). But W.52 is not only the wife's "wish"; it is also her *critical assessment of the husband*—and in the assessment slot similar to the therapist. The wife here appears to be attempting to align with the therapist as a proponent of therapy against the husband. Notice that couple therapy is one of the few communication contexts where it is permissible to discuss another adult's faults to a third party in that person's presence.

The therapist, then, expands on his assessment of T.51 by formulating the wife's goals in a somewhat different way (T.53–55) in his announcement to the husband. The therapist displays his expertise by revealing the wife's implicit goals. This making explicit what is implied is a characteristic therapeutic intervention.

WHAT SHOULD BE THE GOALS OF THERAPY?

From a therapeutic perspective, a person's goals may be unrealistic, too broad, or ill defined (Sluzki, in press). Consequently, the therapist needs to have the clients reformulate goals in a way that can be attained through therapy (Davis, 1986).

In the following transcript, we see the therapist calling on the wife to again formulate her goals for therapy:

(10) (T.85-W.104)

T.85   Uhm (2.5) (.hhh) one way or another you are involved in a: in =
           [   ]
W.86   *Uh   huh*

T.87   = a very particular ritual (2.3) ah right now (   )
           it's a ritual of ah: (1.0) couples therapy, it's a ritual of
           a commitment to a relationship and of approximation up to
           a point

W.89   Uh huh =

T.90   = A statement (.) to each other that you: you want in somehow
           because if not you wouldn't be exposed to all this ah: ah::
           stresses and strains yeah? =

W.91   = Uh huh

T.92   Ah (.) what else do you want in addition to the ritual
           (.) by that I mean perhaps the ritual of therapy itself is a
           very important statement that lodges into ah (.) as ah as ah
           token of love

W.93   Um huh

T.94   Uhm so if that is the case it is satisfied by the mere case
           that you are in therapy no? (.) as well as long as you are here
           you might as well ( ) in addition to that do you want
           something what is that you would like to get as concretely as
           possible

W.95   Well I guess a feeling of just
                       [
T.96   Do you follow me?

W.97   Yea:h
               [

T.98   The risk
            (.)

W.99   Um huh

T.100 Of any change (.) is (.) that you may leave therapy
            (.)

W.101 Um huh

T.102 And if therapy in itself is a ritual (2.0) uhm: (.) then it
            doesn't make sense for you (.) to do- to change too much in the
            direction >whatever direction it may be because you would have
            to leave therapy and therapy itself is a very important ritual<
            (.) a token of appreciation for each other and of love.

H.103 That assessment is one that I- I mean (.) the real purpose of
            therapy is to get out of therapy (.) as soon as possible in
            a way that you'd feel- (da)- you're happier I mean what is the
            end point? you're happier and more content with yourself and
            your- >people you deal with< (.hh) but I think that one of
            the problems with therapy is that people (.) do get caught
            up on the- in the ritual of therapy in itself and so it ah
            perpetuates itself (.) the goals aren't attained because ah
            if they are attained then you leave therapy (.) by definition
            an:d that's a problem >ya know< uhm (.) it's- it's a paradox
            but that's one of the problems with therapy is that you're
            drawn in and held in to the ritual not (.) to the
            goals- not attaining the goals

W.104 But- but only until you can do it on your own I mean it's almost
            like you- you acqui:re the awareness in therapy (.) so you are
            able to handle your own problems (.) you know it's almost
            like you- you learn something in therapy and then you take it
            home and you work on it =

   The therapist identifies the couple's participation in therapy as being a kind of
"ritual" (T.85–87). The therapist's ascription of couple's involvement in therapy
as ritual works to reframe the couple's prior disagreement (not included in the
preceding transcript) and move them away from that recurring argument. In
addition, the therapist positively evaluates the couple's involvement in therapy
as a ritual. Such moves of reframing an apparent problem into a positive
relational statement are a common therapeutic intervention strategy.
   As the therapist expands on his ascription of the couple's involvement in this
ritual, he asks the wife what her goals are "in addition to the ritual" (T.92–T.94).
The therapist marks his request for her goals by asking her to convey it "as
concretely as possible" (T.94). His use of "concretely" suggests a contrast with
her prior presentation of goals as possibly too abstract, too global, or unrealistic.

So the therapist appears to be drawing a contrast between being in therapy for ritualistic purposes and being in therapy to work on attainable goals. This transcript may be seen as the therapist attempting to "negotiate" goals with the couple. That is, the therapist wants the couple, especially the wife, to reformulate her goals in a way that is attainable with therapy.

The wife's response to the therapist's question about her goals in therapy displays an uncertainty as seen by the initial qualifiers "well" and "I guess" (W.95). The therapist's request for the wife's goals may appear initially puzzling to the wife, because she has already presented her goals at the beginning of the session (see transcript [1] [T.03–T.15]).

The therapist recognizes her puzzlement and interrupts her (T.96) in order to explain his question. The therapist proposes that her participation in therapy may be functioning for her as ritual and be an obstacle to her wanting to change (T.98–T.102).

A characteristic two-part sequence of therapeutic interaction is for the therapist to make an observation, assessment, or proposal, and then for the client to comment on what the therapist has said as a second-part response. In the present segment, even though the therapist's observation is addressed to the wife, the husband intercedes (H.103) before the wife can comment and expands on the therapist's observation with a more explicit assessment of the wife's goals.

The husband draws on the therapist's point of therapy as ritual as a conversational resource to *criticize the wife's goal* of continuing in therapy. The husband accomplishes this criticism by contrasting "the real purpose" or "goal" of therapy (to get out of therapy) with getting into the "ritual" of therapy, which prevents her from reaching this goal. That is, the husband cites a commonsense understanding of the goals of therapy—"to get out of therapy as soon as possible" (H.103). By establishing a general statement of what *should* be the goal of therapy and then showing that she is not attempting to achieve these goals, because she is caught up in the ritual, the husband is able to criticize the wife's overlong participation in therapy. The husband does not explicitly mention the wife here but instead uses the general claims (e.g., "the real purpose of therapy is to get out of therapy") and a generalized reference through a second-person plural pronoun (e.g., "you're drawn in and held in to the ritual"). Nonetheless, it is clear from the context of the couple's argument and diverging goals as regards therapy that he is referring to the wife.

The wife responds with a justification (W.104), which displays her recognition of his criticism. The wife's response does not challenge the husband's general statement of the goals of therapy but instead argues for staying in therapy until "you are able to handle your own problems" (W.104). So, the wife can at once agree with the husband's and therapist's warning about the problem of therapy as ritual while at the same time holding on to her claim about the value of therapy in solving problems.

This transcript presents an intriguing case of how goals are *negotiated* in therapy. We saw the therapist contrast the ritual of therapy to attainable goals, the husband develop the therapist's point about the dangers of therapy as ritual in that it precludes attaining goals of finishing therapy, and the wife agreeing with the husband with the important qualification of staying with therapy until you can solve your own problems. Although no agreement is reached, we do see how goals can be evaluated as appropriate or inappropriate and how they can be criticized and defended.

CONCLUSION

We have described what might be called a "discourse of goals in therapy"—how goals are used in the problem–blame–solution structure of therapy. For instance, we saw (a) how the wife presented her goals in her opening telling of problems and ascription of blame through a series of contrasts between their current, undesirable relational state and her desire for improved communication, (b) how the husband agreed with his wife's goals while simultaneously diminishing the severity of their relational problems, (c) how the therapist formulated the wife's goal of bringing her husband to therapy to improve their relationship, (d) how the therapist suggested that the wife reformulate her goals for therapy in addition to the "ritual of therapy," and (e) how the husband and wife could agree on "the goals of therapy" while disagreeing on when such goals are achieved. We do not see any major breakthroughs in this therapy consultation, but we do see how goals are used as an interactional object—as a frame for action that can be presented as one's own or ascribed of another, that can be criticized, reformulated, defended, or explained.

REFERENCES

Bilmes, J. (1986). *Discourse and behavior.* New York: Plenum.

Burke, K. (1936). *Permanence and change.* Berkeley: University of California Press.

Buttny, R. (1990). Blame–accounts sequences in therapy: The negotiation of relational meanings. *Semiotica, 78,* 219–247.

Coulthard, M. (1981). Developing the description. In M. Coulthard & M. Montgomery (Eds.), *Studies in discourse analysis* (pp. 13–31). London: Routledge & Kegan Paul.

Craig, R. T. (1986). Goals in discourse. In D. G. Ellis & W. A. Donohue (Eds.), *Contemporary issues in language and discourse processes* (pp. 257–273). Hillsdale, NJ: Lawrence Erlbaum Associates.

Davis, K. (1986). The process of problem (re)formulation in psychotherapy. *Sociology of Health & Mental Illness, 8,* 44–74.

Geertz, C. (1982). Blurred genres: The reconfiguration of social thought. In *Local knowledge: Further essays in interpretative anthropology* (pp. 19–35). New York: Basic Books.

Gergen, K. J. (1986). Correspondence versus autonomy in the language of understanding human action. In D. W. Fiske & R. A. Shweder (Eds.), *Metatheory and social science: Pluralisms and subjectivities* (pp. 136–162). Chicago: University of Chicago Press.

Gergen, K. J. (1989). Warranting voice and the elaboration. In J. Shotter & K. J. Gergen (Eds.), *Texts of identity* (pp. 70–81). London: Sage.

Heritage, J. (1984). *Garfinkel and ethnomethodology.* Cambridge: Polity.

Labov, W., & Fanshel, D. (1977). *Therapeutic discourse: Psychotherapy as conversation.* New York: Academic Press.

Melden, A. I. (1961). *Free action.* London: Routledge & Kegan Paul.

Mills, C. W. (1940). Situated actions and vocabularies of motive. *American Sociological Review, 5,* 904–913.

Mishler, E. G. (1984). *The discourse of medicine: Dialectics of medical interviews.* Norwood, NJ: Ablex.

Owen, M. (1981). Conversational units and the use of "well. . . ." In P. Werth (Ed.), *Conversation and discourse: Structures and interpretation* (pp. 99–116). New York: St. Martin's Press.

Pepper, S. C. (1942). *World hypotheses: A study in evidence.* Berkeley: University of California Press.

Peters, R. S. (1958). *The concept of motivation.* London: Routledge & Kegan Paul.

Pomerantz, A. (1984). Agreeing and disagreeing with assessments: Some features of preferred/dispreferred turn shapes. In J. M. Atkinson & J. Heritage (Eds.), *Structures of social action: Studies in conversation analysis* (pp. 57–101). Cambridge: Cambridge University press.

Rorty, R. (1979). *Philosophy and the mirror of nature.* Princeton, NJ: Princeton University Press.

Sarbin, T. R. (1986). The narrative as a root metaphor for psychology. In T. R. Sarbin (Ed.), *Narrative psychology: The storified nature of human conduct* (pp. 3–21). New York: Praeger.

Sluzki, C. E. (1978). Marital therapy from a systems perspective. In T. J. Paolino & B. S. McCrady (Eds.), *Marriage and marital therapy* (pp. 366–394). New York: Brunner/Mazel.

Sluzki, C. E. (in press). Therapeutic conversations: Systemic blueprints of a couple's interview. In R. Chasin & H. Grunebraum (Eds.), *Couple therapy: Many approaches to one case.* New York: Gilford Press.

Tedeschi, J. T., & Reiss, M. (1981). Verbal strategies in impression management. In C. Antaki (Ed.), *The psychology of ordinary explanations of social behaviour* (pp. 271–309). New York: Academic Press.

Wootton, A. J. (1981). The management of granting and rejections by parents in request sequences. *Semiotica, 37,* 59–89.

CHAPTER 5

Intergenerational Talk: Goal Consonance and Intergroup Dissonance

Nikolas Coupland
Justine Coupland
University of Wales College of Cardiff

Howard Giles
University of California, Santa Barbara

Karen Henwood
Brunel University

The term *goal,* which we take to refer generally to cognitions prospective of desired outcomes, has no agreed delimitation (cf. Cody & McLaughlin, 1990; D'Andrade, 1987; Harré, Clarke, & De Carlo, 1985; Schank & Abelson, 1977; Tracy & Coupland, in press). There is little consensus as to where we are to locate goals, more locally or more globally, in the structure of interaction. Also, goals can relate to diverse dimensions of outcomes, addressing task, identity, and relational concerns. However we choose to use the concept, goals are empirically elusive. They are neither reliably reproducible outside of the immediate contexts of their employment (but see Cegala et al., 1988; Waldron, Cegala, Sharkey, & Teboul, in press) nor, therefore, amenable to direct observation. This is not to say that goals may not be stable, objectifiable, and representable. We assume that they may be, but only when formulated at a particular level of generality and under conditions of idealization. And then, what is reported as a goal, even by its holder, may be a gross representation of the complex of processes to which behaviors (such as talk) systematically relate. The relationship of goals to discourse cannot, in any case, be captured in any simple formulation, particularly given that discourse is rightly characterized as an active, thoroughly constitutive medium (Fowler, 1985) that is likely to subvert pre-existent goals and to impose as much as to fulfil a goal agenda.

This chapter offers an investigation of the role of goals in an underinvestigated domain of discourse: talk between the generations. Specifically, we examine interactions involving elderly and young-middle-aged females in an audio-/video-recorded corpus. Through quantitative and qualitative analyses, we hope to demonstrate that the goals of the two generation groups involved are quite different but compatible and complementary (*consonant,* in our title), at least in terms of procedural/sequential aspects of talk. We consider the extent of fit between particular apparent priorities for talk across the groups, and we show how the groups align to each other and, indeed, to themselves in the devices and processes they employ in negotiating talk in this context. Then, a second, evaluative group-discussion corpus is introduced, which forces a reappraisal of the "good fit" interpretation of the interactive data. Procedural goals appear, from this second analysis, to have been formulated as part of a network of stereotypically driven beliefs that young people (at least in our data) hold about the elderly, their circumstances, and interactional/other needs. We interpret these later findings as evidence of intergenerational *non*-alignment and comment on its likely implications, assuming that the data are generalizable to at least one set of recurring patterns of intergenerational exchange. First, we briefly outline alternative possible perspectives on the relationships between goals and discourse.

PERSPECTIVES ON DISCOURSE GOALS

We recognize goals to differ, first, as to their *focus* and, second, as to their *scope.* Only when we have established how individual goals might, at least in theory, be delimited can we come on to consider the complexities of goal multiplicity in action (Street & Cappella, 1985).

Theorists have recognized a broad distinction between goals that are directed at or focused on the individual—goals of self-identity or of "being"—as opposed to those that are focused on the environment—instrumental goals (cf. McQuail, 1987). If we recognize "communicating others" as an independent dimension of "the environment," we arrive at a marginally more adequate but still gross three-way classification of goal focus: identity goals, relational goals, and instrumental goals (directly paralleled by Graham, Argyle, & Furnham's [1980] analytic structure).

These simple initial distinctions are useful to our chapter, in that they allow us to specify that our present analysis of intergenerational talk begins by inferring one set of instrumental goals—goals for the procedural management of cross-generation talk—but then seeks to explain how such goals are linked to underlying knowledge structures associated with identity and relational goals, particularly as formulated by young people in respect of the elderly. Therefore, whereas previous models have construed goals exclusively and narrowly as intra- or inter-individually oriented processes, we also critically distinguish identity goals in respect of communicators acting in terms of either their own *personal* capacities or their memberships of *social* categories salient to them and others in context. In the following analyses, it is this *intergroup* perspective (e.g., Gudykunst, 1986; Tajfel & Turner, 1979) that accesses the possibility of conflict underlying apparently compatible procedural goals.

Goals may find widely varying *scope,* in that they relate to either highly restricted, local interactional concerns or, at the other extreme, to highly frequent, general, and even pervasive concerns (Pervin, 1986) well beyond specific contexts of talk. Along this continuum, at least three[1] levels may be distinguished (cf. again Harré et al.'s [1985] tripartite structuring of human social "projects for action"). It is clear that goals may be formulated in relation to individual speech acts and/or "moves" (in the terminology of Sinclair & Coulthard, 1975). Speech–act theory (Searle, 1969, 1979) is built around the observation that utterances in context can be designated as fulfilling, directly or indirectly, local communicative functions in talk. If we take this to be (often but not inevitably) purposeful, we can locate spoken interaction as structured sequences of local goals: an utterance may be designed to make a claim, to challenge a viewpoint, to congratulate, to rebuke, to praise, and so on. In the ebb and flow of interaction, the pragmatic force of individual acts is negotiable and, to a significant extent, contextually determined (Levinson, 1983); so we need to expect goals at this level to be partially represented and often emergent in talk (cf. Hopper & Drummond, in press) rather than prepackaged and fulfilled through talk.

Goals may, at a higher level, be construed as plans for whole social episodes or encounters (see Berger & Bell, 1988): larger scale designs to win an argument, to provide or to gain social support, or to enhance esteem. This is the level at which goals can be apparently specified and objectified most clearly and most exclusively. But, even here, we must recognize that talk is very rarely interpretable as "the fulfilment of" such a goal. Preceding remarks about goal focus suggest that instrumental goals will often be set alongside identity goals and that what we may construe as "the" goal for an encounter necessitates strategic operations, conflicts, and compromises at multiple levels (Street & Cappella, 1985).

At the "highest" level, the term *goal* comes to embrace notions of more

---

[1]At the most microlevel, linguists working with systemic models (cf. Halliday, 1973) argue that language organizes its meanings in three simultaneous dimensions: ideational, interpersonal, and textual, which combine in the construction of clauses. But it is not clear whether the notion of "goal" is applicable at this level of analysis, even though Halliday and associates see linguistic structure as directly reflecting the social purposes to which language is put: linguistic meaning is an extension of the "social semiotic" (Halliday, 1978). Systemicists could, therefore, argue that language use is intrinsically the interrelationship of ideational (or referential or propositional) meanings with interpersonal/relational and textual/sequential frames. Still, the notion of goal is probably better reserved for more focused and more particular outcomes than the Hallidayan clause-level approach is concerned with (but see Ventola, 1987, for an extension of Halliday's theoretical concepts to more macrocontextual dimensions).

enduring socioemotional needs and priorities—some more amenable than others to being delimited and explicitly articulated. (For some, lifetime ambitions may be represented as a discrete set of aspirations; others may hold, no less fervently, a far more amorphous conglomeration of, say, face wants.) In the identity dimension, communicative interaction as a whole needs to be seen as the fulfillment or nonfulfillment of goals that are fundamental to who we are and how we construe and relate to others and to our environments. Group-level processes relating to *social* identity are, again, salient here, as in the work of theorists who see communication as the realization of the prevailing sociostructural circumstances and cultural contexts at hand.[2] It is important, therefore, to allow group-predispositions, preferences, and representations, which may, again, not be articulated explicitly or even represented consciously, into our analyses of discourse goals. For example, in the analyses of elderly self-disclosure that follow, we consider how managing "elderliness" itself establishes a goal agenda for older conversationalists and how construals of old age mediate young people's priorities when evaluating and, perhaps, participating in such discourses.

From the preceding overview, it is apparent that goals inevitably enter the analysis of talk in context and that goal multiplicity is the norm and, indeed, an inevitable quality of talk. Moreover, we should expect goals to be arranged hierarchically (cf. Hawkins & Daly, 1988), with highest level goals often exerting influence over—or, at least, providing a context for—lower level goals "nested" within them, showing either more or less consonance. That said, we should also anticipate influence in the other direction during interaction, with local goals triggering or making salient high-level goals (e.g., for group-identity maintenance or modification).

INTERGENERATIONAL GOAL CONSONANCE

Although they are severely underrepresented in the language and communication literatures, the elderly are an identifiable (although, of course, internally differentiated) social and cultural group (Coupland, Coupland, & Giles, in press; Giles & Coupland, in press). Different traditions of linguistic research have begun

---

[2]The seminal (though empirically discredited) work of Bernstein (1971–1975) established talk as "a quality of the social organization," such that the diverse "coding orientations" of social groups were seen as focal processes in cultural reproduction. Although recent research in Bernstein's particular domain (social class relations in British society) has often distanced itself from his work, his theoretical position has been widely adopted elsewhere (cf. Atkinson, 1985). The language and gender domain, for example, now conventionally argues that female and male communicative styles both determine and are determined by their respective sociostructural positions (Coates, 1986; Maltz & Borker, 1982).

to identify the distinctive characteristics of elderly and (old) age-related speech and language (see Coupland & Coupland, 1990, for a review). At least as important is the emerging finding that talk between the generations has characteristic configurations, that young-to-elderly and elderly-to-young talk can, to an extent, be modeled in terms of recurring generational strategies, sometimes driven by stereotypical formulations of old age and, for that matter, of youth (cf. N. Coupland, J. Coupland, Giles, & Henwood, 1988). The perspective we are developing in our own research is to view intergenerational talk as a forum for the enactment and consolidation of generational beliefs (Giles, Coupland, & Wiemann, in press), attitudes, goals, and aspirations and the occasion of social evaluations and attributions that are significant components of age-groups' identities. Here, we concentrate in particular on elderly and young strategies in the management of self-disclosure of "painful" personal experiences and misfortunes.

We can demonstrate the high degree of fit that can be achieved between elderly and young discourse goals by reviewing analyses of "painful self-disclosure" (PSD) sequences in an interactive data set. This is a corpus of 40 videotaped interactions where pairs of volunteer subjects, women aged 70–87 and 30–40 years, were asked to "get to know one another." Participants,[3] who had never met previously, were given no further instructions and were left alone, knowing that they were being video-recorded, for 8 minutes. The elderly women, most with (grossly characterized) upper-working-class backgrounds, were members of two day centers (nonresidential social centers) in Cardiff, Wales; most lived alone and were widowed. The young women were mostly lower-middle-class and married and were recruited through an advertisement in a local newspaper. Twenty of the dyads were intergenerational (young–old); 10 were peer-young; and 10 were peer-elderly. According to the study design, therefore, each subject participated in two interactions, one within- and one across-generation.

As reported in detail in J. Coupland, N. Coupland, Giles, and Wiemann (1988), we identified all PSD sequences in the data according to a predetermined schema of topic categories: reported bereavement, severe ill health, immobility, loneliness, disengagement, and an assortment of family, financial, and social troubles. All sequences were transcribed (using notation developed from that of Jefferson, as summarized in Atkinson & Heritage, 1984). Of course, we can make no claims as to the intrinsic or actual "painfulness" of the states and events being disclosed, and we use the term PSD as a convenient gloss.

The interactive study (see N. Coupland, J. Coupland, Giles, Henwood, & Wiemann, 1988 for a detailed distributional account) revealed clear genera-

---

[3]Interactions in this corpus are referenced with an "I" prefix to a two-digit number: I01–I40. Participants in these interactions are identified with either "E" (elderly) or "Y" (young) prefixes to two-figure digits: E01–E20; Y01–Y20.

tional differences in amounts of painful self-disclosure. In summary, PSD in the defined sense occurs in 32 of the 40 encounters and accounts for highly variable proportions (between 1% and 57%) of speaking time in each (mean = 13.7%). In these gross distributional terms, PSD is a major component of encounters involving at least one elderly participant, where it occupies far more time (approximately 16%) than in peer-young encounters (approximately 6%). Half of the peer-young encounters, but only 10% of the encounters involving at least one elderly participant, have no PSD. Furthermore, in the cross-generation encounters, almost the whole of PSD is talk about the elderly's (and not the young's) painful experiences. Elderly speakers in the data engage in PSD to roughly equal extents across peer and intergenerational contexts. These findings seem to support the general observation that the elderly speakers in our data are behaving significantly more "disclosively" than the younger women. The distributional evidence suggests the operation of differential goals vis-à-vis self-disclosure, although we need to specify this claim through much more detailed attention to the contextualization of elderly PSD.

Some relevant findings emerge from the analysis of pre-contexts to painful self-disclosures in the data. It is apparent that elderly disclosers here do play a major role in determining their own disclosing. This may seem almost tautological, though our taxonomy of alternative pre-contextual types in the data shows that PSDs can also be triggered by recipients' eliciting behaviors. Again, they can be, in a sense, self-generating, triggered by previous textual happenings with no apparent will on the part of participants to either elicit PSD or to disclose. In fact, more than half the PSDs in the data (53%) are determined interactionally by disclosers themselves rather than being directly or indirectly elicited (26%) or being textually generated (20%). The elderly are responsible for determining slightly more than half the total of PSDs, whether conversing with younger (53%) or older (59%) speakers. The observation that the elderly are behaving "disclosively" is, therefore, supported in the more particular sense of showing a will to disclose in designing their talk, at least to a significant extent, as PSD.

On the other hand, we see it as highly significant that the young participants also *elicit* PSD from their elderly interlocutors to a considerable extent—34% of instances, contrasting with elderly speakers eliciting only 12% of instances from their peers. We take this to be evidence of the young sharing responsibility for the engendering of elderly PSD. The two processes (elderly disclosure and young elicitation) are, of course, not in competition. The young's eliciting role will require particular disclosive acts but, more generally, will legitimize elderly disclosive behavior; conversely, elderly disclosure will establish interactional norms that legitimize eliciting behavior.

This pattern of complementarity does not, however, mean that the younger group's goal here is purely to accommodate the elderly's wishes or norms established in particular interactions. A qualitative focus is revealing. The data contain instances of young women's eliciting behaviors that presuppose interrogatory rights they would certainly not have in peer-young conversations (and which may not, of course, be endorsed by particular elderly conversationalists, either). On one occasion (see N. Coupland, J. Coupland, Giles, Henwood, & Wiemann, 1988), a young speaker (Y10) asks, "Is your husband still alive?" (in a context where there is no on-going PSD talk). Y06 asks E06, "Do you sleep alright when you get to bed?" when previous talk has been on the general theme of reading habits. These are surely intrusive questions in first-encounter conversations, even though we have no access to recipients' (the disclosers-to-be) own evaluations of them. Such questions impose obligations upon elderly interlocutors either to disclose or to prevaricate. Less direct elicitations—questioning strategies that give rise to PSDs less predictably—can also enable painful self-disclosures. When Y11 asks her elderly interlocutor, "Where are your family living now? Are they all fairly close to you or are you quite spread out?", she taps an area of experience that is reported as a "painful" experience. Even indirect elicitation acts can, therefore, be seen as potential threats to the equilibrium of discourse—and threats that are often tolerated by young elicitors.

The younger women, as recipients, show a clear tendency to attune their responses to elderly PSD in respect of the particularities of the on-going disclosure. They signal interest and engagement and thereby often sustain PSD, both in particular and in general terms. Although several options are open to them as makers of next moves to PSD, the young women rarely have recourse to the expression of such shared experiences and, of course, never to generational in-group experiences. Signaling surprise at an elderly PSD, for example, which itself demonstrates engagement with the particular topic being revealed, is a frequent young recipients' next move. If we assume that elderly disclosers of painful experience are disclosing at least partly because of the need for interactive engagement (and the benefits to identity this, in turn, brings), recipient surprise is a valuable endorsement of the newsworthiness of the telling. If the telling is somehow cathartic, surprise is presumably therapeutic.[4]

Extract 1 (from I06)

1 E03 (sighing) and um anyway they had a house then in Bristol (.)

2 Bristol (.) had their own house there (.) but things didn't

3 seem to go (1.0) very well you know (1.0) and er (.) one day

4 he came home (.) and he said um (.) she's gone (2.0) with

---

[4]For similar patterns in the management of age-identity marking and age-disclosure processes in intergenerational talk, see (respectively) J. Coupland, N. Coupland, Giles, and Henwood (in press) and N. Coupland, J. Coupland, and Giles (1989).

5   two little kids ((and))
                    [   ]

6 Y03   (quietly) oh dear and how <u>old</u> were <u>they?</u>

7 E03   well the one was in his arms she he was about um twelve months old
                                                        [

8 Y03   she left

9   the children? she left the ch
                    [   ]

10 E03   yes

11 E03 twelve month old

12 Y03 mm

13 E03 and the little the little girl was (.) four and a half
                                                [

14 Y03   good

15   heavens above and <u>where</u> did she go?

16 E03 she went back home to her mother =

17 Y03   = (tutting) oh dear <u>left</u> the children

In Extract 1, Y03's high-rise intonation contour on the last two syllables of "She left the children?" (lines 8–9), as well as her "Good heavens above!" (lines 14–15) are part of an extensive repertoire of sustaining and attuning recipient moves that the young employ. Sympathy is encoded, either verbally (e.g., "oh, dear" . . . "oh, that's a shame" . . . etc.) or prosodically and facially/posturally at appropriate points. Sometimes, the affective signal is focused on particular items of content, isolated through reformulation of the painful event just disclosed (e.g., in Extract 1, [tutting] "Oh dear left the children" [line 17]) or through explicit evaluative glosses (e.g., in an earlier sequence, "Oh that couldn't have been easy."). Initiations maintaining the topic of an ongoing PSD are also common as young next moves. In Extract 1, "and how old were they?" (line 6) and "and where did she go?" (line 15) explicitly require the teller to elaborate the content of her PSD. There are very many further instances in other interactions, some of which are "Is he still there [in a mental institution]?" (I06) and "How long ago were you widowed?" (I21).

Overall, the various contributions we have shown the young participants making to elderly partners justify labeling them as "facilitators" (Holmes, 1984), particularly of elderly PSD. Their quite frequent role in eliciting PSD runs contrary to what Berger and Bradac (1982) supposed is normative for interrogative behavior among new acquaintances; these authors concluded that "it appears that interrogative strategies which are impersonal, i.e. non-intimate and de-individuated, are more acceptable initially than are highly personal strategies" (p. 82). Moreover, our data deny Berger and Bradac's (1982) subsequent claim that "highly personal internally-focused strategies are likely to inhibit self-revelation" (p. 82). This is not the case when our elderly speakers are questioned on aspects of their personal well-being and experience.

In their major function in supporting on-going PSDs, the young in our data generally fulfill the role that Coates (1986, p. 115) and others have considered prototypically female in intersex encounters, providing, above all, solidarity and support to interlocutors. In the sex-roles literature, this conversational orientation has been considered a powerless role, although we are reticent to classify the young as globally powerless in relation to the elderly here. Although, in terms of amounts of talk and personal focus, the elderly do very clearly dominate, the young are equally clearly dominant in the domain of discourse management, through their eliciting behavior. The relational character of our intergenerational data is very much that of interviews (in the "talk show" mold, not selectional interviews), with the young enabling and sustaining extended spoken performances by the elderly.

PROBLEMATICALITY

At this point, we need to address the question of *why* young women generally adopt such a facilitative orientation to elderly PSD, when there seems to be an intrinsically "painful" element, at least in potential, not only to the telling but also to the *receiving* of negatively valenced, intimate self-disclosures among new acquaintances. There are grounds for predicting that recipiency to elderly PSD is problematical to the young, along one or more of several dimensions. In Brown and Levinson's (1987) terms, painful self-disclosure predictably threatens a recipient's negative face: her rights to unviolated personal space. Simultaneously, the discloser exposes her own positive face (her desire to be approved of/thought well of) by indulging in counternormative self-disclosive behavior (Berger & Bradac, 1982).

At the most basic level, the emotional loading of many of the disclosures we have considered painful inevitably intrudes on recipients' negative face rights, particularly given that our data are first encounters between strangers. Beyond this, young recipients of elderly PSD are forced into selecting among response options, *all* of which bear potential face threats in their own right. If a recipient discourages on-going painful disclosure (perhaps by selecting a pre-closing move or shifting topic onto nonpainful self- or other-topics), there is an immediate threat to her positive face. The discloser may find such recipient response strategies underaccommodative (cf. J. Coupland et al., 1988), socially or even morally deficient: The discloser thinks that the recipient is not resourceful or courageous enough to be recipient of PSD and, incidentally, not as courageous in this respect as the discloser herself is being in threatening her own face through disclosure. If a recipient chooses the options that encourage disclosure (e.g., through eliciting further information or through supportive back-channeling in the manner we have seen the young most typically employ), she accepts the prospective threat to her own negative face: She may have her emotional space invaded once again and possibly to a greater extent. And, of course, there will be a recurring positive face threat in the need to encode further responses.

The preceding represents, at least from a theoretical perspective, a potentially intractable accommodative dilemma (cf. Giles, Coupland, & Coupland, in press). It would not be surprising if the competing considerations of face resulted in *no* desirable—or even tolerable—response suggesting itself to some recipients on occasions. The lack of relevant shared experience we have pointed to compounds this problem, removing the potential for group-solidarity marking that is a perennially available referent for the elderly. It is, therefore, most surprising how rarely the flow of discourse reflects these problems we have projected for recipients.

Extract 2 (from I18)

1 E08   =because when I was a widow you see after eleven years

2   I had three little children you see to bring up I worked
                                    [   ]

3 Y09   mm

4 E08   very hard I done everything <u>cook</u> er parlourmaid <u>every</u>thing

5   I done

6 Y09   mhm

7 E08   well I had to get a living you see=

8 Y09   =oh yes yes (1.0) mm (2.0) oh well (3.0) um (.) I was going

9   to say I'm I've started working again I've got a little

10   daughter and I've just started back to work

A sequence such as the one in Extract 2 suggests that the young recipient (Y09) does experience problems in maintaining the flow of talk. However, the young population in our data seems highly socially skilled in this respect, inasmuch as such instances are very rare. We have little textual evidence of problematicality, therefore, although certain recipient responses to disclosures do seem to suffer an intrinsic inadequacy that we suspect is perceived by recipients themselves (cf. Taylor & Simard's [1975] objective–vs.–subjective criteria for communicational efficiency in interethnic encounters). In I40, the elderly interlocutor (E20) has said she has been widowed for 21 years and now attends a day center. Y20 offers what might be called a "contextualization" move, "So this is really good for you isn't it then to be able to go somewhere like this." The contextualization, even if it is, in itself, appropriate, makes unwarranted assumptions about the elderly interlocutor's particular circumstances and needs. Appreciating this (if she does) will be uncomfortable for the young recipient, who is nevertheless trying to reinterpret disclosed information in a positive light: to "look on the bright side" (cf. Jefferson, 1984, who noted from her own data [p. 363] the propensity of recipients of troubles talk—who are young in our terms—to propound overly optimistic responses).

At this point in the argument, then, we have no coherent explanation for the young women's tolerating of (and, from quantitative and qualitative evidence, their goal of generating) interactional sequences that carry threats to both participants. On the expectation that the answer is to be found at the level of group-predispositions and beliefs, we turn now to the second data-set, the evaluative study, as a basis for further analysis.

INTERGENERATIONAL DISSONANCE

The second data set was gathered as an attempt to expose some of the attributional and evaluative processes that might underlie the strategies of PSD management and recipiency already witnessed (N. Coupland, Henwood, J. Coupland, & Giles, 1990). An evaluative follow-up study was designed in which young women, very similar in age and background to the younger group in the interactive study, listened to 16 diverse audio extracts (each approximately 30 sec. long) chosen from intergenerational encounters in the videotaped study. Details of the design and procedures used in the interactive study were made clear to the groups of listeners before they heard the extracts. Nine of these were from PSD sequences, chosen to represent variously contextualized and developed painful disclosures on topics of ill health, bereavement, and loneliness. The remaining seven were randomly chosen from "nonpainful" sequences of elderly disclosure, including some clearly positive reports (talking proudly about children and grandchildren or current social activities) and some expressions of dissatisfaction or of current difficult (but still not "painful," in our defined sense) circumstances. The listeners were asked to imagine themselves in the roles of the younger women they heard on tape and to describe their thoughts and feelings, what influenced them most, and what was most problematical for them as (supposedly) the younger persons involved. A set of prepared questions was used as a preamble to free discussion on these issues among small groups of women about the extracts they had heard as well as on the theme of elderly PSD in general. Discussions in 11 groups (involving a total of 43 women) were audio-recorded and transcribed.[5]

The follow-up study does not give direct access to motivational and evaluative processes at work in the interactive study. The probable experiential gaps between the young individuals in the two studies, the immediate versus the reflective contexts, the dyad versus the group contexts, and the predictable face considerations in the young evaluators' public presentations of their apparent reactions to the PSD stimuli all conspire to preclude this. Rather, we contend that discourse on the theme of elderly PSD is amenable to analyses not different in kind from those employed in the original study. Although confidence in the overtly simple judgments expressed in the group discussions would be unwarranted, a further interpretive analysis can give a sense of the kinds of attributions of elderly self-disclosure available to young people in either accepting or denying its problematical nature. We are interested in how beliefs and goals vis-à-vis older people are represented in a specific context of talk and, possibly, consolidated and constructed discursively. The group discussions as constituted would arguably predispose specifically intergroup formulations, giving us access to how generational stereotypes can mediate responses to and plans for intergenerational talk. Also, the real-time, reflective evaluative process that we would be tapping into might itself be crucial to the formation and perpetuation of intergroup attitudes.

The preceding discussion has raised the possibility that PSD recipiency may be problematical in several overlapping dimensions. Most generally, we have argued that PSD in the context of our interactive study will impose some affective load upon recipients, who may experience discomfort or embarrassment, frustration or, perhaps, even boredom. The discourse analyses showed little evidence of procedural or sequential difficulty, which we would take to be represented by recipients showing difficulty in finding any plausible next move to PSD. Again, we hypothesized that the accommodative dilemma of responding to PSD might constitute a strategic difficulty; A next move may be found, but it would fail to satisfy recipients' own appraisal of what would constitute a desirable or, at least, adequate strategy at that point in the discourse. In our explorations of the evaluative group-discussion data, we were initially interested in whether participants would overtly recognize problems along any dimension(s) to be associated with PSD recipiency and, if so, which.

In fact, such recognition of specific problems directly associated with re-

---

[5]Participants in the group discussions are referenced by pairs of (fictitious) initials. "R" refers to the researcher leading the discussion groups. Individual group discussions are identified with the prefix "GD."

ceiving PSD is uncommon. There are certainly references to procedural difficulties, but only very rarely of the sort anticipated. VB in DG6 and D8 in DG10 do
comment on the limited range of options open to recipients of PSD by observing
that there is often no option but to give sympathy or to change the subject (which
is itself acknowledged to be difficult to achieve). More often, experienced
procedural problems are said to take the form of expressed dissatisfaction with
the recipient roles of the elderly speakers in the extracts, that they were
interrupting and inattentive listeners (see, e.g., Extracts 3 and 4).

Extract 3 (from DG6)

line

1 R   what was it about the snippets of conversation that you found

2   the most problematic?

3 VB um (.) the fact that the the older person interrupted you all

4   the time (.) whatever you
                    [   ]

5 R   mhm

6 VB you said (.) she wasn't really listening (.) she had her own

7   mind her own thoughts and she was just preparing the next thing

8   she was going to tell you didn't really listen to the question

Extract 4 (from DG7)

line

1 HC oh when they didn't stop and listen to you and they just sort

2   of carried on with what they were saying all the time when you

3   were trying to say something and they would just . . . continue and

4   sort of butt in before you'd finished your question completely
                                        [   ]

5 DR   yeah
                                        [

6 R   yeah

7 HC taking it on to a different tack um that's difficult

Several other discussants raise the problem of powerlessness, that is, being unable to control the developments of topics or themes in intergenerational conversation. PE and GR (in DG4) suggest that sudden changes of topic (as when an elderly speaker in the stimulus recordings chains a PSD on the subject of an abdominal rupture to one on her failing eyesight) are difficult to respond to. HC in DG7 comments that "It is hard to get a conversation to where you want it to go" with older people.

There is, of course, an *affective* dimension to each of the preceding procedurally focused complaints, but specific affective consequences are mentioned very rarely. RT in DG10 responds to a disclosure on loneliness as follows: "She just came across as if she wanted to moan to somebody and that was really embarrassing." RT and KM, in the same discussion, ascribe this to a conscious intent on the part of some elderly people: They are "trying to make you feel sorry for them in some way." But most recognition of the affective impact of PSD is generalized into a discourse of sadness and sympathy for elderly people, living and having lived difficult lives. Extract 5, for example, sees LJ expressing a global response to the condition of being elderly.

Extract 5 (from DG10)

line

1 R   right (.) what . . . did you find influenced you most?

2 LJ   . . . um (1.0) you know if they're having problems with health

3   and this sort of thing then it affects you I think very

4   definitely it does to me anyway (.) um (.) if they're feeling

5   lonely and depressed then that oh that hurts me very strongly
                                                [   ]

6 R   mm

7 R   is there was there a particular snippet there that you . . . can

8   remember in that respect?

9 LJ   um (2.0) I think . . . the emphysema one I think really went home

10   (.) that one um (1.0) and oh the very lonely people (.) I think

11   there were a couple of those who were very very lonely (1.0)

12   I felt sorry for those because you then think of people who are

13   in that situation um and there must be thousands of people like

14   that all over (.) the world

The invocation of the social group ("thousands of people like that all over the world," lines 13–14) appears to mitigate any experience of problems in relation to PSD in particular and, of course, in relation to the particular instances of PSD in the stimulus material. In the group discussions, recognition of problematical elderly life circumstances regularly works to *deny* problems of PSD recipiency (the issue that the researcher was attempting to explore quite systematically in the evaluative study). This process of contextualization is apparent in Extract 6.

Extract 6 (from DG6)

line

1 R   was it just the . . . bereavement that you found might have been

2   difficult to respond to or was there anything else?

3 PE   well no just the general situation of old age . . . I mean it just

4   seems to me that old age is very often a sad situation and I

5   don't think there is an awful lot can be done about it
                     [

6 MS   I didn't find

7   it difficult
     [

8 ML   no

9 PE   I mean I didn't find it difficult either but I think that's the

10   situation it's it's you just accept that I mean when you're

11   talking to old people
     [

12 MS   they like to talk about their husband who passed away seven

13   years ago
     [

14 PE   yes I agree
     [

15 ML   yes

16 MS   they like to have a chat about it

17 ML   yes it's lovely it's yes yes and if you listen
                     [   ]

18 MS   yes

19 ML I mean you don't have to say anything

                             [   ]

20 MS   no

21 ML just let them unburden

In answer to R's question, PE observes that "old age is often a fairly sad situation" (line 4) and that little can be done about it. MS interjects to deny that she finds PSD "difficult" (lines 6–7), and PE seems to feel the need to match MS's denial and redress her earlier statement to some extent. ML even maintains that it is "lovely" (line 17)—to listen to old people talking about lost loved ones— which appears to transform the suggestion of problematical recipiency into satisfaction at some sort of altruistic—perhaps therapeutic—involvement. The discussion at this point works in various ways to deny what we have seen as the essence of PSD talk. It is now glossed as the elderly having "a chat about it," and "liking" to engage in such talk (line 16): An image of talk that is both enjoyable and superficial is constructed in the discussion discourse. Problematicality is subverted to the extent that ML claims "I mean you don't have to say anything" (line 19): Recipients are implied to be free from any significant involvement.

For some discussants, the very generality of what they perceive as undesirable elderly behaviors in talk is used to downgrade the degree of problematicality they cause. In Extract 7 (following), for EB and RW, it is the fact of "those" [modes of talk] being "routine" (lines 7–8) that leads to their view that PSD in not problematic for them as listeners. This is a perplexing claim, until it is made clear by both RW and MC that they accept that elderly PSD is routinely unfounded. Their ageist suggestion is that "you have to take it with . . . a pinch of salt" (lines 19–20) and that some elderly "play for sympathy" (line 23). MC finally invokes the classic inverted-U stereotype of the old as children (cf. Coupland & Coupland, 1990).

Extract 7 (from DG5)

line

1 R is there anyone here who feels that (.) um me asking the question

2 what was problematic doesn't doesn't really resonate with how

3 they felt does anyone feel (.) that they didn't find (.) the ext

4 responding to the snippets snippets of conversation problematic?

5 (1.5)

6 EB on the whole no=

7 RW   =on the whole no because one's come across those before
            [   ]   [   ]

8 EB   routine

9 NL   yes
                                                              [

10 EB   one's come

11   across those before . . .

12 RW well I've got a granny of eighty-five who's continually saying

13   she's lonely she's not lonely at all because there's a visitor
            [   ]

14 R   yes

15 RW just about every hour of the day into the house
                                                   [

16 R   mhm

17 RW but she says she's lonely and nobody comes to visit her
                                                       [

18 R   mhm

19 RW and in some respects you have to take it with a little bit of a

20   pinch of salt=

21 R   =mhm

22 RW um (.) what people say

23 MC yes they play for sympathy they're very much like some some

24   elderly people are very much like young children they want

25   to be the center of attention for as long as possible

A discourse of elderly stereotyping[6] is, in fact, structurally integrated into other patterns of argumentation in the group discussions. Stereotyping here operates at different levels of inclusiveness, with both categorical and less

---

[6]Stereotypes of old age have been widely researched (cf. Braithwaite, 1986; Branco & Williamson, 1982; Brubaker & Powers, 1976; McTavish, 1971; Rosencrantz & McNevin, 1969; Sigall & Page, 1971). The discourse analytic perspective we are adopting here does not mesh well with these predominantly experimental and questionnaire-based studies. They have, for example, tended to use a restricted set of descriptive labels that do not relate easily to ascriptions of the elderly made by particular groups in contexts. See Henwood, Coupland, Coupland, and Giles (1990) for an extended discussion of different traditions of stereotype research and of elderly stereotyping processes in the present evaluative data set.

inclusive characterizations (cf. Henwood, 1987) of the elderly. We find labels such as "cantankerous" (GD in DG3), "depressing" and "moaning" (HP in DG3), "boring" (ML in DG3), "selfish" (KM in DG10), and "rambling" or "rattling on" in conversation (EK in DG5; KM in DG10). Such stereotypical ascriptions are, however, often counterbalanced by less pejorative themes, such as the discourse of sadness and sympathy for old people that we refered to previously. Discussants will often focus on exceptions to stereotype conformity, thereby apparently legitimizing their negative ascriptions to the out-group. In GD4, NL says, "It can be a b rather boring to be with an old person for any length of time and a bit frustrating and you feel a bit resentful of the time you have to spend . . . it's the sort of duty thing." She then immediately restricts the scope of her observations with "It's an exceptional person that makes you feel like that," and the more positive global view is bolstered by another participant's (HP's) contribution that "some of the conversations [in the stimulus material] were quite buoyant . . . it was an elated sort of conversation." Pejoration seems to be in turn enabled by this up-swing; HP adds "but some were very downcasting very sort of moaning type conversations."

The ebb and flow of stereotyping and counterstereotyping in the discussion data seems to reflect a normative constraint, in public discourse in a liberal democracy, that naked categorical assertions about social groups are undesirable. We are prepared to construe a good deal of the more positive ascriptions within the stereotyping talk as a *veneer* of tolerance and liberal sentiment over some generally endorsed beliefs about the elderly as undesirable interactional partners and problematical conversationalists. Of course, as we noted earlier, their actual beliefs are not open to analysis. What seems most significant in the group-discussion data is the readiness with which young discussants appeal to group formulations—positive, negative, or both—in the context of questioning about particular sequences of PSD. The pervasive denial of specific problems associated with PSD recipiency is achieved only through adopting the broader perspective. Such problems (as *we* construed them) are either dissolved into highly general, recognized inadequacies of intergenerational talk or are reduced to an irrelevance by comparison with considerations of the elderly's problematical lives. Either way, the availability of group-salient, stereotypical formulations of old people intervene crucially in what we originally conceived as an exercise of evaluation and response.

OVERVIEW

Intergenerational PSD sequences in conversation can reasonably be seen to constitute an interactional routine (cf. Coulmas, 1981) that is substantially enabled and supported by disclosers and recipients alike. We infer that PSD reflects complementary instrumental goals for cross-generation talk, realized by complementary sociolinguistic behaviors of the sort we have considered. If young and old contributions to PSD discourse reflect "prefabricated" goal structures or communicative sets, an important element of this prefabrication can be traced to underlying identity and relational goals, that we believe are attested in the evaluative data we have discussed: namely, goals that young people hold vis-à-vis the "treatment" of the elderly as a social group. The high degree of instrumental goal-consonance for procedural aspects of talk is, we argue, facilitated by stereotype-consistent beliefs that young people hold about elderly identity and the possibilities and priorities for talk with the old. It is also easy to see, however, the very complementarity of discursive behaviors confirming cross-generational goals and beliefs, which thereby come or continue to be seen as "the way things predictably are."

Future research, while also attending to individual variability, gender, socio-economic, and cultural diversities, could very valuably explore the ways in which elderly groups themselves (and preferably, of course, in situ) rationalize cross-generation encounters and draw out the stereotypes that *they too* doubtless invoke. Without these new data, there is certainly a risk of an unbalanced perspective that arguably takes the elderly, but not the young, discursive strategies at face value. Nevertheless, we feel that the chapter has shown how the recipiency role of the young in respect of intergenerational PSD is, ultimately, highly ambiguous. As we have shown, recipients do a substantial amount of work to bring about interactional patterns that ultimately distance them from their interlocutors. Goal consonance that is apparent in patterns of elderly self-disclosure and young elicitation, mutual tolerance of counternormative and face-threatening intimacy, and the young's repertoire of sustaining and supporting moves may be possible only because young people often access, as well as construct, such negative identities for the old as depressed and depressing and as dull, grouchy, and unreliable conversationalists. Good procedural fit belies complex group-evaluative processes, which are a barrier to healthy cross-generation relations. Perceived "problems" in talk, which seem (to us) to be an inevitable consequence of intimate self-disclosing to strangers, are contextualized and even denied through the establishment of particular (and apparently lower) expectations of interaction with elderly people. Talking to the old is perceived as a time-consuming duty and a necessary therapy rather than as relational development and broadening.

We have witnessed the consolidation of these intergroup orientations and goals as real-time events in evaluative group discussions. The group discussions, where young women overtly rationalize elderly PSD in talk with their peers, may be representative of commonplace in-group discourses through which evaluations of intergroup experiences and goals for future involvement are established. Through this process of transformation, we see problems in one sense denied but in another sense perpetuated and consolidated. The ground is seemingly laid for new initiatives by recipients (in the same or in a later encounter) that guarantee the continuation of intergroup nonalignment. The young come to evaluate elderly PSD positively only through (and at the cost of) perceiving the elderly as a disenfranchised out-group needing special consideration. Recipiency to elderly PSD by the young is only to be regarded positively to the extent that intergenerational conversation is pseudoconsultation. The young seem to accept (in our data, often enthusiastically) their opportunity to make some sort of therapeutic intervention in the lives of the elderly. However appropriate this might be in particular cases, it nevertheless inevitably constrains the roles that older and younger adults can fulfill in intergenerational talk. The more general consequence is the imposition of a rigidly intergroup frame on talk between younger and older adults, which must perpetuate the social alienation that elders so often consider their greatest handicap.

ACKNOWLEDGMENT

The research on which this report is based has been supported by the Economic and Social Research Council (ESRC,UK), reference number G002220022.

REFERENCES

Atkinson, J. M., & Heritage, J. (Eds.), (1984). *Structures of social action: Studies in conversation analysis.* Cambridge, England: Cambridge University Press.

Atkinson, P. (1985). *Language, structure and reproduction: An introduction to the sociology of Basil Bernstein.* London: Methuen.

Berger, C. R., & Bell, R. A. (1988). Plans and the initiation of social relationships. *Human Communication Research, 15,* 217–235.

Berger, C. R., & Bradac, J. J. (1982). *Language and social knowledge.* London: Edward Arnold.

Bernstein, B. (1971–1975). *Class, codes and control (Vols. 1–3).* London: Routledge and Kegan Paul.

Braithwaite, V. A. (1986). Old age stereotypes: Reconciling contradictions. *Journal of Gerontology, 41,* 353–360.

Branco, K. J., & Williamson, J. B. (1982). Stereotyping and the life-cycle: Views of aging and the aged. In A. G. Miller (Ed.), *In the eye of the beholder: Contemporary issues in stereotyping* (pp. 364–410). New York: Praeger.

Brown, P., & Levinson, S. (1987). *Politeness: Some universals in language usage.* Cambridge, England: Cambridge University Press.

Brubaker, T. H., & Powers, E. A. (1976). The stereotype of "old": A review and alternative approach. *Journal of Gerontology, 31,* 441–447.

Cegala, D. J., Waldron, V. R., Ludlum, J., McCabe, B. Yost, S., & Teboul, B. (1988, March). *A study of interactants' thoughts and feelings during conversation.* Paper presented at the Ninth Annual Conference on Discourse Analysis, Philadelphia, PA.

Coates, J. (1986). *Women, men and language.* London: Longman.

Cody, M., & McLaughlin, M. (Eds.) (1990). *The psychology of tactical communication.* Clevedon:

Multilingual Matters Ltd.

Coulmas, F. (1981). *Conversational routine: Explorations in standardized communication situations and prepatterned speech.* The Hague: Mouton.

Coupland, J., Coupland, N., Giles, H., & Henwood, K. (in press). Formulating age: Dimensions of age-identity in elderly talk. *Discourse Processes.*

Coupland, J., Coupland, N., Giles, H., & Wiemann, J. (1988). My life in your hands: Processes of self-disclosure in intergenerational talk. In N. Coupland (Ed.), *Styles of discourse* (pp. 201–253). London: Croom Helm.

Coupland, N., & Coupland, J. (1990). Language and later life. In H. Giles & W. P. Robinson (Eds.), *The handbook of language and social psychology* (pp. 451–468). London: Wiley.

Coupland, N., Coupland, J., & Giles, H. (1989). Telling age in later life: Identity and face implications. *Text, 9,* 129–151.

Coupland, N., Coupland, J., & Giles, H. (in press). *Sociolinguistics and ageing.* Oxford: Blackwell.

Coupland, N., Coupland, J., Giles, H., & Henwood, K. (1988). Accommodating the elderly: Invoking and extending a theory. *Language in Society, 17,* 1–41.

Coupland, N., Coupland, J., Giles, H., Henwood, K., & Wiemann, J. (1988). Elderly self-disclosure: Interactional and intergroup issues. *Language and Communication, 8,* 109–133.

Coupland, N., Henwood, K., Coupland, J., & Giles, H. (1990). Accommodating troubles-talk: The young's management of elderly self-disclosure. In G. M. McGregor & R. White (Eds.), *Reception and response: Hearer creativity and the analysis of spoken and written texts.* (pp. 112–144) London: Croom Helm.

D'Andrade, R. (1987). A folk model of the mind. In D. Holland & N. Quinn (Eds.), *Cultural models in language and thought.* Cambridge: Cambridge University Press.

Fowler, R. (1985). Power. In T. van Dijk (Ed.), *Handbook of discourse analysis* (Vol. 4, pp. 61–83). London: Academic Press.

Giles, H., & Coupland, N. (in press). Language attitudes: Discursive, contextual and gerontological considerations. In A. G. Reynolds (Ed.), *McGill conference on bilingualism, multiculturalism, and second language learning: A tribute to Wallace E. Lambert.* Hillsdale, NJ: Lawrence Erlbaum Associates.

Giles, H., Coupland, N., & Coupland, J. (Eds.). (in press). *Contexts of accommodation: Developments in applied sociolinguistics.* Cambridge: Cambridge University Press.

Giles, H., Coupland, N., & Wiemann, J. M. (in press). "Talk is cheap . . ." but "My word is my bond": Beliefs about talk. In K. Bolton & H. Kwok (Eds.), *Sociolinguistics today: Eastern and Western perspectives.* London: Routledge.

Graham, J. A., Argyle, M., & Furnham, A. (1980). The goal structure of situations. *European Journal of Social Psychology, 10,* 345–366.

Gudykunst, W. B. (Ed.). (1986). *Intergroup communication.* London: Edward Arnold.

Halliday, M. A. K. (1973). *Explorations in the functions of language.* London: Edward Arnold.

Halliday, M. A. K. (1978). *Language as social semiotic.* London: Edward Arnold.

Harré, R., Clarke, D., & De Carlo, N. (1985). *Motives and mechanisms: An introduction to the psychology of action.* London: Methuen.

Hawkins, R. P., & Daly, J. (1988). Cognition and communication. In R. P. Hawkins, J. M. Wiemann, & S. Pingree (Eds.), *Advancing communication science: Merging mass and interpersonal processes.* (pp. 191–223). Newbury Park: Sage.

Henwood, K. L. (1987). *The social psychology of stereotypes: A critical assessment.* Unpublished doctoral Thesis, University of Bristol, England.

Henwood, K. L., Coupland, N., Coupland, J., & Giles, H. (1990). *Stereotypes and problematicality in talk about elderly self-disclosure.* Unpublished manuscript, University of Bristol, England.

Holmes, J. (1984). Hedging your bets and sitting on the fence: Some evidence for hedges as support structures. *Te Reo, 27,* 47–62.

Hopper, R., & Drummond, K. (in press). Goals and their emergence in a relationship turning point: The case of "Gordon and Denise". *Journal of Language and Social Psychology, 9.*

Jefferson, G. (1984). On the organization of laughter in talk about troubles. In J. Atkinson & J. Heritage (Eds.), *Structures of social action: Studies in conversation analysis* (pp. 346–369). Cambridge: Cambridge University Press.

Levinson, S. C. (1983). *Pragmatics.* Cambridge: Cambridge University Press.

Maltz, D. N., & Borker, R. A. (1982). A cultural approach to male–female miscommunication. In J. J. Gumperz (Ed.), *Language and social identity* (pp. 195–216). Cambridge: Cambridge University Press.

McQuail, D. (1987). Functions of communication: A nonfunctionalist overview. In S. H. Chaffee & C. R. Berger (Eds.), *Handbook of communication science* (pp. 327–349). Newbury Park, CA: Sage.

McTavish, D. G. (1971). Perceptions of old people: A review of research methodologies and findings. *The Gerontologist, 11,* 90–101.

Pervin, L. A. (1986). Personal and social determinants of behavior in situations. In A. Furnham (Ed.), *Social behavior in context* (pp. 81–102). Boston: Allyn & Bacon.

Rozencrantz, H. A., & McNevin, T. E. (1969). A factor analytic analysis of attitudes toward the aged. *The Gerontologist, 9,* 55–59.

Searle, J. (1969). *Speech acts.* Cambridge, England: Cambridge University Press.

Searle, J. (1979). *Expression and meaning.* Cambridge, England: Cambridge University Press.

Schank, R., & Abelson, R. (1977). *Scripts, plans, goals and understanding: An inquiry into human knowledge structures.* Hillsdale, NJ: Lawrence Erlbaum Associates.

Sigall, H., & Page, R. (1971). Current stereotypes: A little fading, a little faking. *Journal of Personality and Social Psychology, 18,* 247–255.

Sinclair, J. McH., & Coulthard, M. (1975). *Towards an analysis of discourse.* Oxford: Oxford University Press.

Street, R. L., Jr., & Cappella, J. N. (Eds.). (1985). *Sequence and pattern in communicative behavior.* London: Edward Arnold.

Tajfel, H., & Turner, J. C. (1979). An integrative theory of intergroup conflict. In W. C. Austin & S. Wotchel (Eds.), *The social psychology of intergroup relations* (pp. 33–53). Monterey, CA: Brooks/Cole.

Taylor, D. M., & Simard, L. (1975). Social interaction in a bilingual setting. *Canadian Psychological Review, 16,* 240–254.

Tracy, K. & Coupland, N. (Eds.). (in press). *Multiple goals in discourse.* Clevedon: Multilingual Matters. Also double special issue of *Journal of Language and Social Psychology.*

Ventola, E. (1987). *The structure of social interaction: A systemic approach to the semiotics of service encounters.* London: Frances Pinter.

Waldron, V. R., Cegala, D. J., Sharkey, W. F., & Teboul, B. (in press). Cognitive and tactical dimensions of conversational goal management. *Journal of Language and Social Psychology, 9.* in press.

CHAPTER 6
On Enacting Friendship and Interrogating Discourse

William K. Rawlins
Purdue University

Viable friendships, like all significant relationships, are ongoing communicative achievements, requiring interactively developed expressive and interpretive practices. As a broad category of interpersonal relationship in American culture, however, friendships are distinctively underdetermined by publicly recognized normative features. In contrast to the legal or religious sanctions and prescriptions for marriage, the economic contracts and specifications for professional partnerships and organizational relations, and the certifiable blood ties and expectations of kinship, the duties and rights of friendship are privately negotiated and voluntarily enacted.

Accordingly, whereas other primary relationships are socially grounded in factors that transcend the affected parties' actual communicative practices, the existence and persistence of friendship fundamentally derives from how the friends communicate and the extent to which their treatment of one another is mutually edifying. Although cross words and misunderstandings alone cannot dissolve a marriage, a business partnership, or a blood tie, volatile or unfortunate exchanges may be all that is necessary for two people to turn away from each other and no longer be friends. It is therefore a fragile and potentially capricious relationship.

The contextually negotiated essence of friendship means that given cases may assume a wide variety of social forms. Certain friendships are developed as ends in themselves and thrive on the opportunity for autonomy. Moreover, they aspire to the classical ideal of friendship as constituted by shared ethical comportment, good will, and trust. Without clear institutional guidelines, the stan-

101

dards for behavior within such discretionary bonds emerge from continuously enacted mutual commitments to behaving and interpreting conduct in ways that perform and preserve assumptions of favorable intentions between the friends. The enduring character of these friendships derives from mutually defined responsibilities and discursive practices.

In other cases, friendship may complement or fuse with other socially sanctioned dyads, such as marriage or business associations. Here, the ideals of friendship just mentioned may significantly influence the relational practices of these persons; that is, they may tend to regard and treat each other as friends even as they enact the institutional requirements of their relationship. In contrast, the precise activities and sensibilities of "friendship" within a primary relationship may be articulated and carefully delimited by prevailing social conventions. And, in particularly glib or utilitarian relationships, the notion of friendship may be employed tactically. Here, the moral and positive connotations of calling someone a "friend" are used strategically to define specific affiliations and to transform the tenor of social situations in ways that range from cordial to mystifying or blithely self-serving. The inherently relational and contextual, normative essence of friendship allows for such diverse operationalizations.

Elsewhere (Rawlins, 1989b, 1989c), I have used the term *double agency* to describe the capacity of friendship to course in and out of private and public spheres serving different blends of individual and social purposes. Sometimes, friends may consider it prudent to pretend that they are not friends in a public situation, and such veiling may be pursued to benefit the social order and/or to protect the friendship. Conversely, one or both members of a dyad may feign friendship in public, when their actual purposes for interacting in that context have little to do with friendship. A variety of circumstances may compel friends to choose among a collection of publicly and/or privately generated expectations and exigencies in conducting their friendship (Rawlins, 1989a). Certain actions might celebrate or flaunt the values of the friendship while risking public criticism; other gestures may benefit one person in a public context at the expense of his or her friend's regard. And, obviously, there is comportment that receives similarly favorable or unfavorable evaluations both within the friendship and by members of the larger society. The successful ongoing negotiation of friendship within various social systems, which exhibit diverse public and private demands and evaluative standards, comprises one of its key communicative challenges and exemplary features.

Drawing upon this ideal-typical discussion of the distinctive and mutable location and deployment of friendship in the cultural matrix of interpersonal relationships in America, the present essay has four interrelated objectives. First, I raise a series of questions that friends theoretically must answer to understand and appraise each other's actions and discourse. Next, in developing these questions, I simultaneously and reflexively suggest that they comprise a model for use by investigators and commentators in interrogating any interpersonal discourse. Finally, embodied in those efforts are the arguments that deciphering communicative goals is a highly complex undertaking and that multiple value judgments permeate all examinations and descriptions of discourse, whether they are consciously and explicitly acknowledged or not. There are inherently moral stakes and stances enacted in all production, consumption, and appraisal of discourse.

INTERROGATING THE DISCOURSE OF FRIENDS

Like Ricoeur (1971), I assume that social action is meaningful and can be viewed as textual or discursive in nature and is, therefore, susceptible to reading or interpretation by self and/or others. I pose the following questions as if a person were attempting to understand the actions and/or discourse of his or her friend. Thus, the questions reflect and suggest a generic stance for examining the discourse of friends, which recognizes that the boundaries and possibilities of self and other are implicated in the interaction of friends, the modes of their mutual probing, and the answers they will and will not accept from each other. In turn, these queries also pose analogous analytical quandaries for other investigators of discourse. The order for presenting them is intentional, yet somewhat arbitrary, as the questions are interdependent and presuppose the others to various degrees.

1. What Words Are Uttered, and What Behaviors Are Enacted? Clearly, the identification of these ostensive features of human interaction raises a host of questions in and of itself. For my purposes, I am simply acknowledging that people work from some observable texts in everyday life and in professional investigation, even if the features selected and the interpretations of their meaning and significance differ widely. Even if they constitute a "trivial minimum," there are public referents of and vehicles for our discourse (Rawlins, 1987; Rommetveit, 1980). Interhuman problems and opportunities derive from negotiating sufficiently shared meanings and evaluations of what transpires.

2. What Words Are Not Uttered, and What Behaviors Are Not Enacted? Answering this question patently involves one's expectations of another deriving from a host of personal, relational, and cultural factors in conjunction with one's perceptions of what communicative behaviors have occurred. There is profound variation in the degree to which a person's individual words and behaviors can be foretold or depicted as a selection from a determinate field of options. Even so, expectations and constraints develop in local discursive contexts that render the reflection on what has *not* been done or said in a given instance a significant practical concern in interpreting interaction (Bateson, 1972).

3. Who Is Speaking? Goffman (1981) has usefully complexified the answer to this question by stipulating a "production format" for speaking, including an animator who makes the sounds, an author who writes the words, and a principal who assumes responsibility for the speech. In a given professional instance, for example, one's friend may have to utter certain words (and thereby avoid others) written for him or her by someone else and warranted by an organizational office. Yet, in another context, the animator, author, and principal may coalesce in the friend. Such occasions might be evaluated differently within the friendship with varying results for the friends' subsequent views of each other. In the first case, if one recognizes that a friend is compelled by his or her supervisor to deliver disappointing news formulated by other people, the recipient may excuse or even empathize with the friend's role as animator of the discourse. In contrast, perceiving the friend as responsible for the substance of the message may jeopardize his or her status as a friend.

But there are compounding facets in identifying the speaker/actor. Do the dyad's members typically conceive of and treat each other as uniform selves, or as multiplex, situationally variant ones (Hart & Burks, 1972)? That is, does the friend who is also an employer and/or a spouse necessarily speak as a consistent whole, or can he or she assume diverse, if not contradictory, roles in producing utterances in given instances? Is a variety of "voices" seen as simultaneously influencing every instance of discourse? If so, are certain ones emphasized over others; or are they configured differently? Can they be enacted serially or in a variety of temporal arrangements? Clearly, the particular position taken on who is speaking has seminal implications for appraising his or her discourse in given cases, and the precise construal of the nature of the discourse will imply a conception of its producer's identity.

4. Who Is/Are the Audience(s)? Because interlocutors exist in mutually constitutive relationships, this question is closely related but distinguishable from describing the speaker/actor. Is the other-as-audience conceived and addressed as multiplex or uniform, hierarchically or otherwise composed, and constituted simultaneously or over time? In short, is the speaker, however composed, talking with another person who is holistically conceived or purposefully filleted? In enacting the contexts of their relationship, friends must negotiate the nature and degree of personal integration and diversification presupposed in addressing each other. An individual who thrives on situational variance in discourse might experience the other's refusal to acknowledge alternative personae as unnecessarily constrictive. Similarly, the person who values a consistent enactment of self may resent being addressed differently in changing contexts. Accordingly, Snyder and Smith (1986) indicated that, in their research, close friends were more likely than acquaintances to exhibit similar orientations to friendship as involving either consistent or situation-specific renditions of themselves.

Appraising discourse presupposes or articulates judgments of the presence, absence, degree, and nature of personal and/or social responsibility implied by discursive acts. Thus, supplementing the questions already posed, I submit the following queries as particularly important for assessing one's responsibility in producing "texts."

5. How Conscious or Unconscious Is the Person of His or Her Actions or Discourse? The issue of consciousness is a vital concern, ranging from one's self-awareness of actions in immediate concrete engagements to their role in subverting or reproducing the dominant ideologies of a given cultural era. Here, I am focusing on the former, more restricted sense of consciousness as describing the extent of one's conscious awareness of his or her actions and words in managing the here-and-now, concrete situation. Typically, the more conscious one is of one's actions, the greater is his or her responsibility for them. But, limited in this way, the question is still quite difficult to answer, as thinkers from Freud to Bateson have carefully demonstrated.

My position in raising this question is shaped by pragmatist notions and by Bateson and Johnstone (Bateson, 1972; Johnstone, 1970; Rock, 1979). Such thinkers have argued that most of our everyday activities are conducted with minimal conscious reflection. Much human behavior is habitualized. Bateson (1972) observed:

> Some types of knowledge can conveniently be sunk to unconscious levels, but other types must be kept on the surface. Broadly, we can afford to sink those sorts of knowledge which continue to be true regardless of changes in the environment, but we must maintain in an accessible place all those controls of behavior which must be modified for every instance. (p. 142)

Johnstone (1970) maintained that the conscious and responsible self is instantiated when the individual deals with a problem in his or her world. Even so, problems do not emerge solely as objective properties of situations, independent of a given individual's thoughts and actions; nor are they completely subjective. In Rock's (1979) words, "Problems are qualities of the total situation in which an individual is lodged, not parts of consciousness alone" (p. 69). There is a praxic quality to the production, selection, and management of problems that reveals the individual as a potentially conscious, subjective part of encompassing concrete and interactional circumstances.

Accordingly, certain gross categories might be employed for codifying behaviors in social situations according to their routine or problematical character and degree of conscious engagement. First, there are problematic situations that an individual consciously confronts or avoids. One might label these responsible or irresponsible actions or discourse. Second, there are problematic situations that an individual *un*consciously confronts or avoids. One might call these occurrences fate, luck, or naivete, with only minimal blame or credit implied for the social actor. Third, there are routine situations that an individual consciously confronts or avoids. One might view these in a variety of ways, for example, prudent, strategic, overly cautious, creative, paranoid, and so forth, and hold the individual responsible. Finally, there are routine situations that an individual *un*consciously confronts or avoids. One might call these habitual. Clearly, however, these various judgments rest on someone's perceptions of the problematic or routine character of a given social situation as well as its requisite or manifest degree of conscious attention. One person's problematic situation might be routine for another, and vice versa, with consequent potential for eliciting conscious engagement and attributing responsibility for action. Producing a simple, straightforward answer to a question might engage one individual's full attention; for another, formulating complex propositions might approach a social reflex. Ironically, reflections on the degree of consciousness involved can be critical for evaluating discursive activity regardless of whether the commentator pursues them consciously or not.

6. To What Extent Is the Meaning Attributed to an Individual's Words and Behaviors the Meaning that He or She Intended? Closely associated with the extent and nature of consciousness attributed to a person is the issue of intended meaning, which is the essential enigma of all hermeneutical efforts. Certain formulations emphasize that words (and, by implication, social actions) are, for the most part, intentionally produced with specifiable meanings according to the limitations established by cultural conventions for conversing, assuming sincerity conditions (Grice, 1975; Searle, 1972).

But, of course, other meanings are possible that a given individual cannot control, or superintend. For one thing, an individual may simply be unaware of numerous other possible readings of his or her words or behaviors in a given context. Nothing can totally prevent these multiple interpretations from occurring (Bateson, 1972; Rommetveit, 1980). Further, the individual may unintentionally provide stylistic or nonverbal cues or linguistic phrasings undermining his or her intentional messages. In contrast to one's own intentional "expressions," Ichheiser (1970) has called these meanings, which are assigned by others and which the individual cannot completely control, "impressions"—concepts that are analogous to Goffman's (1959) discussion of "cues given" versus "cues given off."

To complicate matters, the producer of discourse may be insincere in the first place, only pretending sincerity, or being ironical, or lying, joshing, joking, or kidding, or—even more problematically—feigning these latter activities. Further, persons may not be entirely sure of what they feel or think even as they are speaking or acting and may completely change their minds while finishing a lucid account of what they no longer believe (Empson, 1947). Such alterations may occur due to actually hearing what they have said, interactional contingencies, and/or the responses of others.

Thus, even within the most scrupulously adhered to or definitively rendered discursive program of locutionary, illocutionary, or perlocutionary action, the discourse producer's perlocutionary intent can dislodge all bets (Dillon, 1986). One may be perfectly sincere in uttering certain words to make a promise but may also have a radically idiosyncratic perlocutionary intent for the effect one wants to achieve by stating that promise. Or, as mentioned, intentions may change during the performance of discourse in light of accurate or inaccurate reception by others and their consequent responses. Ever so abruptly, then, actual discourse production and consumption involves questions of motives or purposes and decisions about their rightness or wrongness, ergo overarching motivational and evaluative frameworks. The worlds of analytical discourses are enveloped by the "politics of experience" (Laing, 1967).

7. Does This Action or Discourse Benefit or Harm Self, the Friend, and the Larger Social Nexus? This is one way of questioning purposes. In examining spoken discourse, for example, complex assessments may interact with determinations of precisely who is speaking, who is the audience, what is and is not said, how conscious the person is of his or her discourse, and what meanings are intended and received. Multiple readings can occur. I have roughed out a conceptual framework of possible ways of assigning purposes to the behaviors of friends (see Fig. 6.1). Basically, one cross-examines one's initial appraisal of an action as primarily benefiting or harming oneself, the friend, or the encompassing social system by asking whether it also simultaneously or potentially benefits or harms oneself, the other, and the larger society in some fashion.

Because many possibilities accrue, I consider just a few examples from the first row in Fig. 6.1. Someone might say or do something that initially appears to be entirely self-serving (Benefit Self). However, a closer look at the developing situation might reveal that the person also has risked a lot by making the statement or has restricted his or her options in other areas (Harm Self). Moreover, the original action or discourse may also be seen to benefit the friend (Benefit Other) and the larger social order as well (Benefit Social System). Cross-examination thereby vindicates the original impressions of selfish purposes. In another case, further scrutiny of an individual's apparently self-seeking actions (Benefit Self) may reveal consequences that neither benefit himself or herself nor the larger society (Harm Self and Harm Social System) but do serve the friend (Benefit Other). Finally, a disturbing example within the double agency of friendship occurs when a person's behavior seemingly propers himself or herself and embracing social organizations but not the friend. Obviously, this is a bare-bones analytical structure, and decisions are not typically so dichoto-

Cross Examination

Initial Appraisal		Benefit or Harm Self?	Benefit or Harm Other?	Benefit or Harm Social System?
	Benefit Self	Benefit Self	Benefit Other	Benefit Social System
		Harm Self	Harm Other	Harm Social System
	Harm Self	Benefit Self	Benefit Other	Benefit Social System
		Harm Self	Harm Other	Harm Social System
	Benefit Other	Benefit Self	Benefit Other	Benefit Social System
		Harm Self	Harm Other	Harm Social System
	Harm Other	Benefit Self	Benefit Other	Benefit Social System
		Harm Self	Harm Other	Harm Social System
	Benefit Social System	Benefit Self	Benefit Other	Benefit Social System
		Harm Self	Harm Other	Harm Social System
	Harm Social System	Benefit Self	Benefit Other	Benefit Social System
		Harm Self	Harm Other	Harm Social System

FIG. 6.1. Ways of assigning purposes.

mous; but I believe it underscores the complexity of reaching judgments regarding the purposes of a friend's actions, even before the decision is made as to whether they are bad or good and defensible or not.

8. How Should This Action or Statement Be Evaluated? This is the quintessential postmodern quandary, and it poses two problems at once. First, what evaluative standard(s) is/are to be utilized in judging the activity? Second, how does this particular action or discourse rate when so appraised?

Regarding the first issue, Gergen (1985) suggested that actions can be assessed according to global and immutable and/or local and revisable practical, political, moral, and aesthetic criteria. As previously mentioned, friendship by definition involves the contextual negotiation of duties and rights (Paine, 1969).

Yet friendships are typically developed within encompassing social nexuses; they exist alongside, within, in opposition to, or as replacements for more bona fide social relationships. Accordingly, various combinations of publicly and privately defined evaluative standards intersect and compete in judging a friend's behavior. Because of the double agency of friendship, conceptions of appropriate meanings, valued and disvalued purposes, and responsible action can become exceedingly difficult to specify or adjudicate depending on the particular character and circumstances of the friendship.

Thus, the second issue of rating specific actions within friendship involves determining and negotiating precisely which standards of appropriate behavior to apply in the given instance, as well as how the behavior in question stacks up. The general flavor of the enterprise involves enacting a reasonably consistent process of invoking shared standards to ensure *responsible* judgment, but conducting these appraisals in a caring way that comprises an appropriately sensitive procedure of interpreting standards to ensure *responsive* judgment. The justice of friendship feeds on its own rendering.

Whether the behavior in question involves word choice, a manner of speaking or personal comportment, a proposed decision on a course of action, or disputable deeds experienced or witnessed by the other friend, as in all social life, evaluation is part and parcel of friendship. Yet, because of the negotiated and situated character of friendships, selecting and applying evaluative standards is no perfunctory matter. As ideal types, one can view the procedures for judging action within friendship as attempting to combine concern and rationality, responsiveness and responsibility, and insight into particular incidents with consistency in overarching practices. When pursued carefully and caringly, the judgment of friends embodies an ethical praxis for adjudicating the idiosyncrasies of individuals within a mutually constituted moral enterprise. The process embraces a dialectic of subjective intentions and intersubjective conventions.

THE DIALECTIC OF INTENTIONS AND CONVENTIONS

People have difficulty perceiving actions as neutral (Laing, 1971). Obviously, the precise nature of the behaviors seen to require judgment will interact with all of the issues considered thus far in interrogating discourse or social action. Additionally, in regarding questionable occurrences within friendships, one typically asks if these actions that aid or undermine self, other, and/or society were motivated by good or bad intentions. Such conclusions have at least two seminal repercussions between friends. First, the assumption of benevolent as opposed to malevolent motives for a friend's actions may comprise the reflexive essence of managing problematic events within friendship. Friends assume that they mean each other well—or, at least, no harm—and typically have each other's best interests in mind (for example, when criticizing the other's actions or not choosing the other to participate in certain activities). Yet, this assumption is built up and maintained by behaviors and statements by the friends that clearly enact or reflect favorable intentions.

However, friendships are potentially fraught with ambiguity, both in the friends' attempts to interpret each other's words and actions and the significance assigned to their behavior by third parties and/or society at large (Rawlins, 1989a). Such ambiguity in friendship is often compounded by ambivalence (Brain, 1976; Harre, 1977). The intermittent delights or disruptions of fulfilling or disappointing an array of publicly and/or privately produced ideals and realities within a given friendship can threaten stable interpretations of even the most straightforward actions. An important challenge to friends, therefore, is to behave and interpret behaviors in a manner that preserves the assumption of benevolent as opposed to malevolent intentions underpinning each other's actions. The shared convention of perceiving good intentions constitutes an "insurance policy" for the relationship when contradictory conditions may result in ostensibly negative behavior by one's friend. He or she is truly innocent until proven guilty. Accordingly, communicating within friendship involves continual interaction between interpretive and behavioral practices to maintain a mutual definition of the relationship as friendship.

The second, reflexive implication of judgment within friendship derives from recognizing that, as one distills and labels one's and/or another's goals, intentions, or motives, one is simultaneously articulating and constituting both one's own and the other's possibilities for selfhood within the friendship. Accordingly, ascribing intentions, enacting conventions, and negotiating specific contexts interpenetrate in the accomplishment of selves as friends through discourse. Friends acknowledge the "susceptibility to circumstances" (White, 1984) of behaving and experiencing behaviors within their relationship as part of larger social formations. A reciprocity and plurivocity of idealistic and realistic expectations, private and public audiences, and creative and mundane communicative actions inform the revisable conventions for reading friends' intentions. In short, friends are continuously committed to learning how to interpret each other's actions to facilitate suitable judgments and a resonant edifying bond. In this process, intersubjective conventions for interpreting a friend's behavior multiply and diversify to facilitate understanding of spontaneous actions and subjective intentions on his or her part (Burns, 1953).

Such a commitment implies an interpretive stance within friendship that is compatible with Simmel's notion of cultivation (Weingartner, 1965). Simmel considered cultural forms as potential vehicles for human growth and emancipation in contrast to limitation and encapsulation. He argued that a person's behaviors could develop according to two independent logics with respective modes of "being consequent" (Weingartner, 1965). One is the *logic of biography*, wherein the implications of a particular action derive from the subjective dictates of the unfolding of a given individual's engagement with life. At any moment, a person's next action potentially follows the guiding principles of his or her own cultivation (Weingartner, 1965). In contrast is the *logic of form,* wherein "the experiencing subject enters an objective realm which is ruled by its own laws" (Weingartner, 1965, p. 132). Examples of the latter would be grammatical rules or societal dictates or conventions for determining proper language and behavior. According to this logic, an "objective" or public connection between given and subsequent actions exists that does not necessarily reflect an individual's intentions.

Weingartner (1965) observed:

> The two logics, the subjective one of cultivation and the objective one of the form, are independent of each other, while the individual's experience has its place in both. Given any particular experience, in other words, *two* "next" experiences which need not be the same are implied. (p. 132)

Here, the plot thickens. Indeed, two "separate sets of demands" for contiguity or linear coherence are posed by action, namely, carrying out self-initiated objectives and fulfilling societal expectations. But they *may or may not* contradict each other. Interplay transpires between one's own subjective intentions for personal cultivation and the necessary employment of cultural conventions as communal, objective, and logical resources for constituting oneself in society. Manifest forms of behavior and language thus become problematic when viewed as either enactments of what I term *conventions of appearance* or *appearances of convention.*

Conventions of appearance inform such matters as the literal use of words or actions to express or make apparent one's actual intentions. This mode reflects living within or "playing by" publicly recognized rules of expression, that is, redundancies between internally composed forms of thinking and feeling and their social display. A close fit exists between one's own intentions and cultural conventions in given situations. Notice that this fit means that one's individual purposes may nicely accord with dominant social forms both in their experience and in their enactment. It also means, however, that idiosyncratic intentions may be predictably encoded in deviant or routinely mutant cultural forms. Both the everyday and the unorthodox are governed by conventions of appearance when these conventions map individual intentions.

Appearances of convention allow the depths of the surface to emerge with a sheen that makes interiority difficult to perceive. Conventions are employed to disguise or to render ambiguous one's actual intentions. This mode reflects the attempt to transcend or "play with" publicly recognized rules of expression. A complex and subtle relationship exists between one's own intentions and the cultural conventions enacted in given situations. One may appropriate idiosyncratic forms for culturally endorsed purposes, or one may behave or converse conventionally for ulterior or interior motives.

In either mode, continued interaction ultimately presupposes some degree of shared rules or conventions; however, an individual's potential for the cultivation of a personal biography derives from the extent to which the logic of form can be appropriated to fulfill subjective intentions instead of vice versa (Weingartner, 1965). The double agency of friendship uniquely positions friends in the composition of one's biography. First of all, friendship requires a keenly developed sense of how another stylizes his or her being. A person may tend consciously or unconsciously to behave "mock conventionally" or even ultraconventionally in public. Through interaction within friendship, these subjectively developed modes become intersubjectively codified; they are no longer completely privatized. Regarding "mock conventionality," a friend comes to understand why or under what social conditions another tends to duplicate conservative cultural comportment but does so according to idiosyncratic assumptions. Further, a friend may even realize that the other's assumptions and intentions are not unusual but that he or she likes to believe they are. A friend may also recognize that the ultraconventionality of another makes that individual special or unique as a person or communicator. There are few subtexts in his or her world. Mastering the multiplex conventions of another's elusiveness or the "deceptively" pristine rules of his or her straightforwardness is an intersubjective accomplishment that reflexively engenders knowledge of self and other.

Not only is the achievement of such knowledge important in friendship, but so is what one does with it. Does one accept or reject another's enactments of conventions of appearance or appearances of convention? Friends, as double agents, realize that any cultural performance by the other activates the potential for subverting or enhancing oneself, the other, the friendship, or the encompassing social order in a variety of combinations. The friend attempts to judge accordingly. Some behaviors by the friend in the public sphere are approved for maintaining a stance of creative marginality for self and/or the friendship; other conduct is criticized because of its potential for fostering personal alienation within socially endorsed discourse. Sometimes a friend is chided to "straighten up his or her act" in the interest of maximizing opportunities in a public, impersonal realm despite temporary or even long-term risks to the friendship.

The critique of another's articulation and enactment of his or her being by a friend continually violates certain codes and instantiates others. It comprises an involved aesthetic, moral, and practical enterprise. One recognizes that another's style of communicating, however flawed when evaluated by unflinching or "objective" standards, composes and reflects that person's efforts at reconciling intentionality and conventionality, appearances and essences, interiority and exteriority, hostility and affection, and selfishness and altruism. In judging a friend, then, one participates in a mutually pursued shaping of self's, other's and the relationship's possibilities; one embraces an immense responsibility.

CONCLUSIONS AND IMPLICATIONS

Like all discourse, this chapter can be read in many ways; like all authors, I have consciously and unconsciously instantiated multiple motivations and intentions in writing it. I am not able to be explicit about all of them. Even so, I have examined the "double agency" of friendship and some implications of its contextual character for the discursive management of friendships. I have argued that the forms and functions of interaction between friends change because individuals' goals and purposes change in concrete circumstances, and vice versa. Thus, the surface facts of discourse and the interpretive and evaluative experience of producing and consuming that discourse must be situated in actual cultural moments.

Intentions, conventions, and circumstances interpenetrate in the ongoing accomplishment of selves as friends through discourse. Both intention-based and convention-based interpretations of discursive interaction must address and answer to a dialectic of public and private exigencies (Rawlins, 1989b). Further, valuational issues are unavoidable, because various cultural eras and moments of friendship differentially acknowledge public versus private evaluative standards for appraising communicative behaviors (Rawlins, 1989a); and all conventions must be actively produced and reproduced in consort with others.

Accordingly, notions, like goals, motives, and intentions, comprise and reflect descriptive devices that serve specific points of view at certain points in time at determinable levels of description. The relevant observers may include the self-as-communicator, affected others, third parties, scholars of discourse, and/or other social commentators. As we distill and label our own as well as others' goals, intentions, or motives within ongoing interaction, we are simultaneously constituting our own and their "selves" as well as the relationships we will share.

The questions I have posed for interrogating the discourse of friends are intended to reflect the spirit, if not the praxis, of rigorous yet concerned questioning that occurs in friendship viewed as a model of mutually negotiated ethical comportment. My questions imply a stance that is similar to the cross-examination of friends for self-acknowledged scholars of discourse in their investigations of social texts. Its dialectical nature challenges the "heroic perspective" (Spence, 1978) of detached, "scientific," objective, administrative, and/or mock-clinical analyses. It recognizes that neither subjects nor objects are "constituted or even conceivable independent of each other" and that the praxic accomplishment of human existence involves a dialectical enactment of the tension between "the subject structuring aspect of the social structure" objectifying persons and their knowledge-based "conscious activity" revealing them to be subjects (all quotes in this sentence are from Rossi, 1983, p. 320). It also notices that procedures for identifying another person's intentions can be used consciously or not, in starkly different services.

On the one hand, interpretation may be conceived as a minimal task of scrutinizing a text, informed by unequivocal conventions for discovering a specifiable truth. Thus, it limits alternative meanings in the name of compliance or "cooperation" with dominant conceptions of the status quo and not-so-subtle apologies for "normalcy." In contrast, interpretation may be seen to require deep engagement and reciprocity in attempting to grasp multiple possible worlds and diverse truths "opened up" by the text (Ricoeur, 1971). Alternative meanings are invited, probed, and reflected on in the name of tolerance, freedom, and understanding other modes of human experience.

Thus, the interpretive stance of friendship as an ideal-type embodies a particular set of discursive practices for linking the general to the given case (Beiner, 1983). It aspires to both responsibility and responsiveness by emphasizing reciprocal role-taking and empathy over the arbitrary or unreflective imposition of preformed standards of interpretation and evaluation—in short, by attempting to "trade on each other's truths" (Rommetveit, 1980) instead of privileging one's own.

REFERENCES

Bateson, G. (1972). *Steps to an ecology of mind.* New York: Ballantine Books.

Beiner, R. (1983). *Political judgment.* Chicago: University of Chicago Press.

Brain, R. (1976). *Friends and lovers.* New York: Basic Books.

Burns, T. (1953). Friends, enemies, and the polite fiction. *American Sociological Review, 18,* 654–662.

Dillon, G. (1986). *Rhetoric as social imagination.* Bloomington: Indiana University Press.

Empson, W. (1947). *Seven types of ambiguity.* New York: New Directions Publishing Co.

Gergen, K. (1985). The social constructionist movement in modern psychology. *American Psychologist, 40,* 266–275.

Goffman, E. (1959). *The presentation of self in everyday life.* Garden City: Doubleday Anchor Books.

Goffman, E. (1981). *Forms of talk.* Philadelphia: University of Pennsylvania Press.

Grice, H. P. (1975). Logic and conversation. In P. Cole & J. L. Morgan (Eds.), *Syntax and semantics: Vol. 3. Speech acts* (pp. 41–58). New York: Academic Press.

Harre, R. (1977). Friendship as an accomplishment: An ethogenic approach to social relationships. In S. Duck (Ed.), *Theory and practice in interpersonal attraction* (pp. 339–354). London: Academic Press.

Hart, R. P., & Burks, D. M. (1972). Rhetorical sensitivity and social interaction. *Speech Monographs, 39,* 75–91.

Ichheiser, G. (1970). *Appearances and realities.* San Francisco: Jossey-Bass.

Johnstone, H. (1970). *The problem of the self.* University Park: Pennsylvania State University Press.

Laing, R. D. (1967). *The politics of experience.* New York: Pantheon Books.

Laing, R. D. (1971). *Self and others.* Middlesex, England: Penguin.

Paine, R. (1969). In search of friendship: An exploratory analysis in "middle-class" culture. *Man, 4,* 505–524.

Rawlins, W. K. (1987). Gregory Bateson and the composition of human communication. *Research on Language and Social Interaction, 20,* 53–77.

Rawlins, W. K. (1989a). A dialectical analysis of the tensions, functions, and strategic challenges of communication in young adult friendships. In J. A. Anderson (Ed.), *Communication yearbook 12* (pp. 157–189). Beverly Hills, CA: Sage.

Rawlins, W. K. (1989b). Cultural double agency and the pursuit of friendship. *Cultural Dynamics, 2,* 28–40.

Rawlins, W. K. (1989c). Rehearsing the margins of adulthood: The communicative management of adolescent friendships. In J. F. Nussbaum (Ed.), *Life-span communication: Normative issues* (pp. 137–154). Hillsdale, NJ: Lawrence Erlbaum Associates.

Ricoeur, P. (1971). The model of the text. *Social Research, 38,* 529–555.

Rock, P. (1979). *The making of symbolic interactionism.* Totowa, NJ: Rowan & Littlefield.

Rommetveit, R. (1980). On "meanings" of acts and what is meant and made known by what is said in a pluralistic social world. In M. Brenner (Ed.), *The structure of action* (pp. 108–149). New York: St. Martin's Press.

Rossi, I. (1983). *From the sociology of symbols to the sociology of signs.* New York: Columbia University Press.

Searle, J. (1972). What is a speech act? In P. P. Giglioli (Ed.), *Language and social context* (pp. 136–154). Middlesex, England: Penguin.

Snyder, M., & Smith, D. (1986). Personality and friendship: The friendship worlds of self-monitoring. In V. J. Derlega & B. A. Winstead (Eds.), *Friendship and social interaction* (pp. 63–80). New York: Springer-Verlag.

Spence, L. D. (1978). *The politics of social knowledge.* University Park: Pennsylvania State University Press.

Weingartner, R. H. (1965). Theory and tragedy of culture. In L. A. Coser (Ed.), *Georg Simmel* (pp. 122–134). Englewood Cliffs, NJ: Prentice-Hall.

White, J. B. (1984). *When words lose their meaning.* Chicago: University of Chicago Press.

II
Theoretical Dilemmas Linking Goals and Discourse

CHAPTER 7
Some Problems with Linking Goals to Discourse

Janet Beavin Bavelas
University of Victoria

This chapter is concerned with exploring, via the particular case of "goals," some general problems facing theories that use intrapsychic concepts to explain discourse behaviors. The use of the concept of goal to explain face-to-face interaction is an instance of a widely shared paradigm that assumes that the mind causes action, in other words, that an individual's observable behaviors must ultimately be explained by his or her mental processes. (Similar concepts include "intention," "motivation," "cognitive processes," "learning," "personality," and so forth.) This paradigm is typical of psychology as a discipline, including social psychology, but it can also be found in many other social sciences, including communication and linguistics. A minority in each of these fields, including many discourse analysts, focus more on overt communicative acts and generate descriptive rather than inferential theories. What I have to say here has much less relevance for the latter group.

The first modern goal theorists in psychology were Tolman (1932, 1959) and Lewin (1935; Cartwright, 1959). In their theories, goals were external to the organism (whether rat or human); they were "out there" (much like "goal *posts*" in idiomatic use). Although goals might create hypothetical states in the organism, the goals themselves were specifiable conditions or events that elicited and shaped behavior (e.g., Bavelas & Lee, 1978). Goals have more recently been brought inside; they are internal mental entities or processes. It is this shift that has created the theoretical issues discussed in this chapter.

THEORETICAL PROBLEMS

Because many readers who anticipate a critique of mental concepts will immediately free-associate to the label "behaviorist," some clarification in that direction is needed. I distinguish between substantive and methodological behaviorism by separating *what* a theory may include from *how* a theory is to be examined empirically (Bavelas, 1978, chap. 19). In reaction against the introspectionists of the early part of this century, substantive behaviorists such as Watson and Skinner aspired to exclude all nonobservables from their theories (e.g., "motivation" was eliminated in favor of "hours of deprivation," and "learning" was replaced with "prior reinforcement history"). The substance of the theory had to be behavioral. A gentler reaction was that of theorists such as Tolman, Hull, or the Gestalt psychologists (Wertheimer, Koffka, Kohler). In these theories, the explanatory concepts could be nonbehavioral, but they had to be capable of being translated into behavioral methods permitting observable empirical tests of the theory. Most of us are the heirs of these methodological behaviorists, free to generate theories and define concepts as we wish but obliged at some point to find "operational definitions" of concepts and to take these into the sobering domain of observables. It is safe to assume that theorists who are interested in goals are methodological, not substantive, behaviorists. I am not advocating that they become substantive behaviorists; rather, I am describing problems that are inherent in—but by no means insoluable for—methodological behaviorism that includes mental constructs. (Different criteria would be applied for the different problems inherent in a substantive behaviorist position.)

In a classic article, MacCorquodale and Meehl (1948) pointed out some of the obligations incurred by theory builders who choose to use concepts that are not, in themselves, observable. They pointed out that there are at least two kinds of such concepts: First, there are *intervening variables,* which are rather Spartan concepts that "merely abstract the empirical relationships. . . . the statement of such a concept does not contain any words which are not reducible to the empirical laws" (pp. 106–107). The second, more ebullient, *hypothetical constructs,* go much further:

> [they] involve the supposition of entities or processes not among the observed. . . . Concepts of the second sort . . . [involve] words not wholly reducible to the words in the empirical laws; the validity of the empirical laws is not a sufficient condition for the truth of the concept, inasmuch as it contains surplus meaning; and the quantitative form of the concept is not obtainable simply by grouping empirical terms and functions. (pp. 106–107)

Examples from other sciences are "gravity" as an intervening variable and "evolution" as a hypothetical construct.

Obviously, most of the mental concepts used in our theories are hypothetical constructs. The problem is that they have many *surplus meanings*—connotations beyond the empirical measures used in any particular study. They are, in Underwood's (1957) phrase, more an "artistic or literary conception" (p. 55) than a scientific specification. We cannot underestimate the role of the theorist's subjective experience (and his or her appeal to others' subjective experience) in theories that invoke hypothetical constructs, including goals. In our own consciousness, we are aware ourselves of having goals, so we do not question the use of the term; its surplus meanings may even be an advantage in its initial acceptance. The same surplus meanings, however, can create a drastic imbalance between the hypothetical construct as used in the theory and the particular method of its measurement, which is usually much more specific. At worst, there is an inverted pyramid with a large theoretical and conceptual superstructure supported by a narrow data base. The danger is greater the more appealing the construct, because creative speculation and generalization will certainly exceed the empirical base.

(The majority of social scientists seem to treat theories with intervening variables as mere descriptions, rather than proper theories. "Black-box" theories [e.g., Watzlawick, Beavin, & Jackson, 1967, chap. 1], which deal solely with input–output relationships or patterns of behavior, are often seen as incomplete because of an unacknowledged and therefore unquestioned assumption that explanations of behavior must be mental.)

When goals are invoked to explain the production, comprehension, or patterning of discourse, another problem arises. Not only must the concept of "goal" be defined explicitly and clearly, but a model of *the process by which goals are connected to discourse* must be explicated. Just as we all "know" what a goal is, we can all imagine how they affect discourse; intuitive plausibility becomes a disadvantage in the longer term, because the "mere formalities" of tight theoretical connections are likely to have been neglected. For example, a minimum theoretical specification is whether goals operate consciously on discourse ("I have this goal; therefore, I will talk this way."). If so, is this awareness verbal? Do subjects' open-ended self-reports confirm the model? The theory need not equate awareness with verbalizability; there are cognitive models that tap unverbalized cognitive processes and test these by ingenious techniques. But some such model must be chosen and tested.

If awareness is not invoked, another route must be proposed. Moreover, the theorist in this case cannot appeal to introspective experiences, even in examples, when elaborating the theory. It is quite striking how often scholarly discussions of important theoretical issues are advanced by personal authority, such as anecdotes or appeals to how we (the scholars) experience the world. It is as if our standards for a theory are that it describe the world as a group of social scientists see it and that it conform to anecdotes that those social scientists can adduce in support of it. This is *not* the same as a legitimate phenomenological or ethnomethodogical approach because of the inordinate weight given to the opinions of a small group of scholars.

The possibility of multiple goals presents a further requirement, namely, that a subsection of the theory must describe the nature of the *interaction between goals.* Lewin (1938) had such a model, which included detailed predictions for the process and outcome expected when goals conflict. As I describe later, our Victoria group adapted Lewin's model to discourse in the face of conflicting goals (Bavelas, 1983, 1985; Bavelas, Black, Chovil, & Mullett, 1990a, 1990b) and obtained substantial empirical confirmation. The way in which the concept of goal was defined in this work may not match the definition or interests of another researcher, but one lesson is clear: The process was, as it should be, far from a dreary duty. The details that link goals to each other and to discourse should be of great intrinsic interest to the theorist who proposes such a connection. He or she should regard the requirement for details as a welcome one, permitting intimate exploration of a chosen territory. The most interesting questions should be: How would we know that goals affect discourse? What consequences would this lead to? What difference would it make?

A final major theoretical problem is that the essential nature of a mental goal, however defined, is *monadic:* It refers to some process, disposition, motivation, or awareness in an individual. Yet, if such goals are then connected with face-to-face *interaction,* a fundamental disparity of units arises. Goal as a construct located in an individual mind might explain monologue, but even the cleverest and bravest reductionist does not have the alchemy to produce the creative spontaneity of dialogue out of two goals, in separate minds. The problem, of course, is a general one, not limited to theories about goals. Any intrapsychic model of dyadic (or group) discourse faces a chasm between the mind of an individual on the one side and the behavior of a social unit on the other. This does not mean that the problem is insoluable, just that it exists and is too little recognized. Mentally driven theories can hypothesize a start to the interaction, but they must also account for the reciprocity and accomodation that characterize face-to-face interaction. Otherwise, the goals of the two individuals would run parallel, never affecting each other. (The nonmentalistic alternative is to shift the level of analysis to dialogue as a social system whose pattern is its own explanation.)

So far, I have sketched out some minimal requirements for theories that link goals to discourse. Even so, it may seem like a great deal to ask of a theory even before it moves on to data. Perhaps this suggests a more modest course, in which a narrower but specifiable conception of goal is linked to an equally limited aspect of discourse—spending within one's means, so to speak. The alternative is to spend on credit with a broadly defined construct without paying the theoretical or empirical bills.

EMPIRICAL PROBLEMS

The most serious evidential risk for theories that invoke internal constructs is *hidden circularity*. For example, goals determine the discourse, and the discourse is the evidence of the inferred goals; there is no independent evidence for the extra conceptual baggage being carried on board. It is crucial to provide independent, collateral evidence for the concept invoked. To do so, it is necessary to explicate the theory enough that it is possible to say: If goals are driving behavior in this particular way, then when X happens, Y should follow. In other words, the hypothesis must be falsifiable; it cannot account for all conceivable outcomes without being meaningless. Circularity can be found remarkably frequently in theories of mental processes, because the more complex the theory, the harder it is to identify potential circularities. Indeed, the broader the theory appears to be in its application, the more likely that this breadth is being bought with hidden circularity. Even the substantive behaviorists are vulnerable on this point: Why did a behavior occur? Because it was reinforced. How do we know the behavior was reinforced? Because it occurred. To assume that behavior is goal-driven risks the same trap. This problem can be diagnosed, first, by explicit logical formulation and, second, by early attempts at falsification.

All of this implies a pressing methodological necessity to *identify goals empirically,* whether by experimental manipulation, indirect measurement, or subjects' reports after the fact. There are, however, obvious dangers with the last approach. If we provide subjects with our terminology, it may not be possible for them to reply in a disconfirming manner. Too often, the researcher assumes that the subjects have goals and only asks about which ones. This is like offering a ballot with several candidates, but all from the same party. It might seem that this problem could be avoided by manipulating goals or measuring them indirectly, but it must, of course, be established that what was manipulated or measured was really "goal," that is, that there is no alternative interpretation of the independent variable. A tight definition of the term will make all of these tasks possible.

A related issue is the problem of differing operational definitions. If various researchers use various methods for studying goals, are they all really studying the same thing? *Convergent operations* (a variety of methods for measuring the same concept; Campbell & Fiske, 1959) are important, because they establish the breadth of the concept being measured. But this is only true if the measures are used *together* in the same studies often enough to show that they are functionally similar. That is, in the desirable form of multiple operations, measures of the same concept correlate with each other in the same setting. It is quite a different matter when different measures are used (alone) in various studies. In the latter case, we have no evidence that the researchers are, in fact, studying the same concept. Conceptual and operational breadth are assumed but not demonstrated. The remedy in this case is straightforward: Researchers with different measures should include each other's measures in their studies.

Finally, there is the anomaly of labeling some discourse, namely, *methodological discourse,* as not-discourse. When a researcher asks subjects about their goals, whether by interview or questionnaire, this interaction is also discourse; yet it is often seen, instead, as a direct route to the mind. I do not wish to raise here the specter of recursiveness and self-reflexivity; the fact that subjects' replies are discourse does not make them invalid as a source of information. It does mean that we should remain attuned to the context in which the replies are made, instead of treating them as context-free "truth."

ALIENATION FROM DISCOURSE

It is essential to keep in mind the fundamental *difference between (mental) goal and discourse:* One is a construct, the other is observable behavior, and some strange things can happen when they are juxtaposed. Goals in the sense of hypothetical, intrapsychic entities cannot occur *in* discourse. They can affect discourse, or they can be inferred from discourse. To the extent that we begin to "see" goals in discourse, we have pushed discourse aside and replaced it with an inferred construct. We have lost track of what is observed and what is inferred and have begun to believe in the literal reality of hypothetical mental constructs. This reified construct becomes what we think we are actually seeing, rather than the discourse.

Even when the distinction between goal and discourse is maintained, discourse is sometimes pushed aside as *"merely discourse."* In other words, there is often a kind of elitism in favor of constructs, in which goals are considered to be at a "higher" (i.e., theoretical) level, while the actual discourse is at a "micro" level—small and particular, only a means to a higher end. That is, discourse is of interest to the extent that it is a path to the construct; the particulars are not as important as the generality. This Platonic principle rejects the particular instance in favor of the idealized type. In my view, the importance of the emergence of discourse analysis was the legitimization of discourse itself as intrinsically interesting. To the extent that we favor explanatory constructs and mental models over discourse, we have stepped back into more traditional ways and left discourse analysis. It is true that researchers should always seek generality, but not simply by the use of general words. The general term *goal* does not have any real generality until it can be shown *empirically* that many particular instances of discourse can be explained or predicted by this construct.

One way of summarizing several of these problems is to return to the pyramid image. Do we want an inverted pyramid with a very small data base supporting a highly elaborated theoretical superstructure or a stable pyramid with a large observational base supporting modest conceptual inferences? The first is tempting for several reasons, of which two should be emphasized: First, in many quarters, theory building is seen as more elegant, as a more important contribution, than mere observation. Second, the words with which theories can be built are more malleable than data, which can always prove us wrong. We may be able to make words mean anything we want, but data are not usually so cooperative.

My opinion about how we should proceed is probably obvious. We should be more like our natural science colleagues: Biologists, chemists, biochemists, astronomers, and the like pursue problems presented by phenomena; they describe the world first and then try to aggregate these descriptions into theoretical models. To me, the varieties of discourse are like the fauna of our planet—there to be examined, grouped, classified, and explained. The inner workings will come from intense observation and cautious inference.

BUILDING A STABLE PYRAMID: AN EXAMPLE

It is one thing to have an opinion about how research and theory should proceed; it is another thing actually to do it. In a particular project, our everyday choices are affected by many immediate factors that are never mentioned by nonscientist philosophers of science or by theory experts who do not do research. Our long-term project on equivocation (Bavelas et al., 1990b) illustrates these real-life pressures and confusions.

My interest in ambiguous, evasive, odd messages began when I was working with the Palo Alto group in the 1960s. We frequently noticed "disqualified" or "incongruent" communication in the families of schizophrenic patients and saw this as an important part of the situation with which the schizophrenic must cope. An example (from Sluzki, Beavin, Tarnopolsky, & Veron, 1967) is:

Adult son: You treat me like a child.

Mother: But you are my child. (p. 498)

The play on the word "child" seems not playful here but deadly serious, yet there is something perversely elegant about it. It is possible to see it, on the one hand, as a smooth, reasonable transition but, on the other hand, as a malevolent mystification by which the patient's meaning is taken from him and shaped into something else, or (on yet another hand) as mere simpleness or excessive literality.

Such messages kept occurring, and I kept being fascinated by their resonances and multiple meanings—but troubled by something else. Once I tuned in to them, I did not hear these equivocal messages solely from the families of schizophrenics, whom we were studying, but from my own friends and family and from all kinds of apparently "normal" people (including myself). Fortunately, so did my colleagues, and we were able to resist the temptation to label such communication as pathological, or pathogenic, and to see its more general import.

One clue was the observation (Sluzki et al., 1967) that, while the family puts the patient in an impossible position by their communicative style, so does the schizophrenic patient: Analyzed in the same way, his or her messages are equally problematic for the family. This insight was greatly assisted by a well-intentioned project, carried out very naively, in which we sought normal, control families with which to contrast and understand communication in schizophrenic families. In these interviews, we did *not* find the clear, straightforward, congruent standard of communication we expected but rather a good deal of incoherent, tangential communication. Fortunately, rather than concluding that these normal control families were undiagnosed "schizophrenogenics," we took seriously our commitment to the situation as an explanation and asked ourselves, what was the situation for these families?

In brief, they had been asked by their family doctors to be interviewed by a famous psychiatrist because they were normal. What a responsibility! What a set-up! They dared not make a mistake: They could be neither unhappy nor unrealistically happy; they could neither admit to problems nor say that they had no problems; they had to be perfectly honest, natural, and, above all, *normal.* As they tried to thread their way through this mine field (which we had not intended), they sounded very strange indeed (e.g., Watzlawick, 1964; Watzlawick et al., 1967, pp. 76–78). So, by the mid-1960s, we at least understood that such imperfect communication was the product, not of an imperfect mind, but of an impossible situation, a situation in which no direct response would be satisfactory.

Although I then left clinical research for an academic career, these "bad" communications that were not really bad did not entirely fade from my mind. About 10 years later, during an individual study course with a mature student who had adult children, I was challenged to address the issue of always blaming the parents (of schizophrenics or anyone else), and I finally had to take my beliefs seriously: If communication is situational, then it is necessary to give up blaming. If the schizophrenic is not defective but only reacting to the subtle complexities of his or her situation, then so are the parents and family. It cannot be that different laws operate for one side than for the other.

Thus began the "disqualification project." Starting in 1977, we sought to identify the situations in which perfectly normal people would choose or produce messages that were considerably less than perfect. After first finding a method with which to identify and measure such messages (Bavelas & Smith, 1982), we began to list the many everyday situations that leave no alternative other than unclear communication. The result was a list of "binds" in which all communicative alternatives seemed impossible, yet communication was required. For example:

- You have to write a thank-you note for an awful gift from a well-liked friend or relative.

- You are asked for a letter of reference about a friend who was an incompetent employee.

- Two friends who disagree intensely about an issue ask you for your opinion on it.

In all of these cases, it is necessary to reply, yet all of the direct response options would have bad consequences. A disqualified response, which "says nothing while saying something" avoids the worst consequences. At this point, there was nothing worth calling a theory, just a notion about normal, transient, "benign binds" (as opposed to double binds; Bateson, Jackson, Haley, & Weakland, 1956).

Fortunately, I happened to describe our work to Professor Tamara Dembo (who had trained and worked with the German Gestalt school and also with Kurt Lewin). She suggested immediately that our situations were, colloquially, ones that involve "tact" and, more technically, appeared to be avoidance–avoidance conflicts. At last, it was possible to make more than a descriptive statement:

> A bind in our terms is an *avoidance–avoidance conflict,* in which two unappealing choices repel the individual, who will leave the field if possible—in this case, communicationally, by evasive or indirect communication. . . .

> Three premises can be applied to the case of conflict: (1) Situations are represented as valences [i.e., goals] attracting or repelling the person, that is, as eliciting approach or avoidance. (2) The force of the valence, whether positive or negative, is stronger if closer; this is the "goal gradient": A positive valence becomes more attractive as one approaches it, and a negative valence becomes more repellent as one comes closer to it. (3) There is a force or tendency towards movement—either the valences vary slightly, though randomly, or the decision region itself becomes negative. (Bavelas, 1983, pp. 138–139)

This theory accounted for previous results and predicted new ones, for example, that approach–approach conflicts (with two positive goals) would *not* elicit evasive communication. The social consequences of messages became goals with valences that could be positive or, more interestingly, negative. These external goals induce a psychological decision process that includes tension, vacillation, and finally, resolution.

Now we were at a crucial point in theory development. Lewin's theory is very appealing but also highly elaborate. It is a comprehensive theory of personality (cf. Lewin, 1935; Bavelas, 1978, chap. 17), and the conflict portion alone is a monograph (Lewin, 1938). Because Lewin was unusual among personality theories in including the interaction between the individual and the environment, his theory could be applied, more readily than most, to communication. However, the basic features of his theory were definitely intrapsychic; overt behavior was of interest because of what it revealed about intrapsychic processes. Even external features of the environment (such as goals) became part of the psychological life space and had their influence primarily by creating internal tensions toward resolution. We had no data on these internal tensions or, indeed, on any psychic structures or processes, and—being more interested in discourse—we were not keen to turn our attention to them. In short, had we adopted the larger structure of Lewin's theory, we would have created a classic inverted pyramid. It was clear from many colleagues' reactions that this would have been a popular choice, but, partly because a minority of other colleagues (such as Edna Rogers) urged us to "keep the faith," we began to back away from a full-fledged Lewinian theory and take another direction.

Essentially, we took an intervening variable approach. We explicitly labeled our theory as an *adaptation* of Lewin's and stripped it down to the bare, observable essentials (Bavelas et al., 1990b). We put goals back out there in the social environment, as consequences of message choices, and spent most of our time seeking equivocations (as we came to rename them) in the widest possible variety of situations. *Varied replication* became our main interest, because we wanted to show that our limited theory held firmly for its domain. We conducted avoidance–avoidance experiments with subjects writing their own messages (Bavelas & Chovil, 1986). Then we did the same with subjects responding on the telephone or face-to-face, in a total of about 14 different hypothetical scenarios; in some of these, we distinguished empirically between equivocation and deception (Bavelas et al., 1990a). The opportunity arose to do a field experiment that created a "real" conflict for politicians (Bavelas, Black, Bryson, & Mullett, 1988) and also to conduct some purely observational field work with politicians and reporters, with the aim of extending our theory into this particularly equivocal dyadic interaction. In other words, we sought generality by extending the data base for our relatively simple theory.

The difference between the route we took and the one we almost took became sharply clear to us when we examined a particular aspect of our data, namely, *latencies* (Bavelas, 1985, p. 205; Bavelas et al., 1990b). An avoidance–avoidance conflict is created for our subjects when they are actually asked the experimental question (e.g., "How do you like the gift I sent you?"). When the experiment is conducted with spoken (rather than written) communication, it is possible to measure response latency, which is the time between the end of the question and the beginning of the subject's reply. It is well established in Lewinian theory (Barker, 1942) that avoidance–avoidance conflicts produce longer latencies than do approach–approach conflicts or nonconflict conditions. According to the theory, this is because of vacillation between the two alternatives, caused by the goal gradient. Imagine that you are the subject and are considering a brutal truth ("I don't like the gift you sent"). As you come psychologically closer to saying this, it becomes more negative, so you change to the other possibility, a lie ("I love the gift!"). But coming closer to that alternative inevitably makes it more negative (and the first choice less so), so you reverse again. Even though this would happen very fast, it should take measurable time, producing a longer latency, and indeed, this is what we obtained. In all such experiments, the latencies were in the predicted direction, and, in most cases, the difference was statistically significant. These "empty moments" are, in the full Lewinian theory, envelopes that hold the intrapsychic process of vacillation, and they are probably as close as we will ever come to seeing this process. It was very tempting to interpret them as such.

By this time, however, we had a rule of always looking for a discourse-focused interpretation when tempted by an intrapsychic one. This was partly to maintain theoretical consistency but equally to force ourselves to see new phenomena rather than just more instances of old theories. The alternative explanation for the latencies was suggested mostly by the lay judges who scaled our messages for equivocation. They noticed the pauses and interpreted them *as part of the message*. Hesitating before saying something negative is a way of encoding reluctance. Someone who unhesitatingly told a friend, "You look awful," would seem eager to hurt that friend, whereas appearing to have it dragged out of him or her conveys, "I hate to say this but. . . ." As a 19th-century writer observed, "Well-timed silence hath more eloquence than speech" (Tupper, 1854, p. 90).

In the end, what we say about equivocation is detailed but limited, compared to many other theories, but we are very confident about its empirical validity and replicability. On a personal note, that kind of solid confidence feels good— not as heady as high-flying speculation but more lasting.

REFERENCES

Barker, R. G. (1942). An experimental study of the resolution of conflict by children: Time elapsing and amount of vicarious trial-and-error behavior occurring. In Q. McNemar & M. A. Merrill (Eds.), *Studies in personality* (pp. 13–34). New York: McGraw-Hill.

Bateson, G., Jackson, D. D., Haley, J., & Weakland, J. H. (1956). Toward a theory of schizophrenia. *Behavioral Science, 1,* 251–264.

Bavelas, J. B. (1978). *Personality: Current theory and research.* Monterey, CA.: Brooks/Cole.

Bavelas, J. B. (1983). Situations that lead to disqualification. *Human Communication Research, 9,* 130–145.

Bavelas, J. B. (1985). A situational theory of disqualification: Using language to "leave the field." In J. Forgas (Ed.), *Language and social situations* (pp. 189–211). New York: Springer.

Bavelas, J. B., Black, A., Bryson, L., & Mullett, J. (1988). Political equivocation: A situational explanation. *Journal of Language and Social Psychology, 7,* 137–145.

Bavelas, J. B., Black, A., Chovil, N., & Mullett, J. (1990a). Truths, lies, and equivocations: The effects of conflicting goals on discourse. *Journal of Language and Social Psychology, 9,* 129–155.

Bavelas, J. B., Black, A., Chovil, N., & Mullett, J. (1990b). *Equivocal communication.* Newbury Park, CA: Sage.

Bavelas, J. B., & Chovil, N. (1986). How people disqualify: Experimental studies of spontaneous written disqualification. *Communication Monographs, 53,* 70–74.

Bavelas, J. B., & Lee, E. S. (1978). Effects of goal level on performance: A trade-off of quantity and quality. *Canadian Journal of Psychology, 32,* 219–240.

Bavelas, J. B., & Smith, B. J. (1982). A method for scaling verbal disqualification. *Human Communication Research, 8,* 214–227.

Campbell, D. T., & Fiske, D. W. (1959). Convergent and discriminant validation by the multitrait-multimethod matrix. *Psychological Bulletin, 56,* 81–105.

Cartwright, D. (1959). Lewinian theory as a contemporary systematic framework. In S. Koch (Ed.), *Psychology: A study of a science, Vol. 2, General systematic formulations, learning, and special processes* (pp. 7–91). New York: McGraw-Hill.

Lewin, K. (1935). *A dynamic theory of personality. Selected papers.* (D. K. Adams & K. E. Zener, Trans.). New York: McGraw-Hill.

Lewin, K. (1938). The conceptual representation and measurement of psychological forces. *Contributions to Psychological Theory, 1* (4, Serial No. 4).

MacCorquodale, K., & Meehl, P. E. (1948). On a distinction between hypothetical constructs and intervening variables. *Psychological Review, 55,* 95–107.

Sluzki, C. E., Beavin, J., Tarnopolsky, A., & Verón, E. (1967). Transactional disqualification. Research on the double bind. *Archives of General Psychiatry, 16,* 494–504.

Tolman, E. C. (1932). *Purposive behavior in animals and men.* New York: Century.

Tolman, E. C. (1959). Principles of purposive behavior. In S. Koch (Ed.), *Psychology: A study of a science. Vol. 2. General systematic formulations, learning, and special processes* (pp. 92–157). New York: McGraw-Hill.

Tupper, M. F. (1854). Of discretion. In *Proverbial philosophy* (p. 90). London: Thomas Hatchard.

Underwood, B. J. (1957). *Psychological research.* New York: Appleton-Century-Crofts.

Watzlawick, P. (1964). *An anthology of human communication: Text and tape.* Palo Alto: Science and Behavior Books.

Watzlawick, P., Beavin, J., & Jackson, D. D. (1967). *Pragmatics of human communication.* New York: Norton.

CHAPTER 8

Message Design Logic and the Management of Multiple Goals

Barbara J. O'Keefe
University of Illinois at Urbana-Champaign

Many communication theorists have assumed that the relationship between messages and goals is relatively simple: A communicative task is defined by a specific objective or set of objectives, and for any task there is one general sort of message that is employed to do the job—it is the action that "counts as" getting the job done. Something like this image of message design can be found, for example, in analyses of communication based on speech–act theory (e.g., Bach & Harnish, 1972; Searle, 1972).

And, in fact, it is often the case that, given a communicative task to pursue, virtually every speaker addresses that task in a similar way with relatively equal ease and success. For example, Linde and Labov (1975) observed that apartment descriptions appear to be produced to a uniformly applied formula, which leads people to reason in very similar ways about what information to communicate and how to communicate the information.

However, not all communicative tasks elicit uniform performance from different individuals. Some tasks lead people to produce very different kinds of messages, with differing degrees of success. A great deal of research on interpersonal behavior has been directed at describing the range of messages produced for key interpersonal tasks such as compliance gaining, resisting influence, comforting, and regulating behavior (for reviews, see Burleson, 1984; O'Keefe & Delia, 1982; Seibold, Cantrill, & Meyers, 1985). Obviously, such diversity in message design poses a puzzle for any simple theory of the relationship of communicative actions to goals: Why does message diversity occur, and why does it persist when some messages are plainly more effective than others?

Stimulated by the work of Brown and Levinson (1978), a number of theorists have been led to argue that heterogenous responses to communicative tasks reflect the operation of multiple and competing goals (see, e.g., Baxter, 1984; O'Keefe & Delia, 1982). Even though a communicative task may be defined by one primary objective, such as gaining compliance, the speaker may have other objectives that must be attended to as well. Whereas for any particular goal, one set of message types might be optimal, it is seldom the case that any particular type of message will be well designed to meet *all* the objectives an individual might pursue. Hence, message diversity results from the situational relevance of multiple goals: Because individuals are balancing the competing claims of multiple goals, they must assign some priority ranking to the different goals they wish to accomplish; and as different speakers strike the balance among competing goals at different points, they are led to produce different types of messages.

Both Brown and Levinson's account and the work that has been stimulated by it are based on the assumption that messages are rationally designed to meet communicative objectives. This chapter argues that the range of observed variation in message design presents standard rational models, such as Brown and Levinson's, with various anomalies; it advances the claim that to explain observed variation in communicative performance, one must appreciate not only that goals can differ but that conceptions of rational message design differ as well.

The chapter has three sections. The first section outlines the standard rational model of message design, as represented in Brown and Levinson's (1978) analysis of politeness. The second section discusses the limitations of the standard rational account. The third section offers an alternative to the standard rational account, which elaborates the idea that some variations in message design are attributable to variability in the concepts of communication that individuals employ in designing messages.

A RATIONAL MODEL OF MESSAGE DESIGN

Brown and Levinson (1978) argued that the various forms of politeness within a language could be understood as rational resolutions of goal conflicts that naturally arise when a speaker undertakes a face-threatening action: To achieve his or her goal, the speaker needs to be clear, but being clear will mean being more face-threatening; and conversely, to save face, the speaker must sacrifice getting the point across.

Brown and Levinson's analysis is quite persuasive, both in its details and in exemplifying a general technique for message analysis. A rational model like Brown and Levinson's offers a principled explanation of the existence and use of variations in politeness forms. In previous work on face protection and identity management (e.g., Gross & Stone, 1964; Scott & Lyman, 1968; Weinstein, 1969), researchers have constructed lists of face-managing strategies but have failed to adequately explain why message variations occur and why there should be diversity within a given situation in the types of messages produced by different individuals (for an elaborated discussion of this point, see O'Keefe, 1987). Brown and Levinson's model offers a unified account of why messages differ, why they take the specific forms they do, and why they are differentially successful in being clear and polite.

In Brown and Levinson's account, message variants arise from the coordinated exploitation of two linguistic resources: indirectness and face-relevant elaboration. Indirectness is a message property that can be defined and analyzed independently of its use as face protection. Although analyses of indirectness by different theorists differ in details, most would agree that indirectness essentially consists of communicating by implication. A speaker says one thing, which, under the circumstances, would warrant the inference that the speaker means to communicate a second intention or idea as well. But, theoretically, communication by implication is less certain to achieve its goals than direct communication, since the hearer may or may not make the correct inference. Consequently, indirect communication can be seen as less efficient than direct communication: It is less likely to make the desired point clear to the hearer.

Indirectness can be exploited to good effect in dealing with face-threatening situations. In Goffman's (1967) formulation, which serves as the foundation for Brown and Levinson's analysis, face is defined as "the positive social value a person claims for himself" (p. 5). Face is created and sustained in and through communication with others; it is an aspect of the "front" an individual puts forward. In short, face is the person as publicly defined and represented, the self that is "on the record." The inner self remains implicit and is "off the record," not part of one's public identity. Theoretically, then, only explicit communication can pose a serious threat to face—that which remains private and unspoken does not become part of one's public identity. By keeping face-threatening intentions unspoken and "off record," indirect messages can communicate potentially face-threatening intentions without necessarily giving offense, whereas "on-record," direct communication commits the face-threatening action of making those intentions public.

What this means is that indirectness can be exploited rationally in the service of an individual's goals. Being more direct makes it more likely that one will get one's point across, but creates increased possibilities for face threat; being indirect reduces face threats but may fail to get the point across or secure the hearer's acknowledgment of the point.

However, indirectness is not the only resource individuals can call on in designing messages to avoid face threats. They have a second verbal resource as well: face-relevant elaborations, which Brown and Levinson have called "forms of redress." Because face is a symbolic entity that is created through communication, it can be manipulated symbolically. A person can give "face" by offering verbal descriptions, accounts, or reassurances to another. These forms of redress can be appended to face-threatening actions in an effort to offer the other face even as it is taken away by the primary act being performed by the speaker. Obviously, it is more efficient to simply perform a face-threatening act baldly, with no redress, but adding in redress mitigates the face threat by giving face in return.

As with indirectness, forms of redress can be exploited in a rational process of designing messages to reflect the priority given to one's goals: As a speaker gives higher priority to saving face, he or she should be more likely to employ forms of redress; the lower the priority given to saving face, the less likely a speaker should be to use redress.

By assuming that speakers design their messages rationally to reflect their goals, but that they sometimes are faced with multiple, competing objectives, Brown and Levinson were thus able to provide a principled explanation of a number of important facts about message design: (a) in many situations, there are many ways of being polite and there are degrees of politeness; (b) messages vary in face threat and protection; and (c) frequently, speakers do not produce those messages that seem best adapted for achieving their primary goals, but rather employ inefficient messages.

In sum: Brown and Levinson's detailed analysis of the rational exploitation of indirectness and forms of redress provides an exemplary account of the adaptive properties of interpersonal messages, of the fit between messages and the jobs they are meant to do. Forms become more polite as lower priority is given to clear communication and a higher priority is given to saving face; the priority given each goal is a function of situational variables; hence, messages vary because situations vary and cause different priority to be given to clarity and face protection.

INDIVIDUAL DIFFERENCES IN MESSAGE DESIGN

It is easy to see how Brown and Levinson's formulation can account for the appearance of fundamentally different kinds of messages across a particular communicative task. For example, one might argue (as Baxter, 1984, has proposed) that the range of compliance-gaining message strategies identified by diverse research programs essentially reflect a common differentiation of message types in terms of the priority given to the face wants of the addressee. That is, across the range of compliance-gaining situations, a range of messages will be observed, with variations in messages basically reflecting differences in indirectness and redress associated with politeness. As the specifics of the compliance-gaining situation shift, so does the relative priority given to clarity and face protection.

However, there is also substantial evidence that, even within a specific situation, it is frequently the case that different individuals will produce different messages. Research on the development of person-centered communication skills (for summaries see Burleson, 1989; O'Keefe & Delia, 1982, 1985) suggests that individuals addressing the same specific communicative task can vary systematically and dramatically in the degree to which they produce messages that show respect and consideration for the message recipient.

For example, in one recent study (O'Keefe & Lambert, 1989), we asked college students what they would say in the following situation: A friend (Terry) who has frequently cancelled plans to go out with you calls again to say that, rather than going with you to a movie tonight, as you had planned, he or she must attend a meeting; Terry asks whether you can go to the movie tomorrow night. Some of their replies to Terry are shown in Examples 1 through 6 (following). Although all the messages express the speaker's disapproval of Terry's behavior, they vary in a number of features: how much verbal abuse is heaped on Terry, whether some degree of understanding is expressed, whether the speaker agrees to see Terry in the future or refuses, how the friendship figures in the message, and so on:

1. No, Terry, we can't make it tomorrow night because I've wasted my time waiting for you. I've tried to be understanding about your hectic schedule but you aren't being understanding to me. As a friend you owe it to me to keep your commitments with me instead of throwing me aside every time something comes up.

2. Terry, I understand you have obligations and responsibilities but you have to be fair to your friends. Because I'm a good friend, I won't blow you off as much as you've blown me off. Just remember: in life—friends are *the most* valuable people to you. Since your meeting is not till 8:00 p.m., let's go out for a walk right now and talk. No excuses!

3. Terry, I think we need to talk about why you haven't had time for me lately. I could understand if you had to break an engagement with me once in a while but all of the time gets a little old. If you don't have time to go out then don't make plans in advance and let me know when you have time for me.

4. Okay, but are you sure you can make it tomorrow night or are you going to cancel out on me again? Lately Terry, you have placed our friendship second to your meetings and activities. I don't even remember the last time we went out together, do you? I have no plans for tomorrow night but I'm not going to make tentative plans only for you to cancel them. Give me a call tomorrow around 7:00 and tell me if you want to go out.

5. Terry couldn't you have scheduled your meeting at another time? I realize that your activities are very important to you, but it's becoming quite obvious

that these activities and everything else come before me. Or maybe that's not the case, you just think that no matter what happens, I'll be by your side. Well, to be honest with you, I'm getting hurt every time you cancel on me because I feel like you just don't care anymore! I want to be there to support you and your activities, but I can't unless you're here to support me, too—!

6. Terry, this has happened a few too many times. I understand that you have meetings, etc., but you need to get organized. I can't revolve my life around your schedule. You know that. I understand about tonight. However, if you had a book of previous dates, or something, you would have realized that you did have a meeting. It's too late now. I'll go to the movie tomorrow night if you know absolutely that you will be there. I'm not mad at you, I just want you to become more organized.

Although Brown and Levinson (1978) did not attempt to account for the existence of such individual differences in message design, it is easy to see how their framework might be extended to do so, by positing that individuals differ systematically in the ways they assign priority to instrumental goals and to the face wants of speaker and hearer. For example, Kline (1985) conducted a series of studies in which she investigated the relationship between cognitive complexity and politeness. Working within Brown and Levinson's framwork, Kline developed a method for classifying regulative messages in terms of the degree to which the hearer's needs for respect and autonomy (positive and negative face wants) were satisfied by the message producer. She found that those who scored higher in cognitive complexity were more likely to use polite messages. But in a followup experiment (Kline, 1985), she found that when individuals were explicitly instructed to satisfy the hearer's face wants, the effects of cognitive complexity on face protection were moderated because those who scored lower in cognitive complexity elevated the levels of face support they provided. This research suggests that one consequence of cognitive complexity is an increasing concern with face wants, which in turn leads to the production of increasingly polite messages.

However, there is reason to believe that individuals differ not only in the priority they give to different goals but also in the method they use in managing multiple goals. In a study I conducted in collaboration with Greg Shepherd (O'Keefe & Shepherd, 1987, 1989), we asked people who were known to disagree strongly about a topic to discuss the topic and try to persuade each other. Their messages were classified in three ways. First, we classified the messages in terms of the kind of basic posture an individual adopted toward the conflict—whether the message expressed agreement or disagreement with the position advocated by the message recipient. Second, we classified the messages in terms of how the basic posture was expressed—whether the message was explicit in taking a position or conveyed agreement or disagreement only by implication.

An individual's decisions about whether to agree or disagree and how to express agreement/disagreement define a set of goals that are being pursued and traded off: Someone who explicitly agrees is trading off being clear about his or her own position and avoids threatening the face wants of the other person. Someone who explicitly disagrees is able to clearly express his or her own views but commits an overtly face-threatening action. Someone who conveys agreement or disagreement implicitly resolves the trade-off between clear communication and face by trading off the possibility of continuing the conversation, by refusing to say anything to which they will be committed. Following this analysis, we were able to classify messages in a third way, according to their method of goal reconciliation, the way in which the goals that an individual traded off were addressed in the message.

We found that individuals employed three basic methods of managing subsidiary goals, that is, the goals that are traded off by the basic posture and manner of expression (this in contrast to the dominant goals, those secured by the basic posture and manner of expression). The first method, selection, reflects the practice of simply trading off subsidiary goals. Individuals who employ selection make no effort to address the goals that are traded off. "Selection" takes different forms, depending on the basic posture and manner of expression, but the following were all taken as instances of selection:

- listening to the other person's argument and giving only back-channel responses and no real uptake (implicit agreement)

- explaining one's own viewpoint in a nonargumentative manner, avoiding "clash" with the other person by failing to give uptake to the other's contributions (implicit disagreement)

- explicitly agreeing or disagreeing with what the other person said (explicit agreement or disagreement)

Individuals who employed "separation" strategies addressed subsidiary goals in a separate and discrete part of the message, as an "add-on" that was not integrated with the primary action being performed. This basically involved redressive elaborations added to the basic message, such as compliments, hedges, apologies, accounts, and so on, designed to satisfy the goals traded off by the basic posture and manner of expression. So, for example, the following kinds of messages were categorized as embodying instances of separation:

- complimenting the other person on his or her argument, but then criticizing it or rejecting it (explicit disagreement)

- agreeing with the other person, but then mentioning issues "won" by the speaker or areas of sustained disagreement (explicit agreement)

- refusing to discuss the assigned topic or give uptake, then either apologizing for noncooperativeness or offering an account for it (implicit agreement or disagreement)

- hedging or qualifying agreement or disagreement (explicit agreement or disagreement)

Finally, individuals who employed "integration" strategies adopted modes of self-presentation and communication that "defused" the basic posture and manner of expression they adopted; by explicitly manipulating the meaning of their behavior, these individuals avoided the trade-offs that would ordinarily be associated with agreeing or disagreeing, being implicit or being explicit. For example, the following kinds of messages were categorized as embodying integration:

- explaining a failure to argue with the partner as deriving from the partner's greater commitment to and expertise with the assigned issue, and professing a desire to be instructed in the issue (implicit agreement)

- characterizing the interaction as an opportunity for both parties to learn more about the assigned topic by exchanging opposing views (explicit disagreement)

- acting toward the situation as though it is a problem-solving exercise in which the common interest of participants is to find a compromise solution that they can both accede to (explicit agreement)

- treating the interaction as an opportunity for two people to become better acquainted with each other through exploration of their beliefs about the topic (implicit disagreement)

The identification of these three different techniques for dealing with subsidiary goals (selection, separation, integration) suggests that Brown and Levinson's (1978) analysis is incomplete. Based on their analysis of indirectness and forms of redress, Brown and Levinson argued that there are a variety of situations that motivate people to perform intrinsically face-threatening actions (FTAs) and that there are four basic strategies for dealing with intrinsically face-threatening situations: (a) do the FTA baldly; (b) do the FTA with redress; (c) do the FTA off-record; and (d) don't do the FTA. In the abstract, this scheme appears complete and exhaustive.

But there is at least one way of dealing with subsidiary goals—the method we called "integration"—that clearly resists classification into any of these categories. Integration basically involves defining the communication situation to avoid awkward or unwanted implications normally associated with one's actions (e.g., lack of respect for the hearer's views would ordinarily be implied by an attack on the hearer's views). Use of integration generally results in a change in the surplus meaning of the actions performed to accomplish one's goals. For example, contextualizing agreement and disagreement as acquaintance strategies does not alter the way in which they contribute to the logical development of a topic in a discussion, but does alter their value as face-threatening actions. Although it may appear that both selection and separation represent kinds of politeness techniques that Brown and Levinson have described, there is no strategy in their scheme that corresponds even roughly to what we observed and called "integration."

LIMITATIONS OF THE STANDARD RATIONAL MODEL

The question is, can the Brown and Levinson model—or one like it—be revised or extended to account for the kinds of messages we classed as employing integration? This section argues that a standard rational analysis is limited in its ability to account for the observed range of individual variability in message design. Not only does such an analysis fail to adequately account for the "integration" method of dealing with subsidiary goals, but it also provides an incoherent analysis of the "selection" method.

It should be noted at the outset that those who employed the "separation" method of dealing with subsidiary goals acted in ways that fit Brown and Levinson's model fairly neatly. They chose to pursue the goal of persuasion by advancing assertions and trying to get the other person to agree; the objective assigned to them (persuade the other) seemed to lead inevitably to the performance of a particular communicative act with a particular point. Certainly, such people varied in the kinds of messages they produced: Some used indirect actions, some used redressive forms in their messages, and so on. But these message variations are all easily understood as instantiations of Brown and Levinson's four basic politeness strategies. Moreover, people in this study were asked to rate their partners' behavior for politeness and persuasiveness, and our results supported the view that use of such conventional politeness forms does, in fact, produce a tradeoff of clear and effective communication against face support (O'Keefe & Shepherd, 1987, 1989).

Anomalies of Integration

What we called "integration" appears to involve a qualitatively different way of reasoning about message design. Consider the individuals in our study who defined the situation as cooperative rather than competitive. These individuals treated the situation as one in which the relevant outcome to be sought was a cooperative resolution of the conflict between the wants of the two parties. Such individuals diligently pursued the goal of securing agreement, but they defined and organized agreement as a common understanding achieved jointly rather than as a backdown of the other party. And the achievement of such agreement was brought about not through the performance of some particular act that sought agreement but through forging a common world of discourse with the partner.

Brown and Levinson's analysis assumes that face wants are managed through manipulating two linguistic resources—directness and redressive elaboration. But such a consensus-seeking approach employs neither of these to manage subsidiary goals. Obviously, attempts to reach consensus do avoid performing any face-threatening action, since the agendas of both speaker and hearer are affirmed. But it does not make sense to call this an instance of avoidance (i.e., "Don't do the FTA") because there was no FTA to be performed. Hence, although no FTA is committed, consensus-seeking does not involve avoidance of the FTA. Nor does it seem to be a case of indirectness: In indirectness, the FTA is performed but off-record; whereas with this approach, the FTA is not performed at all. And, of course, no on-record FTA is performed. So whatever this approach represents, it reflects a message design process different in kind from the one Brown and Levinson have described.

It is a message design process that cannot be described within their model or any model that assumes that communication situations consist of a set of fixed parameters that dictate goals, which, in turn, dictate actions. Brown and Levinson's analysis is based on the assumption that people alter their communicative actions to fit the communicative situation, but individuals who use consensus-seeking and other forms of integration do just the opposite—they alter the situation to fit the action they want to perform.

The existence of integration as a method of dealing with subsidiary goals also suggests an interesting puzzle: If it is possible to approach a situation like the one we studied in a way that makes face threat irrelevant, why would anyone choose to pursue an intrinsically face-threatening line of action? The only answer Brown and Levinson can give is that avoiding the FTA trades off efficiency in communication and thus makes it more difficult for the speaker to achieve his or her personal agenda. But, in fact, pursuing a cooperative course of action has just as much potential to produce agreement as the alternative course of pursuing a backdown. Indeed, in several recent studies (Bingham, 1988a, 1988b; O'Keefe & McCornack, 1987; O'Keefe & Shepherd, 1987, 1989), messages employing integration were judged as most effective in managing face issues but were not rated as ineffective in advancing the speaker's own aims. One study (O'Keefe & McCornack, 1987) found they were actually more effective in achieving both the dominant communication goal and face protection).

From the standpoint of Brown and Levinson's analysis, it should not be possible to avoid the tradeoff between clear communication and face threat; but some of the people we have been studying clearly manage to do so. If some people can find a way out of the dilemma, then anyone should be able to find this path, because communicators share the same linguistic resources. The fact that they do not poses an interesting problem for theories of message production.

The Paradoxes of Selection

Those who employed integration as a method of dealing with subsidiary goals used unconventional means and were uncommonly effective. By contrast, those who employed selection were both unconventional and ineffective. For example, some of these individuals dealt with the conflict situation by lying; when the partner introduced the assigned topic, they blatantly lied about their position on the issue, misrepresenting their views as in agreement with the partner (we know they lied because they reported their beliefs on a pretest questionnaire). Other subjects wouldn't discuss the issue or anything else, refusing to give uptake to their partners. Others made incoherent contributions that introduced irrelevant personal topics. And so on.

How can the use of uncooperative messages be understood as a rational response to the goal-management demands of this situation? That is, how can this behavior be accommodated within an analysis such as Brown and Levinson's? The most straightforward suggestion is that these are all instances of avoidance (i.e., "Don't do the FTA").

But that suggestion preserves Brown and Levinson's category scheme at the expense of the assumption of rationality: All of these "avoidance" behaviors are radically uncooperative by conventional standards. Lying, being irrelevant, refusing to get the point, and so on involve gross flouting of every standard of cooperative conduct in conversation (see Grice, 1975). They do not involve withholding the FTA, in any normal sense; there is no point to be made and hence no intrinsically face-threatening action that follows from getting the point across. Instead, these uncooperative acts involve withholding communication itself. It hardly seems rational that individuals would perform such radically uncooperative acts, with their attendant costs, simply in the interest of not disagreeing with another person; this is especially striking when one considers the number of different, utterly conventional ways there are to disagree or talk about conflict politely.

In short, this too seems to be a form of behavior that stands outside the kind of analysis Brown and Levinson have offered. At the very least, it seems to embody a very different sense of rationality than the one that Brown and Levinson assumed.

Summary

Although Brown and Levinson have offered a convincing analysis of conventional forms of politeness, their analysis cannot be extended to account for any but the conventionally polite and cooperative separation strategies that people used in their face-to-face arguments. The question is, how can the full range of variation in messages be described and explained?

I believe the answer lies in recognizing that much of the variation in messages elicited by complex communication situations cannot be accounted for simply in terms of the priority given to different goals; some of the variation is associated with individual differences in the bedrock assumptions communicators make about how to pursue goals through communication. Brown and Levinson's conventional communicator acts as though, given a situation and a goal, there is a natural line of action that ought to be pursued in order to achieve that goal, and such a communicator follows the conventions of cooperation that make such a system of exchange work. These conventional communicators appear to reason from ends to means.

The uncooperative communicators we observed seemed to design their behavior on a different basis: The conventional basis of communicative conduct was disregarded, and they oriented purely to whether they were willing to reveal their thoughts and feelings to the partner. Hence, their actions were designed defensively rather than planfully and reflected a self-oriented design (Don't reveal yourself) rather than an other-oriented design (Don't do the FTA). Their behavior raises the question of what leads a person to view a communication situation such as this one as an occasion for self-exposure rather than an opportunity to influence the addressee. Certainly, we can imagine the circumstances in which the threat of self-exposure would lead anyone to at least consider lying or behaving in some other uncooperative fashion; but, in the situation we examined, everyone already knew the person's views, because they were indicated on the pretest and publicly reported to the subjects as part of the experimental induction. In such a circumstance, what leads a person to avoid conflict through radically uncooperative acts, such as lying or refusing to give uptake?

Similarly, behavior of the more sophisticated communicators who sought consensual solutions raises questions for a rational account of their behavior. The basis on which they appeared to select a line of action differed markedly from the more conventional actors. Whereas the conventional communicators selected an action to perform whose point matched the goal they sought to achieve, and the action was supported and defended on conventional grounds, the consensus-seeking communicators appeared to begin with the notion that agreement is brought about as a consequence of defining a mutually acceptable alternative. This might be achieved by compromise or by convincing the other person that a particular alternative is mutually desirable. But the action pursued to achieve the desired end seemed to follow from the situation-specific assessment of what it would take to reach agreement with the particular addressee, rather than from an assumption about what action is conventionally designed to get agreement independent of the addressee. The performance of these communicators raises the question of what permits some, but not all, communicators to realize that a situation such as this one need not involve an FTA? And, if they are reasoning on a different basis than the more conventional communicators, what form of reasoning allows the more sophisticated communicators to design the kinds of messages they use?

THE LOGIC OF MESSAGE DESIGN

Individual Differences in Reasoning About Messages

My theory of message design logic (O'Keefe, 1988) is designed to explain why people's messages can display such markedly different views of relevance, appropriateness, and effectiveness. On the basis of studies of individual differences in message production across a number of different genres, I have argued that individuals may employ any of three different sets of beliefs about message design ("message design logics") in producing and understanding messages. Each of these three message design logics can be understood as a constellation of related beliefs and operations: a communication-constituting concept, a conception of the functional possibilities of communication, unit formation procedures, and principles of coherence. The three message design logics identified in my original formulation are called expressive, conventional, and rhetorical.

An *expressive* message design logic reflects the view that communication is a process of expressing and receiving encoded thoughts and feelings. Characteristically, those who use an expressive logic fail to distinguish between thought and expression; in producing messages, they "dump" their current mental state, and they assume that others produce messages the same way. Expressive communicators do not generally alter expression systematically in the service of achieving effects, nor do they ordinarily find anything other than "literal and direct" meaning in incoming messages.

A *conventional* message design logic is based on the view that communication is a game played cooperatively, according to social conventions and procedures. Within conventional logic, thought and expression are related in a less isomorphic way, because expression is subordinated to the achievement of other instrumental goals. Language is still treated as a means of expressing propositions, but the expressed propositions are specified by the social effect one wants to achieve (utterance content is specified in the sense that uttering a given set of propositions under certain conditions counts as performing an action that is associated in sociocultural practice with the effect that the message producer wants to achieve; for example, uttering a certain kind of proposition under the right conditions counts as performing a request, and performing a request is a way to get certain wants satisfied simply by exploiting conventional obligations among persons). Conventional communicators treat communicative contexts (the roles, rights, and relations that situations contain) as having fixed parameters (that is, they take social structure—roles and norms—to be both manifest to all and relatively inflexible) and design messages by performing what they take to be the contextually appropriate actions.

A *rhetorical* message design logic reflects a view of communication as the creation and negotiation of social selves and situations. The rhetorical view subsumes knowledge of conventional ways to achieve goals within the view that social structure is flexible and created through communication. Rather than seeing selves and situations as fixed by convention; and rather than seeing meaning as fixed in form and context, self, situation, and meaning are bound together in dramaturgical enactment and social negotiation. For the rhetorical communicator, social reality is created by what and how something is said or written, and so messages are designed to portray a scene that is consistent with one's wants; the discourse of others is closely interpreted to determine the nature of the drama and the perspective they are enacting.

Differences in performance attributable to differences in design logic are clearly displayed in Examples 7 through 12 (following). These messages were produced in response to the Group Leader problem. The Group Leader problem has been used extensively in our studies of interpersonal competence. This problem asks people to say how they would handle a situation in which they, as the leader of a class project group, must deal with a procrastinating group member who has requested an extension just before a major project deadline. This scenario has several features that lead it to elicit different messages from individuals whose design logics differ. First, the procrastinator, Ron, is represented as having repeatedly failed to conform to the group's decisions and procedures; this leads people to have a negative impression of Ron and a number of salient beliefs about his past conduct that are not particularly relevant for dealing with the present situation. Second, the group is portrayed as having a particular organization and set of commitments that might or might not be subject to renegotiation but that are relevant to dealing with Ron's failure to perform; the ways that the group's arrangements might be altered to secure a good outcome are fairly easy to see and plainly advantageous. In short, the presence of salient but irrelevant and negatively valenced beliefs about Ron's past behavior and the desirability of reorganizing the situation make this scenario especially useful for detecting differences in design logic.

An expressive message design principle leads people to produce a Group Leader message that is sparse, ineffectual, and highly affective in tone. The two most identifiable properties of expressive messages are a lack of editing (so that socially unacceptable content or tenuously relevant content is included in the message) and a failure to engage the immediate task to be accomplished in the situation (so that messages may focus exclusively on past transgressions, rather than present problems, or perform some action that is emotionally satisfying but interferes with task accomplishment). Examples 7 and 8 display these properties:

7. You stupid ass fucker. Why did you wait so long to tell us you were getting behind on your part. You fucked up all our grades. I'm getting you out of this group. Everybody feels the same way. I hope you have fun when you take the class next semester.

8. Ron, I can't believe you haven't finished your research. You have been inconsiderate to the group all along. Several members even suggested that you be taken out of the group but we decided to give you a chance. Now what are we supposed to do? It was your responsibility and you backed out. I'm afraid that I'm going to tell the TA that you haven't done your share. I will be so mad at you if we get a bad grade on this—I need an A in this course.

Conventional messages reflect a view of message design as a matter of mentioning the feature or features of the context that, given the existing structure of rights and obligations in the situation, should serve as reasons for the message target to perform as required. The application of this message design logic produces a second type of message. In contrast to expressive messages, conventional messages generally predicate some future goal-related action of the message target. Conventionally designed messages often mention contextual conditions that are either prerequisite to the performance of the desired action or backing for the leader's demand that the action be performed. Messages 9 and 10 exemplify this design logic:

9. Ron, you idiot, this speech is due next week and you are not getting anything done. Now number one you owe it to other people in the group who have spent a great deal of time and energy working on this to at least do your part. Number two you have been slacking off all together on this project, I hope you realize you will be getting an individual grade—and at this point I seriously doubt that it will be a high one. There is no excuse for this laziness, and I really don't appreciate it, so get going now, and have that material prepared by tomorrow.

10. I would ask Ron if he had serious family problems or was he just blowing us off. If he had serious problems, I would ask him to call the T.A. and tell him/her the situation with our group. If he was blowing us off, I would talk to my T.A. and explain the problem. If Ron had serious problems I would encourage him to talk to someone. I would ask him to please consider what he is doing to our group. If he was blowing us off, I would insist he get his butt to the library and research.

Finally, a rhetorical design logic leads people to produce a third type of message. In rhetorical messages, the conditions described in the scenario are treated not as givens but as resources that can be called on in transforming the situation to facilitate goal attainment. The linguistic mechanisms through which these transformations are effected are motivational appeals, rhetorical labeling, explicit redescriptions of the context, and the like. In the course of talking about one thing (what Ron should do), the rhetorical communicator elaborates the message in such a way as to reconstitute some important set of features of the situation (own identity, Ron's identity, Ron's motives, the group's procedures, and so on). Messages 11 and 12 exemplify this approach to message design:

11. Ron, I'm sorry you won't have everything ready by tonight. Can you give me some good reasons I can tell the group? I know you've been having problems all along and that's obvious to the rest of the group too. You need to be able to see how your personal problems have interfered in the group's completion of the project. I'll be the first to sympathize with you but now we'll have to come up with some concrete solutions. You can't expect someone else to take over your research workload.

12. Well, Ron, it's due next week and we have to get it all to the typist. OK, if it's not done it's not. Tell you what. Why don't you jot down your main ideas so that we can include them in the introduction and conclusion. Also, tell me when you think your section should come in the whole project. Then get it to my apt. by 10:00 the next day because I have to get it to the typist by 2:00. Is this okay? I'll just explain to the group that you'll have it done but not by meeting time. We all want a good grade, so if you need the time to make your part better, go ahead. But if I can't get it to the typist in time, you'll have to type it. Alright, take it easy.

This problem has been used in several investigations (e.g., O'Keefe, 1988; O'Keefe & Lambert, 1989). We have found that generally around 85% of the messages people produce are easy to classify as reflecting one of these three design logics. The remaining 15% or so are not so easy to classify, due to (a) the message embodying structures that are very infrequently employed by the general population and hence not familiar to the coders or (b) the message being ambiguous in a way that makes it difficult to decide what values the message takes on the relevant dimensions of classification. We have, however, developed systematic procedures for assigning even unusual and ambiguous messages to one of these categories.

The Management of Multiple Objectives

Each message design logic offers methods for managing complex goal sets, in which mutually inconsistent sets of goals coexist. Consider the classic dilemma of the potentially face-threatening action, in which a speaker's wish can only be satisfied at the expense of the hearer's face wants. A message producer who employs an expressive design logic will be faced with the desire to express the wish (which would be inconsiderate) and the conflicting desire to be polite and considerate. This person does have a way of expressing his or her own wants while also attending to face wants, and that is through editing the message or being less than frank or distorting the truth a bit. Hence, "Be tactful" is the expressive solution to face-threatening situations.

There are also conventional solutions to face-threatening situations, that is, solutions derivable from a conventional message design logic. These essentially involve off-record communication and the incorporation of conventional politeness forms (e.g., apologies, compliments, hedges, excuses) in messages. The conventional answer is, thus, "Be polite."

Finally, it is possible to deal with face-threatening situations by transforming one's social self or identity. If one assumes that selves are socially constituted, then they are changeable through taking on a different character in social interaction. This is the rhetorical solution—to cast oneself or one's partner into a role in a new drama in which there is no conflict of interest or implication of shame. Within a rhetorical message design logic, it is possible to deal with multiple and conflicting goals by redefining the situation. The rhetorical answer is, "Be someone else."

From this reasoning, one can see that the differences in goal management strategies observed in face-to-face arguments (O'Keefe & Shepherd, 1987) reflect differences in communication-constituting concepts, since selection, separation, and integration correspond precisely to the three message types that are generated by the three different message design logics. It should be apparent that the kinds of message designs and communicative choices that appear puzzling and irrational from the standpoint of Brown and Levinson's model are quite rational when viewed from a different standpoint: the standpoint of the theory of message design logic. When Shepherd and I (O'Keefe & Shepherd, 1987, 1989) observed communicators who employed selection and integration as methods of managing subsidiary goals, what we were seeing were communicators who exhibited, on the one hand, an expressive message design logic and, on the other hand, a rhetorical design logic.

In a situation such as the one that Shepherd and I studied, an expressive communicator can be expected to notice the conflict between views and (especially when the expressive communicator wants to be polite) to refuse to articulate disagreeable ideas; in short, an expressive communicator can be expected to edit—to refuse to contribute, to lie, or to distort. On the other hand, a rhetorical communicator can be expected to approach the situation with an information-gathering, consensus-seeking posture that does not necessarily involve face threat, to anticipate face threats and manage the context to defuse them, and to treat the other as a resource rather than an obstacle to gaining agreement.

Notice, thus, that Brown and Levinson's analysis seems to nicely illuminate the alternatives of a conventional communicator but offers a ham-handed treatment of actions designed on the basis of nonconventional principles. Hence, the central limitation in Brown and Levinson's analysis can be seen: It embodies only one conception of rationality in communication, when alternative conceptions are possible. And the contribution of the theory of message design logic is that it permits messages that reflect diverse implicit conceptions of communication to be understood as rationally designed to meet the producer's ends.

CONCLUSIONS

This chapter has argued that, although a rational model offers an appealing kind of explanation of individual and situational differences in message design, such models are generally limited by the assumption that there is one way of designing messages that represents *the* rational way to associate messages and goals. But to account for the observed range of variation in message production, it is necessary to recognize that individuals can differ systematically in their concepts of message design and, consequently, employ systematically different methods of associating messages and goals. In short, rational analyses of message design should recognize and model the alternative rationalities that can underwrite communication.

It should be emphasized, however, that even a rational analysis that is sensitive to individual differences in message design logic is just an explanation of why messages differ in form and effectiveness. That is, a rational analysis should not be taken literally as a model of message production. One assumption that has been endemic in the study of message production is the assumption that the description given to message structures will serve, in a fairly straightforward way, as a description of the underlying processes that produce the message. This assumption is quite apparent in most research on communication strategies: The work typically begins with the identification of "natural kinds" (types) of messages; such message types are generally referred to as strategies; and message production is quite explicitly described as a process of "selecting" among the strategies that people are then presumed to have in their heads (for analyses and critiques of such research, see O'Keefe, 1987; Seibold et al., 1985). Because the term *strategy* implies some sort of psychological process going on, it invites researchers to assume that message types have (or ought to have) psychological reality *as types*.

In contrast, a message-design-logic formulation suggests that message types are not mirrored in the head; instead, message designs are the product of the interaction between and individual's sense of relevance and the demands of the communicative event. We observe different message types because (a) the requirements of events differ, and (b) individuals construct different concepts of communication, which endow them with different conceptions of relevance.

Hence, just as it has been a mistake to assume that the image of a "strategy" repertoire will suffice as a model of cognition, so it would be a mistake to take my analysis of message design logic and message goal structure as a picture of the cognitive processes underlying communication. Like all rational goal analyses, it provides a systematic analysis of message variations and accounts for message design as a rational adaptation to situational requirements. It displays a central aspect of performance that an actual model of message production should be required to reproduce. But it would be premature (and, to me, counterintuitive) to suppose that anyone has a neat package of beliefs that correspond to a concept of communication or a neatly defined set of motivations that correspond to goals. The intent of my analysis of message design logic, then, is to provide an improved analysis of functional design and so provide a better foundation for a model of message production.

REFERENCES

Bach, K., & Harnish, R. M. (1972). *Linguistic communication and speech acts.* Cambridge, MA: MIT Press.

Baxter, L. A. (1984). An investigation of compliance-gaining as politeness. *Human Communication Research, 10,* 427–456.

Bingham, S. (1988a). *Interpersonal responses to sexual harrassment.* Unpublished doctoral dissertation, Purdue University, West Lafayette, IN.

Bingham, S. (1988b, November). *Message design logic, communication competence, and the management of multiple situational demands.* Paper presented at the annual meeting of the Speech Communication Association, New Orleans, LA.

Brown, P., & Levinson, S. (1978). Universals in language usage: Politeness phenomena. In E. Goody (Ed.), *Questions and politeness* (pp. 56–311). Cambridge, England: Cambridge University Press.

Burleson, B. R. (1984). Comforting communication. In H. Sypher & J. Applegate (Eds.), *Communication by children and adults: Social cognitive and strategic processes* (pp. 63–105). Newbury Park, CA: Sage.

Burleson, B. R. (1989). The constructivist approach to person-centered communication: Analysis of a research exemplar. In B. Dervin, L. Grossberg, B. O'Keefe, & E. Wartella (Eds.), *Rethinking communication: Vol. 2. Paradigm exemplars* (pp. 29–46). Newbury Park, CA: Sage.

Goffman, E. (1967). *Interaction ritual: Essays on face to face behavior.* Garden City, NY: Anchor/Doubleday.

Grice, H. P. (1975). Logic and conversation. In P. Cole & J. L. Morgan (Eds.), *Syntax and semantics: Vol. 3. Speech acts* (pp. 41–58). New York: Academic Press.

Gross, E., & Stone, G. P. (1964). Embarrassment and the analysis of role requirements. *American Journal of Sociology, 70,* 1–15.

Kline, S. L. (1985). Social cognitive determinants of face support in persuasive messages (Doctoral dissertation, University of Illinois at Urbana-Champaign, 1984). *Dissertation Abstracts International, 45,* 3238A–3239A.

Linde, C., & Labov, W. (1975). Spatial networks as a site for the study of language and thought.

Language, 51, 924–939.

O'Keefe, B. J. (1987, November). *Models of functional communication competence: A rational alternative to strategy repertoires.* Paper presented at the annual meeting of the Speech Communication Association, Boston, MA.

O'Keefe, B. J. (1988). The logic of message design: Individual differences in reasoning about communication. *Communication Monographs, 55,* 80–103.

O'Keefe, B. J., & Delia, J. G. (1982). Impression formation and message production. In M. Roloff & C. Berger (Eds.), *Social cognition and communication* (pp. 33–72). Beverly Hills, CA: Sage.

O'Keefe, B. J., & Delia, J. G. (1985). Psychological and interactional dimensions of communicative development. In H. Giles & R. N. St. Clair (Eds.), *Recent advances in language, communication, and social psychology* (pp. 41–85). Hillsdale, NJ: Lawrence Erlbaum Associates.

O'Keefe, B. J., & Lambert, B. (1989, November). *Effects of message design logic on the communication of intentions.* Paper presented at the annual meeting of the Speech Communication Association, San Francisco, CA.

O'Keefe, B. J., & McCornack, S. A. (1987). Message design logic and message goal structure: Effects on perceptions of message quality in regulative communication situations. *Human Communication Research, 14,* 68–92.

O'Keefe, B. J., & Shepherd, G. J. (1987). The pursuit of multiple objectives in face-to-face persuasive interactions: Effects of construct differentiation on message production. *Communication Monographs, 54,* 396–419.

O'Keefe, B. J., & Shepherd, G. J. (1989). The communication of identity during face-to-face persuasive interactions: Effects of perceiver's construct differentiation and target's message strategies. *Communication Research, 16,* 375–404.

Scott, M. B., & Lyman, S. M. (1968). Accounts. *American Sociological Review, 48,* 46–62.

Searle, J. (1972). *Speech acts.* Cambridge, England: Cambridge University Press.

Seibold, D. R., Cantrill, J. G., & Meyers, R. A. (1985). Communication and interpersonal influence. In M. L. Knapp & G. R. Miller (Eds.), *Handbook of interpersonal communication* (pp. 551–661). Beverly Hills, CA: Sage.

Weinstein, E. A. (1969). The development of interpersonal competence. In D. A. Goslin (Ed.), *Handbook of socialization theory and research* (pp. 753–775). Chicago: Rand-McNally.

CHAPTER 9

What Drives Social Action?

Jenny Mandelbaum
Rutgers University

Anita Pomerantz
Temple University

Conversation analysts aim to make sense of sense-making—to explicate the methods through which everyday interactants produce discourse. This involves the close examination of tape-recorded, transcribed everyday conversations. Some of the topics studied by conversation analysts include how interactants take and give up turns (Sacks, Schegloff, & Jefferson, 1974), orient to sequences (Schegloff & Sacks, 1973), repair their own and others' talk (Schegloff, Jefferson, & Sacks, 1977), issue invitations (Drew, 1984), seek information (Pomerantz, 1988), and tell about their troubles (Jefferson, 1980).

Throughout these and other studies, we (as conversation analysts) are fundamentally interested in participants' concerns, orientations, and enterprises. At the same time, however, we have resisted addressing the question of intention. We often have written about participants' orientations and concerns in almost behavioristic ways, giving discourse features as evidence of proposed orientations and concerns. We have often proposed actors to be concerned about discourse features, as opposed to being concerned about pursuing actions. Traditionally conversation analysts have described participants' concerns in terms of their orientations to features of conversation. For instance, participants are portrayed as being concerned about whether or not a particular turn is to be understood to be the reason for the call, or whether and how the conversation is to be closed, and so forth (Schegloff, 1986; Schegloff & Sacks, 1973). These orientations are formulated as participants' answers to the question, "Why that now?"—why is he or she saying that thing at this particular point?

Whereas conversation-analytic studies have tended to downplay or be inexplicit about the role of intentions, studies in speech communication have frequently unquestioningly treated interaction as wholly intentional and goal-driven. As Craig (1986, p. 257) has noted, the assumption that human behavior is goal-oriented is pervasive in many fields. Much of the work on goals in the speech communication field seems to be influenced by cognitive science models of action (e.g., Schank & Abelson, 1977). This work implicitly, and sometimes explicitly, takes the position that discourse is constructed in such a way as to enable interactants to achieve goals. If it is a routine goal, actors will have a familiar script to play out in order to achieve the goal. If not, a plan will be formulated for engaging in behavior that will lead to the satisfaction of the goal. According to this view, interaction is seen to be designed by a pre-existing goal. (For instance, cf. Rule & Bisanz, 1987; Canary, Cunningham, & Cody, 1988; Dillard, 1990, re: compliance-gaining goals. See Manusov, 1989, for a useful review.) Actions that are not in concert with that goal are sometimes described as "digressions" (Jacobs, Jackson, Hall, & Stearns, this volume).

Conversation analysis's tendency to disattend or be inexplicit about participants' concerns, and speech communication's tendency to regard all of social action as goal-driven, suggest the need for a closer look at what drives social action, if indeed "driving" is the appropriate metaphor. Conversation analysis's particular strength is its ability to identify details of social action by looking closely at interaction. In this chapter we address the question of participants' intentions in social action from a (our) conversation-analytic perspective. Drawing inferences from analysis of a fragment of conversation, we propose that, rather than generally being planfully driven by goals, social action sometimes is shaped by various types of concerns. We also note, however, that there are taken-for-granted features of interaction, and some more formal properties of it, that influence how social action is organized. In this chapter, we show how a close look suggests that social action is worked out between participants in an ongoing way, rather than driven by goals.

In order to answer the question, "What drives social action?", we discuss a telephone conversation in which it is rather clear what the participants were trying to achieve. One participant was asking for help, and the other was declining to help. This conversation provides us with materials for illustrating the distinctions we wish to make. Whereas some discourse choices were responsive to primary, multiple and contingent, or prerequisite concerns, other discourse choices were influenced by taken-for-granted considerations or by other properties of social interaction. Below we clarify the proposed three concerns and two other influences by showing how they are manifested in conversation. Before turning to the telephone call, we briefly outline some of the issues raised by these distinctions.

First, we emphasize that we are dealing with *inferred* concerns. Our data are the details of interaction. This approach does not permit us to determine what a participant "actually" is concerned about. Indeed, we take it that such information is currently very hard to obtain. Even self-reports of "actual" concerns are mediated by the situation in which they are solicited and may simply provide an account of what a participant remembers himself or herself to have been concerned about when prompted to think about it by a researcher. We inferred the mental states of the interlocutors from patterns in their interaction.

Second, level of awareness or consciousness of concerns is another cognitive matter to which we have no direct access. As noted above, when we propose that someone had a concern, we are involved in a process of inference. Similarly, we inferred probable consciousness or absence of it from various features of the participants' behavior. Although these participants made their concerns apparent for one another and acted in ways that indicated that they were at least somewhat aware of what they were achieving, we mark as problematic the answers to (a) how "aware" or "conscious" participants are, and (b) the affects of their awareness (or lack of it) on their actions.

The following telephone call[1] provides us with data for exploring an answer to, "What drives social action?"

0		Ring
1	Sheila:	Hello?
2	Ronny:	'lo Sheila,
3	Sheila:	Yea[:h]
4	Ronny:	[('t's) R]onny.
5	Sheila:	Hi Ronny.
6	Ronny:	Guess what.hh
7	Sheila:	What.
8	Ronny:	.hh My ca:r is sta::lled.
9		(0.2)
10	Ronny:	('n) I'm up here in the Glen?
11	Sheila:	Oh::.
12	Ronny:	hhh
13	Ronny:	A:nd.hh (0.2) I don' know if it's: po:ssible, but
14		.hhh see I haveta open up the ba:nk.hh
15		(0.3)

---

[1]We wish to thank Manny Schegloff for providing the data and for his contributions to the analysis. We are also grateful for his feedback on a late draft of this chapter. See appendix for transcription symbols.

16 Ronny: a:t uh: (.) in Brentwood?hh =

17 Sheila: = Yeah:- en I know you want- (.) en I whoa-

18   (.) en I would, but- except I've gotta leave

19   in about five min(h)utes. =

20 Ronny: [=Okay then I gotta call somebody else.right away.

21 Sheila: [(hheh)

22   (.)

23 Ronny: Okay? =

24 Sheila: = Okay [Ron   ]

25 Ronny: [Thanks]a lot. = Bye-.

26 Sheila: Bye:.

We offer five distinctions to help us better understand what drives the social action in this fragment of talk. These include primary concerns, multiple and contingent concerns, prerequisite concerns, taken-for-granted sustained achievements, and unmindful actions.

PRIMARY CONCERNS

We infer that Ronny's primary concern here was to get help (most likely a ride) and that, in order to satisfy this concern, he called Sheila. The inference that this was Ronny's primary concern is based on the following features of his talk. The call was organized around getting help. It was his first and only official business after identification was achieved. Ronny's talk was limited to what was necessary for determining whether or not Sheila could help him: He identified the answerer as Sheila and himself to Sheila (lines 2–5), he indicated he had news to tell (line 6); he reported a problem that Sheila might have helped him to solve (lines 8, 10, 13–14, 16), and he closed the call immediately upon learning that Sheila could or would not help him out (line 20).

These details suggest that this was a single-purpose call. One could hypothesize that there was an additional motive to the request. In the way that friendships may be tested with requests (Baxter & Wilmot, 1984), Ronny might have been testing whether Sheila was prepared to put herself out for him in time of need.[2] We do not know enough about the doing of secret tests to say whether or

---

[2]We are differentiating Ronny's making the request to test Sheila's friendship from an effect that compliance with or refusal to a request may have on a relationship. More specifically, although

not this is likely. We see nothing in the discourse, however, to indicate that Ronny was concerned with testing the relationship.

MULTIPLE AND CONTINGENT CONCERNS

In writing of "dialectical goals," Craig (1986) pointed out that "people often face the need to do more than one thing at the same time" (p. 264). For example, in asking for someone's help, participants often are concerned both with getting the help they seek and with not imposing on the other more than is necessary. Likewise, in declining to help friends, participants often are concerned both with not committing themselves to perform the help-tasks and with not engendering negative reactions.

We propose that both Ronny and Sheila were dealing with multiple concerns. More specifically, we propose that, when Ronny and Sheila enacted their primary concerns (i.e., getting help and declining to give help, respectively), there were additional concerns attached to those enactments. Next, we describe in detail how Ronny asked for help from Sheila in a way that minimized the degree to which he was imposing on her. This concern not to impose can be seen as an additional concern that came about contingently, that is, upon finding that he needed to turn to someone for help. Sheila declined to help Ronny while displaying a sympathetic and friendly attitude toward his asking. This concern to be sympathetic and friendly also can be seen as a contingent concern that came into being when Sheila chose not to help Ronny.

A characteristic of Ronny's talk that makes available his contingent concern is its neutrality with respect to what he wanted. He began with "Guess what," which indicated news but did not suggest whether the news was good or bad. He told his problem, without stating the upshot of it: "My ca:r is sta::lled . . . ('n) I'm up here in the Glen? . . . see I haveta open up the ba:nk.hh . . . a:t uh: (.) in Brentwood?hh." Thus, Sheila was put in a position of "inferring" why he was reporting the situation to her. By describing a problem without making an explicit request, Ronny gave Sheila a chance either to volunteer to help or to treat what he said as news. Sheila treated it as news in line 11 by indicating, with her "Oh::.," that she had just been informed by what he said (see Heritage, 1984, re: change of state tokens). In reporting an event that can be heard as a "trouble" or "problem," Ronny most likely was counting on Sheila's understanding of problems as needing solutions. In telling her the trouble or problem, he made available to her that she might help him, but he did not directly indicate an action

---

Sheila's not having given help (or giving help had she done so) may or may not have had consequences for how Ronny viewed their friendship, that is quite separate from whether he made the request as a test of her friendship.

that he would have liked Sheila to take in response to his problem.[3] Thus Ronny gave Sheila an opportunity to offer the help or not, rather than putting her in a position of having to respond yes or no to an explicit request.

In addition to not making an explicit request for help, Ronny gave Sheila an "out." In saying, "A:nd.hh (0.2) I don' know if it's: po:ssible" (line 13), Ronny was displaying an awareness that Sheila may have to turn him down. Ronny offered a basis that Sheila might have for not helping him that minimized the potential offensiveness of her not helping him out. He proposed not that she would not want to but that she may not be able to, that is, that it would not be her choice. Hence he was making it easier for Sheila to not help, should that be the option she was selecting.

We are arguing, then, that through the way that Ronny constructed his talk, he showed Sheila that he had concerns that were attached to getting help. The way that he constructed his talk shows that he was also concerned with not imposing on Sheila. In reporting his problem without officially requesting help, Ronny enabled Sheila to volunteer to help him. In naming an inoffensive basis for her not helping him, he may have made it easier for her to decline to help. Thus, he attempted to actualize his primary concern in a way that was sensitive to his concern of not imposing on her.

Our account of what motivates Ronny here is based in details intrinsic to the talk, as is usual in conversation-analytic inquiry. It is also possible to posit a more social psychological explanation for the phenomenon. As the following social psychological explanation indicates, though, it may be difficult to ground this explanation in the details of the talk.

Rawlins (1983a, 1983b) proposed a "dialectic" of friendship, in which friends are torn between the contradictory impulses of the freedom to be independent and the freedom to be dependent. Rawlins says, "While each person is free to pursue individual goals and interests separate from the other and without the friend's interference or help, each retains the liberty to call on the other for assistance, should it be necessary" (1983a, pp. 259–260).

In friendships, tensions often arise between wanting to help a friend, on the one hand, and wanting to pursue one's own concerns, on the other. In asking a favor of a friend, interactants often are sensitive to this dilemma and attempt to minimize the expected inconvenience, avoid having the friend sacrifice personal priorities, and/or insure that the friend perceives that he or she can say no. Ronny's concern for getting help (his primary concern) carries with it a contingent concern of not overly imposing on Sheila.

Ronny again displayed this contingent concern in dealing with Sheila's

---

[3]See Drew, 1984, for a similar method used with respect to making and turning down invitations. Drew noted that, when a speaker offers a report and leaves the recipient to draw the upshot of the report, this is a device a speaker may use to avoid making "rejecting" the talk's official business.

declination to help. In lines 17–19, Sheila "anticipated" what Ronny was calling for and offered a reason for not helping him:

17   Sheila: =Yeah:- en I know you want- (.) en I whoa-

18   (.) en I would, but- except I've gotta leave

19   in about five min(h)utes. =

In response to her giving a reason, Ronny right away accepted her refusal. He did not question or challenge her reason. He did not plead, cajole, threaten, promise, or make any appeals designed to make her change her mind. Rather, he immediately accepted the reason and announced his intention to solve the problem another way:

20   Ronny: [=Okay then I gotta call somebody else.right away.

Ronny's abandoning his attempt to get help from Sheila may have been related to his not wanting to put pressure on her to do something that she did not want to do. This concern might have emerged in that he was attempting to solicit Sheila's help, where Sheila's giving help may involve some degree of sacrifice on her part.

To reiterate, Ronny's alertness to the possibility of imposing was suggested in the ways in which he made the request in the first place and dealt with her response to it. He presented the matter in a way that allowed her to volunteer, and, once she indicated a problem with giving the help that she inferred he wanted, he was very quick to accept her position.

Deriving our observations from this conversation we have argued that a favor asker may orient to the presumed imposition or cost of the recipient's compliance by providing a choice and giving a legitimate out for the recipient. In addition, a favor asker may orient to the presumed imposition in deciding whom to ask. If one imposes to some degree on the selected target when soliciting help, then one selects a target where that imposition is more or less appropriate to the relationship. Ronny selected Sheila as a target for his request. When Sheila indicated unwillingness to help, Ronny quickly moved to report that he would select another target. The multiple concerns of getting help while not "overly" imposing would seem to affect both the selection of the target and the manner in which help is sought.

Similarly, we infer that Sheila had contingent concerns in turning down Ronny's request for help. Although Sheila clearly was concerned with pursuing her own activities, she turned him down in a way that showed friendliness toward him and a sympathetic attitude toward his problem. In lines 18–19, she turned down his inexplicit request in a way that claimed a willingness to have done the favor but for circumstances:

18   Sheila: . . . en I would, but- except I've gotta leave

19   in about five min(h)utes. =

Sheila cojoined a claim of willingness ("en I would") with a claim of uncontrollable circumstances ("I've *gotta* leave in about five min(h)utes" [emphasis added]). With this format, she treated his request as legitimate, that is, as one that was appropriate for him to ask of her. In other words, in her refusal she implicitly claims that she was an appropriate target for the request, despite the refusal. Additionally, she may have displayed a sympathetic attitude toward his request by producing the refusal with disfluency, that is, behaving in a way that was interpretable as a show of discomfort at turning him down.

Both Ronny's and Sheila's enactments show that contingent concerns accompanied their primary concerns. Faced with the prospect of "needing to get help" or "turning down a request," interactants may experience additional concerns, such as not imposing or offending the cointeractant. These additional concerns shape the way the actions are carried out.

A qualification is necessary here: We have called "not imposing" and "maintaining a friendship" contingent concerns because they manifested themselves in the enactments of Ronny's getting help and Sheila's declining to help, respectively. Presumably, a contingent concern in one circumstance may be a primary concern in another.

PREREQUISITE CONCERNS

Assume that an actor has a primary concern and engages in some interaction in an effort to satisfy that concern. Some of the behaviors displayed are shaped by his or her attempting to satisfy the primary concern (e.g., getting help). There also are behaviors that are shaped by contingent concerns (e.g., not overly imposing). Still other behaviors are products of yet another kind of concern: concerns that emerge by virtue of getting into the position of attempting to satisfy the primary concern. We call these prerequisite concerns.

A prerequisite concern is one that is a prerequisite to achieving the business of the conversation. For instance, prerequisite to Ronny's getting help from Sheila is for Ronny to reach her. We assume that Ronny was oriented to whether Sheila was home or not, because his being able to reach her was a prerequisite for his seeking help from her. We do not know whether Ronny presumed that Sheila would be home, thought it likely, or was indeed concerned about catching her. In the discourse that we have from the start of the phone call, we see no display of this concern.

We offer another example of a prerequisite concern. In order for Ronny to try to get Sheila's help, he had to know that she knew that he was the caller. Had she shown that she recognized his voice, he would have known that she knew his identity. As it turned out, she did not show that she knew who was calling (line 3):

0   Ring

1   Sheila: Hello?

2   Ronny: 'lo Sheila,

3   Sheila: Yea:h

In line 3, she confirmed her own identity without offering to identify the caller. In response to Sheila's just confirming her own identity, Ronny identified himself (line 4):

2   Ronny: 'lo Sheila,

3   Sheila: Yea[:h   ]

4   Ronny: [('t's) R]onny.

5   Sheila: Hi Ronny.

Ronny's specific concern to be recognized emerged after Sheila's behavior in line 3 suggested that she may not have recognized him. Although in some phone calls the interactants unproblematically recognize each other's voice, in other phone calls, interactants may become concerned with being recognized and/or recognizing the other by voice (Schegloff, 1979, 1986). In this case, we suggest that Ronny's concern about whether Sheila recognized him may have emerged when her talk exhibited some doubt about it.

The two prerequisite concerns that we discussed are Ronny's possible concern with whether Sheila was at home and Ronny's emergent concern with whether Sheila recognized him as the caller. Both are offered as concerns that Ronny may have dealt with before being able to seek help from Sheila.

TAKEN-FOR-GRANTED SUSTAINED ACHIEVEMENTS

Throughout this chapter, we have been fighting with, and hedging on, whether using phrases like, "The interactant's apparent concern was . . ." or "A concern emerged . . ." implies that the actors were aware of the proposed concerns. We now want to mark out one area in which interactants generally are not aware. That area involves achieving the taken-for-granted aspects of our lives.

Erving Goffman (1967) distinguished between circumstances in which obliga tions and expectations are met without thinking or feeling them and circumstances in which obligations and expectations are felt:

> In fact, most actions which are guided by rules of conduct are performed unthinkingly, the questioned actor saying he performs "for no reason" or because he "felt like doing so." Only when his routines are blocked may he discover . . . that his failure to perform them can become a matter of shame and humiliation. Similarly, he may so take for granted his expectations regarding others that only when things go unexpectedly wrong will he suddenly discover that he has grounds for indignation. (pp. 49–50)

In line with Goffman's argument, we suggest that when actions or relationships are routine, established, and/or unproblematic, participants accomplish these actions or relationships without specifically having a concern for accomplishing them.

As an example, Ronny and Sheila interacted as friends with some common knowledge of each other's circumstances. Some of the behaviors that they enacted help sustain a sense of themselves as friends with common knowledge of each other's circumstances.

Ronny and Sheila used address terms for each other. Although address terms are available as "tie-signs" (Goffman, 1971, chapter 5) for outsiders to infer the relationship between the parties, Ronny and Sheila most likely would take for granted their ordinary address terms for each other. Doing so is part of achieving a sustained friendship.

One way in which we "do" having a stable relationship is to be able to produce appropriate address terms and references without their becoming objects of our attention. This should be regarded as an achievement—something to which participants pay some attention—however, it is usually unreflexively achieved in established relationships and is not usually a matter for concern. It is generally assumed rather than being something to which participants pay active attention; however, there are circumstances where such taken-for-granted actions become concerns. For instance, in a developing romantic relationship between individuals of unequal status, the transition to first-name address terms may be the object of considerable attention and concern. (cf. Garfinkel, 1967, for a detailed treatment of the achieved character of social life).

In the conversation between Sheila and Ronny, first names were used in identifying the parties to the call. Ronny's self-identification as "Ronny" indicated his expectation that Sheila should have been able to recognize him from his first name. He addressed her as Sheila, claiming an entitlement to call her by her first name.

The way in which Ronny made place references, for example, "the glen" and "the bank," also indicated his expectations regarding Sheila's knowledge. In telling the problem he was facing, he made reference to "the bank," that is, to a place that Sheila could recognize as the one he was talking about. Selecting an appropriate reference, then, is an achievement.

Sheila did not respond for three tenths of a second, at which point he added, "a:t uh: (.) in Brentwood?hh."

13   Ronny: A:nd. hh (0.2) I don' know if it's: po:ssible, but

14   .hhh see I haveta open up the ba:nk.hh

15   (0.3)

16   Ronny: a:t uh: (.) in Brentwood?hh =

By expanding the reference, he treated her nonimmediate uptake as indicating her not having been able to understand the previous reference (Pomerantz, 1984). Whereas we are often unaware of the process of selecting reference terms that are appropriate to the knowledge presumed of the recipient, when trouble emerges we tend to become more aware (cf. Sacks & Schegloff, 1979, re: procedures for references to persons). That is, there are circumstances in which recognition of a taken-for-granted reference ("the bank") turns out to be prob- lematic, and then getting recognition of the referent may become a concern.

The reference forms that Ronny used suggest the access Ronny and Sheila had (and were expected to have) to one another's worlds. These references provided Ronny and Sheila (and us, as analysts) with a loose sort of guide to the level and nature of their relationship. That is, by choosing these references, Ronny instantiated the nature of their relationship. However we would not say that this was something that they necessarily were consciously or planfully doing or were actively concerned with. Rather, the selection of these place references would have been taken for granted and would only arise as an active concern in situations of uncertainty or trouble (cf. Schegloff, 1972 re: the organization of place reference).

UNMINDFUL ACTIONS

Questions about the extent to which people are aware or conscious of their actions have been raised by several researchers (see, e.g., Langer, 1978, re: "mindlessness"; Berger & Roloff, 1980, re: "thoughtful" and "thoughtless" speech). Langer and others have proposed that we are able to perform actions mindlessly because, in some situations, we follow scripts for actions (cf. Benoit & Benoit, 1986, for a review and assessment of this position).

Langer (1989) described several different kinds of mindlessness. For our purpose here, we concentrate on the phenomena of individuals being unaware of what they are doing and/or how they are doing it. She wrote, "In the routine of daily life we do not notice what we are doing unless there is a problem" (1989, p. 43).

One circumstance in which an actor may be mindless is when he or she performs a task expertly. Langer argued that when we become experts, we assume that we can perform the given task, and we do perform it, yet we no longer know how we perform it: ". . . if we know a task so well that we can perform it 'expertly' (mindlessly), these steps may no longer be consciously available. . . ." (1989, p. 20). She argued that becoming conscious or mindful of each step may incapacitate the expert.

Another circumstance in which a person may be mindless is when he or she performs a sequence of routine activities. Whereas the person may well be aware of his or her actions while initiating the sequence, once started, he or she may go on "automatic pilot." Langer illustrated this with the following anecdote: "William James tells a story of starting to get ready for a dinner party, undressing, washing, and then climbing into bed" (1989, p. 43).

One kind of communicative behavior that frequently is repeated and certainly may become routine is greetings. By closely examining greetings and openings, Schegloff (1986) has pointed out that even something as routine and often repeated as the opening of a telephone call is an achievement throughout. Although "mindlessness" suggests an actor's lack of awareness on some level of an action that he or she performs, analysis of the details of those actions reveals their achieved character.

Unmindful actions are those we "find ourselves having done." Often, they are the unintended consequences of an action. An example may be when a speaker finds that he or she has insulted another without realizing it. Goffman (1959) referred to such actions as "faux pas," where a speaker, for instance, calls someone with a history of psychological problems a "nut" and does not realize until afterwards that it may be understood as being more than just playful. Similarly, people may come to hear unintended meanings in their utterances. The following example is from a field note. Upon warming meatballs a person said, "These meatballs aren't too hot." Apparently, upon hearing the two possible meanings of "hot," they added, "I should warm them up some more" so as to clarify which of the two available meanings they wish to direct their interlocutor to. The added unit of talk clarifies the possible double entendre of "hot," showing it to refer to temperature rather than quality. In this way, a semantic property of the word "hot" (it has at least two available meanings in this context) may result in our doing an action (criticizing the taste) without realizing until afterwards that we have done it.

In the meatball illustration, the unmindful action became an object of attention when its perpetrator showed herself to have noticed it. Often, though, unmindful actions may pass completely unnoticed. Some unmindful actions appear to be produced by characteristics of talk and the way these characteristics operate on speakers. For instance, Sacks (1972) noted structural features of talk that provide for the routine occurrence of unintentional and often unnoticed puns in narrative terminations. Jefferson (1977) analyzed what she and Sacks called the "poetics" of talk, where subsequent words appear to be touched off by the sounds and meanings of prior talk. Although puns and "poetic" features of talk may sometimes be intentional many are unintentional and apparently not attended to. This suggests that some features of talk exert an influence on how interaction is done without participants being aware of them. Features of this kind can be subject to analysis by examining interaction.

CONCLUDING DISCUSSION

As the preceding discussion indicates, much can be inferred from the details of talk. From looking at the conversation between Ronny and Sheila, we were able to infer Ronny's primary concern and suggest how he shaped his behavior in order to achieve it. From features of the discourse, we inferred Ronny's and Sheila's contingent concerns that accompanied their primary concerns. We suggested the possibility of prerequisite concerns that are dealt with to enable participants to be in a position to act on their primary concerns. We showed how taken-for-granted sustained achievements may explain how some action comes about and may become concerns at certain junctures. Finally, we saw how some actions may be unmindful and may become concerns only in their aftermath, if at all.

Of course, we did not have access to inside the participants' heads, particularly to their moment-to-moment states of awareness. Our concern is that, in our lay usage, the terms *concerns, goals,* and *orientations* conjure up a picture of the actors' awareness. We offer the preceding distinctions as a reminder that we should not overemphasize the role of awareness in the production of social action. As we have argued, some behaviors are explainable as directed to satisfying concerns, whereas others may be completely unintentional.

Our discussion of primary concerns, multiple contingent concerns, prerequisite concerns, taken-for-granted sustained achievements, and unmindful actions suggests that, in order to understand what drives social action, we need to be alert to the details of interaction. Using these details, we (like participants) may infer various ways in which action moves forward. We attempted to infer concerns and other forces that influence how social action is shaped by attending closely to the details of talk. We had fairly high confidence regarding some of our inferences; with others, we offered mere possibilities.

The data-based distinctions we have been able to make between different types of actors' concerns, on the one hand, and different ways in which actors perform social action, on the other, suggest that it is sometimes possible for conversation analysts to clarify their local uses of terms such as *participants' orientations* or *participants' concerns*. We often have resolved questions of awareness and consciousness by treating the interactants' awareness as irrelevant for our analyses. The accounts we have provided here suggest that some aspects of interaction do seem to be organized by virtue of interactants' primary concerns, that they are aware of these concerns, and that these aspects may be subjected to analysis. Distinguishing these features of interaction from the taken-for-granted character of other actions in talk seems worthwhile if we are to attempt to account fully for how we interact with one another.

Our analyses have demonstrated the achieved character of strategic, mindful, unmindful, and taken-for-granted actions and have indicated that we can become informed about how the various sorts of actions are achieved by examining the details of interaction. Proposing a possible difference between these types of actions enables and encourages us to explore further whether we can specify in more detail what may be involved in having a conscious project in contrast with other kinds of action. Although Ronny's conscious project appears to have been to get help, in all likelihood, he would not have consciously attended to all of the many actions, strategies, and communication that he employed as he attempted to get help (e.g., his choice of term of address as "doing being a friend"). We hope to find out more about how pursuing a conscious project is different, if it is, from performing an action without awareness.

The distinctions we have been able to make also call attention to some of the subtleties of how we construct our social action. On the basis of the conversation examined here, interactants who have primary concerns may have contingent concerns affecting their discourse choices. How multiple concerns play out after interactants fail in their initial attempts to satisfy primary concerns is a matter for future investigation.

For some interactions, a primary concern might be very influential. However, we suggest that our distinctions account more fully for how moment-by-moment interaction proceeds.

What we have shown is derived from one brief conversation. It should not be taken as an exhaustive account of the forces driving social action. Rather, we hope to have provided a sample of the kinds of answers that close analysis of everyday interaction might offer to the question, "What drives social action?".

REFERENCES

Baxter, L. A., & Wilmot, W. W. (1984). 'Secret Tests': Social strategies for acquiring information about the state of the relationship. *Human Communication Research, 11,* 171–201.

Benoit, P., & Benoit, W., (1986). Consciousness: The mindlessness/mindfulness and verbal report controversies. *Western Journal of Speech Communication, 50,* 41–64.

Berger, C., & Roloff, M. (1980). Social cognition, self-awareness, and interpersonal communication. In B. Dervin & M. Voigt, (Eds.), *Progress in communication sciences* (Vol. 2, pp. 1–49). Norwood,

NJ: Ablex.

Canary, D., Cunningham, E., & Cody, M. (1988). An examination of goal types, gender, and locus of control in managing interpersonal conflicts. *Communication Research, 15,* 426–446.

Craig, R. (1986). Goals in discourse. In D. Ellis & W. Donohue (Eds.), *Contemporary issues in language and discourse processes* (pp. 257–273). Hillsdale, NJ: Lawrence Erlbaum Associates.

Dillard, J. (1990). The nature and substance of goals in tactical communication. In M. Cody & M. McLaughlin (Eds.), *Psychology of tactical communication* (pp. 70–90). London: Multilingual Matters.

Drew, P. (1984). Speakers' reportings in invitation sequences. In J. M. Atkinson & J. Heritage (Eds.), *Structures of social action,* (pp. 129–152). Cambridge, England: Cambridge University Press.

Garfinkel, H. (1967). *Studies in ethnomethodology.* Englewood Cliffs, NJ: Prentice-Hall.

Goffman, E. (1959). *The presentation of self in everyday life.* Garden City, NY: Doubleday.

Goffman, E. (1967). *Interaction ritual.* New York: Anchor Books.

Goffman, E. (1971). *Relations in public.* New York: Basic Books.

Heritage, J. (1984). A change-of-state token and aspects of its sequential placement. In J. M. Atkinson & J. Heritage (Eds.), *Structures of social action* (pp. 299–346). Cambridge, England: Cambridge University Press.

Jefferson, G. (1977, June). *On the poetics of talk.* Paper presented at the Boston University conference on Ethomethodology and Conversation Analysis, Boston, MA.

Jefferson, G. (1980) *End of Grant report on conversations in which "troubles" or "anxieties" are expressed (HR 480512).* London: Social Science Research Council (mimeo).

Langer, E. (1978). Rethinking the role of thought in social interaction. In J. Harvey, W. Ickes, & R. Kidd, (Eds.), *New directions in attribution research* (Vol. 2, pp. 35–58). Hillsdale, NJ: Lawrence Erlbaum Associates.

Langer, E. J. (1989). *Mindfulness.* Reading, MA: Addison-Wesley.

Manusov, V. (1989, May). *How can you resist me? Compliance resistance among friends.* Paper presented at the annual meeting of the International Communication Association, San Francisco, CA.

Pomerantz, A. (1984). Pursuing a response. In J. M. Atkinson & J. Heritage (Eds.), *Structures of social action* (pp. 152–165). Cambridge, England: Cambridge University Press.

Pomerantz, A. (1988). Offering a candidate answer: an information-seeking strategy. *Communication Monographs. 55,* 4, 360–374.

Rawlins, W. K. (1983a). Negotiating close friendship: The dialectic of conjunctive freedoms. *Human Communication Research, 9,* 255–266.

Rawlins, W. (1983b). Openness as problematic in ongoing friendships: two conversational dilemmas. *Communication Monographs, 50,* 1–13.

Rule, V., & Bisanz, G. (1987). Goals and strategies in persuasion: A cognitive schema for understanding social events. In M. Sanna, J. Olson, & C. P. Herman (Eds.), *Social influence: The Ontario symposium* (Vol. 5). Hillsdale, NJ: Lawrence Erlbaum Associates.

Sacks, H. (1972). On some puns with some intimations. In R. W. Shuy (Ed.), *Monograph series on language and linguistics, 25* (pp. 135–144). Washington, DC: Georgetown University Press.

Sacks, H., Schegloff, E. A., & Jefferson, G. (1974). A simplest systematics for the organization of turn-taking for conversation. *Language 50* (4), 696–735.

Sacks, H., & Schegloff, E. A. (1979). Two preferences in the organization of references to persons in conversations and their interaction. In G. Psathas (Ed.), *Everyday language* (pp. 15–21). New York: Irvington.

Schank, R., & Abelson, R. (1977). *Scripts, plans, goals and understanding.* Hillsdale, NJ: Lawrence Erlbaum Associates.

Schegloff, E. A. (1972). Notes on a conversational practice: formulating place. In D. Sudnow (Ed.), *Studies in social interaction* (pp. 75–119). New York: Free Press.

Schegloff, E. A. (1979). Identification and recognition in telephone conversation openings. In G. Psathas (Ed.), *Everyday Language* (pp. 23–78). New York: Irvington.

Schegloff, E. A. (1986). The routine as achievement. *Human Studies, 9*, 2–3, 111–151.

Schegloff, E. A. & Sacks, H. (1973). Opening up closings. *Semiotica, 8* (4), 289–327.

Schegloff, E. A., Jefferson, G., & Sacks, H. (1977). The preference for self-correction in the organization of repair in conversation. *Language, 53* (2), 361–382.

CHAPTER 10

The Two-Way Relationship Between Talk in Social Interactions and Actors' Goals and Plans

Robert E. Sanders
The University at Albany, SUNY

Let us regard the standard conception of the relationship between actors' goals and talk in social interactions as being Cushman's action-theoretic perspective—that actors first form a goal and then talk in a way that is instrumental to attaining that goal (Cushman & Craig, 1976; Cushman & Whiting, 1972; Sanders & Cushman, 1984). This is most explicit in Cushman's use of the "practical syllogism" (Von Wright, 1971) as the template for communication rules. With regard to talk, the practical syllogism has as its major premise a statement that *the actor has some goal;* as its minor premise a statement that *the actor has a belief about what needs to be said to attain the goal;* and as its "conclusion" the proposition that *the actor says that which he or she believes is instrumental to attaining the goal.*

But the practical syllogism is too simple. For one thing, although it is of secondary concern here, it glosses the confounding effect of the cognitive processing needed when actors have more than one goal at a time, especially competing ones, and/or when actors' beliefs about how to attain a goal encompass alternative methods whose costs and benefits differ in terms of practicality, efficacy, and social acceptability. These matters raise additional empirical questions about how actors integrate or select among multiple goals (O'Keefe & Delia, 1982; O'Keefe & Shepherd, 1987; Tracy, 1984) and how alternative means to ends are assessed (e.g., the criteria institutions use to evaluate their current methods for attaining goals or to adopt new ones), and so on (Cushman & King, 1989; Galbraith, 1973).

The other way in which the practical syllogism is too simple is that it does not take into account that, when actors engage others in social interaction in order to attain their goals (either to get their help or, at least, their consent), the process of social interaction itself may induce actors in medias res to change their goals and/or their plans. This is of direct concern here.

The other(s) whom the actor engages to attain his or her goal(s) may not respond as he or she expected when the plan was made or, worse, may have separate, perhaps opposed, goals of their own. *If, as an interaction progresses, an actor projects that plans and/or goals formed in advance are ineffective or unattainable in that interaction, he or she may revise them, perhaps several times in a single interaction, in order to improve the chances of attaining a desirable outcome* (or avoiding an undesirable one).

From this perspective, the relationship between goals and talk in interactions is *not* unidirectional (where first, goals and plans are formed and then they are carried out through talk in social interaction). It is *interactive,* reciprocal, and perhaps cyclic. Talk in social interactions may not only arise from antecedent goals and plans, but goals or plans may arise in medias res as a result of antecedent talk in the current interaction.

Cushman (Cushman & Pearce, 1977; Cushman & Whiting, 1972; Donohue, Cushman, & Nofsinger, 1980) avoided this issue of the directionality of the relationship between goals and what actors say and do by restricting the domain of the analysis to "standardized usages"—ways of attaining particular goals that have been standardized and are normatively preferred (e.g., courtroom procedures, service encounters, a family's customary practices). Given a standardized usage, the relationship between goals and talk in interactions *is* unidirectional: Once a goal is formed, talk follows, "scripted" before the fact.

For present purposes, it does not matter whether we say it is common or rare for interactions to comprise standardized usages (this is partly an empirical question, partly a definitional one). As long as we consider that there are at least *some* interactions that are *not* founded on standardized usages, or that deviate from such usages, we have to reject the categorical view that goals come first and talk, in social interactions, second. And it happens that a variety of naturalistic data do reveal idiosyncratic (nonstandardized) components in interactions, even when nominally standardized usages are involved (e.g., Atkinson & Heritage, 1984; Cronen, Pearce, & Snavely, 1979; Pearce & Cronen, 1980), as well as exhibiting the efforts of individuals in social interactions to adjust what they said and did to attain a priori goals when unanticipated developments arose in medias res (e.g., Sanders, 1987, pp. 13–21, and the following illustrative case).

My purpose here is not just to claim that goals and plans are potentially emergent and changeable in the course of any social interaction. My purpose is to show how this enriches our picture of the "competence" that actors must have in order to attain goals through social interaction.

The potential for having to change goals or plans while interactions are in progress means that the successful attainment of goals through interaction depends on more than the soundness of an actor's a priori beliefs about what to do in order to bring about particular "effects."[1] For actors to be able to assess the likely success of current plans for attaining desired outcomes, they have to be able to project at particular junctures whether the current interaction is progressing towards or away from desired outcomes and why. To make such projections, actors have to "know" about Interaction, that is, about the way interactions are organized and constrained, so as to be able to calculate the effect on the probability of certain outcomes of past contributions to the interaction (or contemplated future contributions). This "knowledge" enables actors to revise those goals and plans whose success is dependent on the progress of the current interaction.

"Knowledge" about Interaction not only enables actors to adjust goals and plans based on the way the current interaction is progressing; it may also foster goals or plans that would not have arisen from a priori beliefs alone about how to bring about particular effects. Goals or plans formed *during* and *because of* the way an interaction progresses may not be ones that would have occurred to the actor beforehand. Rather, new goals may become salient only when the actor projects in medias res that those are attainable *based on the progress to that point of the present interaction.* Likewise, new plans may become salient only when the actor projects what could be said or done *relevantly,* with *socially desirable meanings,* that would increase the chances of having the desired (or a desirable) outcome in that interaction.

Note that this view of the interactive relationship between goals and talk in social interactions challenges the broader assumption that the only bases for the goals and plans that individuals form are experiential and dispositional (psychological and sociological). Rather, we have to consider that there also are "communicative" (at least interactional) reasons for goals and plans, concerning what can relevantly be said in the interaction at each juncture and the social desirability of its meaning in that context.

My purpose here is to make explicit systemic aspects of social interactions that enable actors to make decisions from turn to turn about what goals (outcomes) are attainable and what is likely to be effective in attaining them (see Sanders, 1987, for an extended defense of the claim that interactions have such systemic aspects). But it will enhance the intelligibility of this project if a context for it and a detailed illustration are provided first.

---

[1]The beliefs I refer to are any that enable the development of plans *before* or *apart from* the way the current interaction unfolds, including beliefs about the habits and dispositions of the other(s) in the interaction, the customs and normative obligations within groups and institutions the interaction involves, and even conventions about what to say or do to elicit particular responses from others in the community, such as scripts for, say, getting food in restaurants or money in banks, or conversational devices, for example, to make indirect requests.

KNOWLEDGE ABOUT INTERACTIONS THAT IS
INSTRUMENTAL TO ATTAINING GOALS

Again, the thesis here is that for actors to be able to monitor and correct for the outcome(s) towards which the present interaction is headed, *for any interaction,* no matter how conventional or how novel, actors have to "know" about *internal relations among the components of interactions that progressively constrain outcomes as an interaction progresses.*

Let us define a *constraint* as a feature or property of some entity (e.g., an interaction) that alters the effects—or, more precisely, alters the relative probabilities of effects—that forces would have if exerted on that entity in the absence of that feature or property. The motion of a kite under forces exerted by the wind is thus "constrained" if it is connected by a string to someone's hand, if it has a tail, and so on (i.e., the probabilities as to the specific way the wind will affect the kite's motion are altered).

This applies to the way in which current utterances influence next utterances (and, from there, influence the progress of interactions). Suppose, for example, that a child were told certain rules of etiquette (Utterances$_1$) and it were found that this did not have a determinate effect on the child's saying, for example, "please" and "thank you" (Utterances$_2$) when making requests or receiving gifts. However, if it were found that Utterances$_1$ did change the *relative probability* of Utterances$_2$ under certain social conditions, we could say that being told rules of etiquette did not "cause" polite speech but, instead, changed the child's cognitive "properties" in such a way as to *constrain* his or her speech when certain social "forces" were exerted.

Now let us say that there are formal relations among components in interactions—both structural relations and meaning relations—that delimit what is relevant and also delimit how utterances and behaviors can be interpreted at any juncture during the progress of the interaction towards an outcome. In that case, *knowledge* of these properties of interactions would be a cognitive property that constrains what actors say and do, insofar as it changes the relative probability of specific utterances or behaviors at a particular juncture (Sanders, 1989).

Let us say that utterances are constrained by structural relations in interactions whenever an utterance of one type creates a "slot" for a particular kind of uptake (e.g., adjacency pairs). Filling that slot appropriately would be unremarkable, but not doing so is a notable omission that makes salient and warrants inferences about the actor's goals and interpersonal intentions. To the degree that such inferences pose a social risk for an actor, and the actor is thus motivated to avoid them, such structural relations constrain actors' utterances.

Utterances may also be constrained by meaning relations between them, in two ways. First, utterances are disambiguated—are assigned a specific interpretation—in terms of which one(s) of their possible meanings is relevant to antecedents (and/or consequents) in the interaction (Sanders, 1987). Hence, to the degree that an actor produces an utterance that is not relevant to the interlocutor's, or whose intended meaning is not relevant, the actor risks being understood in an unintended and possibly undesired way and, perhaps, making salient and warranting inferences about his or her goals and interpersonal intentions.

Second, *grounds of coherence,* or what Reichman (1985) described as context spaces, typically form in interactions (a consistent basis of relevance across some set of utterances). These are usually coincidental with an agenda and bounded by the initiation and resolution of the agenda. Once a ground of coherence forms, then, at each turn, actors have the option of continuing it with a relevant utterance or producing an utterance that is not relevant to that ground of coherence—perhaps to change the topic, introduce a new agenda, digress, and so forth. To depart from the current ground of coherence may involve a risk of being understood in unintended ways and a risk of promoting unwanted inferences about his or her goals and interpersonal intentions—or even his or her competence (Tracy, 1982). It depends on whether the agenda underlying the current ground of coherence has been resolved and, if not, whether a departure from that ground of coherence introduces a new agenda that will help resolve the prior one.

In either case, insofar as transgressing a ground of coherence poses a risk of unintended interpretations or unwanted inferences, it is more probable that the respondent will produce relevant utterances than not. "Knowledge" of the types of meaning relations that create grounds of coherence thus constrains what is said (Sanders, 1987).

AN ILLUSTRATIVE CASE STUDY[2]

The transcript of the interaction to be examined here was the source of data for Pomerantz' (1984) analysis of a remediation device and was provided to me by her. This interaction took place in a telephone call between two nurses (apparently acquaintances but not co-workers): Q (who asked the other whether she wanted to take on a private-duty nursing case) and R (who said "no"). Much of

---

[2]A single interaction is rarely an adequate source of data on which to base claims about the methods and devices used by interactants to coordinate their participation in locally managed, mutually accomplished practices. But a single interaction is the only appropriate datum to support claims about the way the separate goals and plans of participants progressively interact (e.g., articles by Schegloff, 1988/1989; Clayman & Whalen, 1988/1989; Nofsinger, 1988/1989; and Pomerantz, 1988/1989 on the instance of Dan Rather's "interview" of George Bush on CBS news).

the interaction can be punctuated into a succession of appeals by Q for R to take the case and a corresponding succession of justifications by R for saying "no."

The focus of the analysis here is on R's having adopted a succession of plans during the interaction to attain the same goal(s). Of particular interest is, first, that each successive plan was put into operation shortly after Q's responses made evident that the prior plan failed and, second, that most of these plans benefitted from the "mistakes" of the past by producing stronger constraints on Q to accept that R cannot/should not take on this full-time private-duty case. Both the "timing" of new plans and their "improvement" on prior, failed plans indicates that R could and did monitor the interaction for its progress towards her desired outcome and revised her plans for attaining that outcome accordingly.

Before proceeding, it will be useful for expository purposes to give a name to R's and Q's respective goals in this interaction. Of course, their goals can only be inferred from their talk, and that, in turn, makes it unlikely that any two analysts would characterize R's and Q's respective goals in exactly the same way; but for the analytic purposes here, it does not matter if we get their goals exactly right, as long as we agree that R's several plans (with one possible exception) were different means of attaining the same goal(s).

Q's talk in the interaction is consistent with either of two distinct goals, and, without knowing more about her prior dealings with R or with the family of the patient, we cannot know which goal she had (if not both). Her talk recurrently put pressure on R to take the case, and so we can infer that it was her goal to induce R to take the case, but it is also possible that this was either for the overarching purpose of obtaining quality care for the patient or, alternately, the purpose of helping R out by getting her placed in a secure, full-time, well-paying job.

As to R, it is reasonably clear from the outset that she had the goal of having Q eliminate her from consideration as a nurse for this patient. Note R's having said "no" twice, baldly, in response to Q's initial query about whether she would be interested in the case:

(1) [SBL:1:1:10:R, 1–8]

1   Q: . . . inna steadⵏy:: i-(0.9) uh: ehrw seven day a week (.)

2   jo:b, (0.9) ca:se?hh

3   (.)

4   R: Sev'n days a week,

5   Q: Ah hah?

6   R: ↓No:.

7   Q: hhYou wouldn't.h

8   R: ↑No(h)o

But R must have wanted more than that, considering her tolerance (even complicity) for letting the conversation dwell on this issue and letting Q continue to pressure her for a considerable length of time, despite R's having said "no" right from the outset. The explanation for R's tolerance for the continuation of talk on the matter suggests itself from the fact that both R and Q finally did treat the matter as settled when Q, late in the conversation, concurred for the first time with R that she was "right" to turn down the case. The fact that R did not treat the matter as settled until then indicates that R's goal was precisely to get this concurrence from Q—perhaps because R did not want to have it left unresolved whether Q "excused" her for saying "no" or instead judged her as "unprofessional" or uncaring. We will, therefore, characterize R's goal(s) in this interaction—at least subsequent to the exchange in Extract (1)—as being to (a) turn down the case (b) with Q's concurrence.[3]

R'S SEVERAL PLANS FOR SAYING "NO" WITH Q'S CONCURRENCE

Each of the plans that R put into operation to attain her goals had this common denominator: They consisted of talk that created meaning relations in the interaction such that Q was constrained (it was relevant) to concur with R that R could/should not take the job. Furthermore, each successive plan (with one exception) strengthened the constraint on Q to produce that response.

---

[3]It is conceivable that R changed her goal during the interaction. Her first saying "no" baldly suggests that she initially had as her goal just to let Q know that she did not want the job. The goal of getting Q to concur with R's decision may only have formed after that, perhaps because it became salient to R—based on Q's unresponsiveness (or perhaps Q pronounced "uh huh" at line 9 with judgmental tone or stress, "uh *huh*")—that a possible outcome of the interaction was that Q would judge R negatively for having said "no." However, in personal correspondence, Pomerantz, Sigman, and Tracy have each independently questioned whether there is evidence for claiming that R's account at line 13 arose from a change in her goals, rather than from a normative obligation to offer an account for saying "no." Although it does not matter for purposes of the analysis whether we say that R changed her goal or not, it is relevant to the central idea here that she could have done so, and it seems to me that the inference that she did revise her goal is supported by the fact that she said "no" baldly twice without offering her account in either of those turns but instead waited through nearly 2 seconds of filled and unfilled pauses before producing the account. That the account was offered for strategic reasons rather than from a normative obligation is also supported by R's repeatedly giving accounts for saying "no," each more elaborate, well past any point where the account could be said to have been normatively called for.

Plan 1 (lines 13-76): Offering an Account for Saying "No"

R's first plan to take herself out of consideration for the private-duty position, with Q's concurrence, was to use an account of a circumstance that prevented her from taking on the case, making it relevant and thus constraining Q to agree that she should not do so. R put into operation three successive versions of this plan, each revision coming after the current plan failed, that is, when Q did not concur with R's saying "no" at the point at which R made it relevant for her to do so.

R's first plan has some resemblance to the method examined by Drew (1984) of turning down a request indirectly by "reporting" circumstances that would prevent complying. However, in this instance, the request had already been turned down baldly, so that R's use of an account at that juncture would not be a way of saying "no" indirectly; it appears to be a tactic for eliciting Q's concurrence with R's having said "no".

It is worth noting that the use of an account to attain Q's concurrence with R's having said "no" is an inherently unreliable tactic. Although offering an account would make it relevant for an interlocutor to concede the point and drop the matter, it makes it equally relevant for the interlocutor to pursue the matter further in order to (a) find a way to help solve the problem that is preventing complyiance or (b) establish a need for compliance that outweighs, either practically or morally, whatever is standing in the way. Q responded to R's accounts in the latter ways rather than the former, desired way until the end.

Plan 1a: An Account Followed by the Initiation of Closing.   R's first version of this plan was to give a brief account after saying "no" (lines 13–14):

(2) [SBL:1:1:10:R, 8–23]

8   R: ↑No(h)o,

9   Q: Uh-huh,

10   (0.9)

11   R: Uh :<
               [

12   Q: (Wh't)

13   R: I uh I wou:ld if iks if it weren't fer the children. But

14   it's too much fer me.

15   Q: Uh huhh. 'h Ye ah well,
                         [   ]

16 R: (ah hah),

17   (.)

18 Q: I: know you said something about chu< (.) preferred not

19   working weekhe:nds,hh

20 R: Ya:h Ah ha:h?

21 Q: But uhm (0.6) 't (0.6) uh this: uhm

22   (0.7)

23 R: 'tlk It's sweet of you tuh think ↑of ↓me though↓

Note that an additional tactic of R's was to move to closure in line 23 once Q seemed to have conceded the point (lines 18–19), and, in particular, note that R appended the counterindicative "though" to her closing (line 23: "It's sweet of you tuh think ↑of ↓me though↓"). This marked her utterance as coming *after*, that is, as presupposing, its having been settled that she would not be taking on the case. Although use of the tag "though" may have just been symptomatic of R's thinking at that point, it may also have been one further tactic to legislate the matter as being settled—by speaking in a way that presupposed it (Lewis, 1979).

Regardless, Q talked over that tag in time to interrupt the closing and cancel the presupposition and (relevantly) offer a solution to R's "problem":

(3) [SBL:1:1:10:R, 23–28]

23 R: 'tlk It's sweet of you tuh think ↑of ↓me though↓
                                    [   ]   ]

24 Q: .hh W'of cour se

25   eh-eh-ih if you found someone: uh,hh to re↑lieve you

26   evrih weeke:nd it w(h)'d b(h)e: (h)alri:ght,=

27 R: That's i::t. Bu t that's the ↑trick you se e:,
             =[[   ]   [

28 Q: .hhh   Mm h m,   Mm: hm,

Plan 1b: An Enriched Account.   R did not put a revised plan into operation until Q—who went on after line 28, Extract (3), to tell R something about the case—serendipitously revealed a fact at line 43, Extract (4), that made it relevant for R to offer a second, enriched account of why she could not take the case:

(4) [SBL:1:1:10:R, 40–50]

40 Q: 'hh And uh:m (0.3) It isn't hard wo:rk,h 'hhhh hh
[[

41 R: (0.3) I see.

42   Ennu where is this.

43 Q: < Out'n Montecito. On Alst'd Roa: d.h
[

44 R: Oh::. An' that's ↑quite

45   a drive from heeuh too: 'hhh Well you know eh sev'n days

46   a week is jus 'too much for me, I can't ↑do it with (.)

47   children. 'hh Eh ez ↑you say if I: c'd find some(b'ddy)

48   to re↑lieve me on the weekend.

49 Q: Mm-hm?

50 R: But that's the trouble.

It is noteworthy, first, that R, having discovered an additional reason why she should not take the case, phrased it as she did and interjected it where she did (lines 44–45: "An' that's ↑quite a drive from heeuh too:"). R's having embedded that statement/reason in an "and . . . too" construction marked her assertion as corroborative of and in addition to something prior. But, in this instance, the "something prior" to which R's statement was linked was not to the immediately prior descriptive/suasory talk about the case; it was to R's distantly antecedent account of why she could not take on the case (which Q had undermined 10 turns before).

Thus, in addition to the original problem she cited (not wanting to work weekends because of her children) and the subsequent problem that she cited in response to Q (that it would be a trick to find a reliable weekend replacement), R cited this markedly additional problem—that the job is a long drive from R's home. Unlike the initial account in Plan 1a, R's enriched account left Q little that she could relevantly say to help "solve" R's problems: The new fact of a long drive was incontrovertible, and the two prior problems had not been successfully overcome (caring for her children on the weekend, the problem of finding a weekend relief nurse). In this way, Plan 1b constrained Q more than Plan 1a to approve of/agree with R's ruling herself out of consideration for this job.

Plan 1c: Initiate Closing with an Account Appended. One indication that Plan 1b did exert a greater constraint on Q is that it rendered her inarticulate and weakly acquiescent for 3.5 seconds after line 50, Extract (4). However, R did not take the floor at that juncture to initiate a new topic or a closing. This enabled Q eventually to take the floor and resume talking about the case, this time to start establishing a need for R to take on the case:

(5) [SBL:1:1:10:R, 59–76]

59   Q: Their u-They: u-they have'n exc'llent nurse there no:w but

60   she's 'hhhh uh:m let (0.2) th'm know some time ago thet

61   uh:: sh-she'll be leaving I think October firs:t.

.

.

.

70   Q: So they('d) wunt to replace her. 'hh An' I thought'v

71   you: the- (.) the (hus°b'n°)
                            [

72   R: Well it's very kiⅰ:nd'v you. End I:

73   mean if it (.) It would of bean lovely. < Ah mean en if it

74   wehrn't thet ah have so many home responsibi lities =
                                                          [

75   Q: (   )

76   R: = of the children. (.) You know,

Plan 1c strengthened the constraint on Q to concur with R's taking herself out of consideration by giving the account as *part of a closing.* Further, the closing included an expression of regret in the past subjunctive (line 73: "It would of bean lovely"), thereby again legislating through presupposition, as in Plan 1a, that the matter was settled. Finally, the initiation of closing *prefaced* the account—lines 72 & 73, extract (5)—instead of coming in normal order after the account, as in Plan 1a. By prefacing the account with a closing this time and, particularly, by marking that so as to presuppose that the matter was settled, R constrained Q to respond to the fact of the closing, not the account. This made it relevant for Q to concede the point (though not necessarily to concur), rather than to further attempt to solve R's problems with taking the case or establishing a need for R to do so.

Note that Plan 1c was not put into operation just when it became evident that Plan 1b had failed (when Q went on at line 59 to present a need for R to take on the case, disregarding R's enriched account in Plan 1b of why she could not do so). Rather, Plan 1c was put into operation at the first point at which it was relevant for R to close—when Q told R at line 71, Extract (5), "I thought'v you:," it was then relevant for R to talk about herself and not the case and, also, (serendipitously?) to initiate closing.

Plan 1c also failed, but this has to be attributed less to a deficiency in the plan than to Q's resistance and her willingness to risk the social costs of being uncooperative with R's agenda. Q's response disregarded R's 'closing + account' altogether, did not even make a back-channel response to it. Instead, she made a further, more intense, direct appeal to R—that special qualities were needed on the case (lines 77–79) and because "it is really import'nt" (line 83). It was at that juncture that R put an entirely different plan into operation.

Plan 2 (lines 85–137): Take Control of What Gets Talked About

R took control of talk about the case by initiating a cross-examination of Q about it (obviously, with Q's cooperation). This was exhibited by a lengthy series of question–answer pairs. While this plan has in common with R's other plans that it constrained Q against continuing to pressure R, this plan did so by giving R control of what it was relevant to talk about, and also differed from R's other plans in not placing constraints on Q to concur with R's having said "no." It is not clear whether this plan differed in these ways because R changed her goal(s) at this point (e.g., she may have become curious about the case or started to rethink whether to take it on); on the other hand, her goal(s) may have remained unchanged, and she just hoped to unearth more information about the case that could be used to strengthen her account of why she could/should not take it.

One other possibility—also consistent with R's goal(s) elsewhere in the conversation—is that the plan here was not just to take control of talk about the case but for R to provide herself the opportunity to tell her own version of what this case involved (she evidently had heard about this patient already). In telling her version, R implied that the patient's condition ("quite permanently [brain] damaged") resulted from the family's having decided to transport her to a Los Angeles hospital, thus delaying treatment, instead of getting immediate treatment by a local doctor in the local hospital. If this was what R intended to insinuate, it may have been as a preface to offering a new account for saying "no," this one being that the family was likely to second-guess and interfere with the patient's treatment.

Whatever R's goal may have been in connection with Plan 2 (to divert Q from resuming her effort to recruit R; to unearth more information that R could use to bolster her reasons for not taking the case; or to downgrade the family, and thus the work situation, in order to constrain Q to concur with R's having said "no"), it need not and did not accomplish any of them. Instead, Q undermined R's control of their talk after R presented her version of the case:

(6) /SBL:1:1:10:R, 133–149/

```
133   R:   An'it (0.3) An'it left'er (0.4) quite permanently damaged I
134        s  uppose
              [
135   Q:          .tk
136          Q:  A:pparently,
137          (.)
138          Q:  Uh ↑he is still hopeful.
139          (.)
140   R:   The husb'n.
141   Q:   Ah hah end yih never jus' (.) eh yih js' never saw such
142        devotion in yer li:fe. 'hhhh And uh:
143   R:   (Was) this (their) first marr↑iage? uh I  (      ) it wz
                                        [                ]=
144   Q:                                          N o : ,
145   R:   =thei r seco nd?
               [    ]
146   Q:            it's: i-No they'd only been ↑marrie(.)d less than
147        two yea:rs.
148          (0.9)
149   R:   Isn't that s:a::d.
```

Q's introduction of pathos at line 138 (the husband's "hope"), and her expansion on that at lines 141–142, is uncooperative with R's cross-examination format (the prior question had been about the patient's condition, not the husband's feelings). When R again asked a factual question (at lines 143–145), also possibly directed at finding something negative about the patient's family situation, Q again did not answer it but introduced more pathos instead (lines 146–147). At that juncture, R stopped cross-examining Q. Evidently, she considered that Plan 2 had failed to constrain Q in the intended way. (Note that if R's prior telling of her version of the case's history was prefatory to her casting aspersions on the patient's family, Q headed this off in Extract (6) by dwelling on the loving and devoted attitude of the husband towards the patient, his wife.)

After Plan 2 was abandoned, R began two other tactics but did not follow through sufficiently to warrant their analysis here as distinct plans. She first suggested that Q herself take on the case, and when Q was unresponsive to this,

R repeated (for a fourth time) the account in Plan 1 for feeling unable to take on the case. When Q was again unresponsive, R went on to Plan 3.

Plan 3 (lines 207–227): Citing a Conflict with an Existing Obligation

Plan 3 was to offer an account of *objective conditions* that *blocked* her from taking on the case, in contrast to her previous accounts of the *subjective conditions* that made her *feel unwilling* to take on the case: R informed Q that she currently had a job, at a hospital, part-time. In addition, R introduced this as "news," not as another account, by using a "pre-announcement" form (line 207: "Yih know w't I:m doing right no:w?"). By offering this as "news" and not as an account, R again presupposed that the prior issue of her taking on the case was already settled, that the previous account(s) had been enough. But R also used this "news" to corroborate (and reiterate) her earlier accounts—she said she elected to take that part-time job even though the pay was low because the hours were right, averting the problems (that R had cited in her accounts) to be expected from a full-time job.

This tactic constrained Q to concur with R's having ruled herself out of consideration more than Plans 1a–1c had, partly because R again talked so as to presuppose that the matter was already settled—but also because this "news" was that R had a prior obligation (albeit not a binding one) and that it solved personal problems that would only be reinstated if she took on the private-duty case. That made irrelevant both further talk about how to solve R's problems and talk that morally pressured R to take on the private-duty case anyway.

However, this plan failed, too. Q only made back-channel responses and then changed the topic by responding to a component of R's immediately antecedent utterance ("it's just too mu:ch") and not to the "issue" in that segment (R's present employment). Q said that she "just hadda thou:ght"; she remembered a nurse who might want to work only on weekends. Note that the potential availability of someone to substitute for R on the weekends seriously eroded all of R's previous accounts for saying no. This put R in a particularly weak position, because she had said twice previously that she would take the case except for the problem of finding a replacement on the weekends.

Plan 4 (lines 252–272): Announce Not Taking the Job as a Current Decision

R put Plan 4 into operation after Q had talked for several more turns about this other nurse:

(7) *[SBL:1:1:10:R, 249–278]*

249	Q:	En has this (.) has'er fa:m'ly, ('heeuhh (.) / 0.8) u-uh:
250		(0.9) But she's (reallih) she's a fi:ve yea:r, (1.2)
251		graduate,
252	R:	But I ↑think ah:ll (1.0) stick with this: pie:ce et Saint
253		Francis ((name of the hospital)) for awhile becuz (1.0)
254		ah mean ah'm sure of my (.) days there.
255	Q:	Ye:s ah-h ah.
256	R:	Uh an:d uh I've: gone temporarily onto this (because I've
257		been suffering fr'm) 'hh ruinous ba:ck pai:n.
258	Q:	Ye:s,
259	R:	And uhm (0.9) uh:: (.) uh ↑I've had uh some little
260		problems w'th my children en ah found thet it was: (0.7)
261		↑jus:t (.) jus'too ↑mu:ch.
262		(0.7)
263	Q:	Ye:s. =
264	R:	= to work full time,
265	Q:	°Ah-huh,° =
266	R:	= 'h An:d uhm 'hhh so I'm ↑not making much money right now
267		but the hours suit me.
268	Q:	Mm hm, =
269	R:	= An' I think I'll jus'stick with it ez long ez ther
270		willing t'keep me o:n tha t bas is.
		[ ]
271	Q:	Ye:s. .hh well thet yes ↑ that's
272		↓far more import'nt.↓
273		(.)
274	R:	Hm:?
275	Q:	That's ↓far more import'nt.↓ 'hhh hh
		[
276	R:	↑We:ll u- uh it i:s. =
		[

277 Q: to- hh

278 R: =really becuz (.) it wrecks my other li:fe you kno:w?

In this segment, R first announced as a "current decision" that she would keep her present job (therefore not take on the case) and supplemented that with an account of the decision. R's "current decision" to not take on the case certainly was not a current decision, in fact. But announcing it as one—now coming after and in response to Q's various appeals to the contrary—constrained Q more than previously to treat the matter as settled. It would only be relevant as an "unfriendly" act to respond to a *decision* to not comply with a request by trying to overturn it.

But constraining Q in that way to respond to the matter as settled did not also produce a constraint to concur with the "decision." It is thus not surprising that R went on from her announcement of a "decision" to follow up with a reiteration of her earlier accounts (beginning with a new hardship at line 257, "ruinous ba:ck pai:n"). Because the accounts in this instance pertain only to the goal of getting concurrence, the decision already having been made, Q could have achieved nothing more by withholding concurrence in response to R's account than to be understood as an unsympathetic moral critic. She did, at that juncture, concur, and that did effectively settle the matter.

METATHEORY ABOUT GOALS OF INTERACTION

The concern in this section is to characterize the formal (systemic) basis on which actors can incrementally "decide" what to say and do during interactions to attain their goals. Note that the usage of "goal" here excludes goals whose attainment does not depend on the way a social interaction progresses and ends. For example, the goal of imparting a particular item of information to someone can often be attained without having an interaction at all, and the goal of having a discussion on some matter with a colleague can be attained regardless of what the outcome of the interaction is.

Let us consider that, in the simplest case, a goal can be attained through interaction in two consecutive turns at speaking. Following Edmondson (1981), we can say that an actor can first initiate an agenda, that is, produce a message (which may or may not be topic initial) whose pragmatic meaning introduces a new demand on others, not just to respond but to respond in a particular way. Then, his or her partner may produce a message that directly resolves the agenda by satisfying the demand it introduced (e.g., A: "Can you give me a ride home this evening?" B: "Sure, glad to."").

We can then formalize the notion "goal of interaction" as follows. First, an *interaction* will be defined as a sequence of two or more messages produced by two or more participant actors such that each participant produces at least one constituent message (where the participants are linked by a channel of communication such that no "next" message can be produced before each participant has gotten the message(s) produced beforehand). Again following Edmondson (1981), the sequence of messages that constitutes an interaction must include one that creates an initial state, IS, an agenda-setting message, and one that functions as a closure state, CS_i, by resolving the agenda.[4]

Now consider that, following any message that initiates an agenda, a branching network of possible message sequences follows according to a set of principles of relevance (e.g., Sanders, 1987, pp. 79–100). For any initial message, IS, any of an n-tuple of messages, {M}, can relevantly follow, and for each member of {M} a further n-tuple of messages, {M'}, relevantly follows, and so on, until an n-tuple of closure states, {CS}, is reached. From that perspective, each successive message in an interaction is one option among a set of alternative possibilities, functionally a selection, regardless of whether the actor who produced the message is aware of it. This is graphically represented in Fig. 10.1.

The further an interaction progresses along some particular pathway between IS and CS_i, the more other possible pathways and the closure states in {CS} that follow from them become irrelevant. Of particular importance in addition, as an interaction progresses along some pathway, the more what is said and done will be interpreted on the basis of its relevance to what has previously been said and done.

It follows from this that the progression of messages in interactions constrains what follows, progressively narrowing the possible outcomes of the interaction. This provides an increasingly better formal, or systemic, basis for actors to project the likely outcome(s) of the current interaction and to make "decisions" at each turn about what to say or do to increase the relative probability of reaching a particular outcome. These "decisions" may be subjectively felt anywhere along a continuum from intuitions about what to say or do, or not say or do, to fully conscious deliberations about means to ends (Sanders, 1987, pp. 229–239; forthcoming).

The formally possible branching network between IS and {CS} thus models a decision tree that maps an actor's preference schedule onto probabilities along each pathway of the network and valuations of states at each node (Sanders, 1987, pp. 175–206). However, this is not to suggest that an actor's actual messages will therefore represent optimal choices (or even relevant options) in the fully elaborated, formally possible branching network that links IS to {CS}.

---

[4]For present purposes, an "interaction," bounded by IS and CS_i, may be self-standing or be a structural division within a larger interaction. This entails that we define a *structural division* of an interaction as an *embedded* interaction (it comprises an initial state and closure state) that begins after a prior IS has been produced among the same participant actors, either before or after closure has been achieved regarding the prior IS.

Turn 1 Turn 2   Turn 3   Turn N

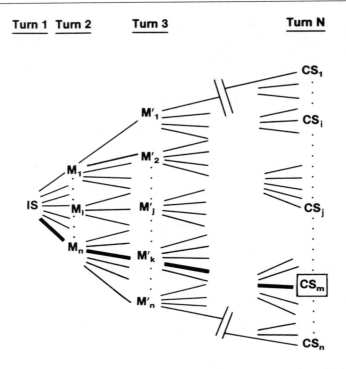

FIG. 10.1. The closure state within a box (CS_m) represents the actor's goal, with the highlighted pathway representing one progression in an interaction from which that goal, or closure state, follows.

For example, it is a debatable point whether R's use of accounts in the preceding case study was the optimal way at that juncture, among alternative possibilities, to attain her (apparent) goals of making herself unavailable for the job that Q wanted her to take and having Q approve of and/or agree with this.

Actors may not be consistently attentive to the entire array of formal possibilities, or even more than just a fragment of them—because of memory and processing limits, or mindset, coordination problems with others in the interaction, motivation, distractions, and so on. Nor should we overlook that there are, almost certainly, social differences between actors as regards the distribution of rights to manage the present agenda, control of the floor, and so on, as well as individual differences as to information-processing capacity, performance abilities, time, and experience needed to optimally or even adequately formulate messages to constrain the progress of the current interaction along a pathway that directly and uniquely ends at the targeted state, CS_i. In any case, it is an empirical question that has been of interest in studies of decision making for some time what the correspondence is in any instance between formally optimal choices and actual choices, and it is a theoretical problem to explain discrepancies (Sanders, 1987, pp. 176–183).

We can now define a *goal of interaction* as a targeted or desired closure state, CS_i, among the *n*-tuple of *possible closure states* {CS}. Defined in that way, a goal of interaction creates a preference for one pathway among alternate possible pathways between IS and {CS}.[5]

MULTIPLE GOALS

Multiple goals are attained whenever an actual interaction arrives at two or more outcomes by including two or more messages that are each members of the same *n*-tuple of closure states, {CS}. Of particular interest here is that, regardless of the wants of actors, only certain ways of attaining multiple goals are formally possible.

Attaining Multiple Goals

Two or more goals can be attained *simultaneously*. This can happen either when the message that *achieves* closure is ambiguous so that on each alternate reading it constitutes a different closure state or when an ambiguous message is an *antecedent* from which two or more closure states follow on each of its alternate readings.

Two or more goals can be attained *sequentially* within a single interaction. This can happen either when *messages* have separate components from each of which different closure states relevantly follow or when *interactions* have separate components in which different closure states can relevantly be attained. This latter condition occurs either when one interaction is embedded within another or when an interaction has a closure state from which an actor can relevantly "loop back" into that same interaction to an earlier juncture along some pathway, to attain a new closure state (as when a discussion leads to some conclusion, and then someone "loops back" from that conclusion to an earlier premise, and the discussion proceeds from there to an additional conclusion).

---

[5]An actor can also have the negative goal of averting one or more possible outcomes, rather than attaining some outcome in particular. But whether the actor's goal is to avoid a possible closure state or to attain one, a goal of interaction produces discriminations between preferred and dispreferred branchings along pathways between IS and {CS}.

Competing Goals

The concern here is when goals—different members of the same n-tuple of closure states—are *formally* opposed, that is, when they compete because they are not relevantly attainable *in the same interaction,* not because of actors' psychological, interpersonal, or role conflicts about them. In general, two or more goals are formally opposed in an interaction when messages that attain them, or from which they follow, are contraries. Because goals formally compete as a function of opposition between the meanings of messages that constitute closure states in an interaction, or from which closure states follow, actors can reconcile competing goals by adjusting the meaning relations among closure states and/or the messages that fall along pathways between IS and {CS}.

I have proposed elsewhere (e.g., Sanders, 1987) that the specific interpretation of utterances and behaviors is a function of the basis of their relevance to antecedents (or consequents) in an unfolding discourse or dialogue. In that case, the specific interpretation of a particular message (an entry in a dialogue or discourse) can be controlled by linking it to or detaching it from certain antecedents or consequents. This can be accomplished by embedded sequences that add antecedents or consequents that foster the desired interpretation of particular messages or by withholding certain entries that would foster undesired interpretations.

Thus, by revising the content, style, or delivery of one or more messages, and/or by embedding additional components within the branching network between IS and {CS}, actors can void the meaning opposition that entails competition *in the interaction* between particular goals. Whether actors do so is probably dependent on such idiosyncratic factors as their motivation, attentiveness, performance skills, personality traits, and so on.

POSTSCRIPT

A concern with actors' goals is unavoidable in studies of human communication. The proposition that what actors say and do in any instance is contingent on their goals is true by definition, insofar as we regard human communication as a form of social action and not (in contrast to much animal communication) the production of biological or conditioned responses that have fixed stimulus values for others.

But unless we are careful to avoid it, a concern with goals of communication can easily divert our attention away from talk and social interaction itself. Our interest instead becomes the psychological and perhaps sociological antecedents of social interaction—the formation of goals and plans *prior to* interaction, individual differences in that process, situational influences on it, and so forth.

This not only overlooks the role of talk and social interaction in the formation, assessment, and reformation of goals and plans; it overlooks the intricacy of the performance problem that communicators face who have to navigate towards their own goals while being responsive, at the same time, to the concurrent efforts of others to attain theirs.

However, once we accept that goals and plans may be formed or reformed in the process of social interaction, the psychological and sociological foundations of goals and plans prior to interaction occupy a diminished place in studies of communication. We are led to shift our attention to the *performance* of actors as successively creating and responding to the progress of the interaction towards particular outcomes and to the *formal (systemic) properties* of social interaction that actors must rely on to monitor, turn-by-turn, whether their goal(s) are attainable and to assess and revise their plans for attaining them. The foregoing case study and metatheoretical framework for it are intended as a step in this direction.

ACKNOWLEDGMENTS

The original version of this essay was written while I was Visiting Professor at the University of Iowa. My thinking on this topic was greatly stimulated by discussions there with Greg Shepherd and Mollie Condra. I am indebted to Stuart Sigman, Anita Pomerantz, and Karen Tracy for their comments on prior drafts of the current version.

REFERENCES

Atkinson, J. M., & Heritage, J. (Eds.). (1984). *Structures of social action.* Cambridge, England: Cambridge University Press.

Clayman, S. E., & Whalen, J. (1988/1989). When the medium becomes the message: The case of the Rather/Bush encounter. *Research on Language and Social Interaction, 22,* 241–272.

Cronen, V. E., Pearce, W. B., & Snavely, L. M. (1979). A theory of rule-structure and types of episodes and a study of perceived enmeshment in undesired repetitive patterns ("URPs"). In D. Nimmo (Ed.), *Communication yearbook 3* (pp. 225–240). New Brunswick, NJ: Transaction.

Cushman, D. P., & Craig, R. (1976). Communication systems: Interpersonal implications. In G. R. Miller (Ed.), *Explorations in interpersonal communication* (pp. 37–58). Beverly Hills, CA: Sage.

Cushman, D. P., & King, S. S. (1989). The role of communication in high-technology organizations: The emergence of high-speed management. In S. S. King (Ed.), *Human communication as a field of study* (pp. 151–162). Albany, NY: SUNY Press.

Cushman, D. P., & Pearce, W. B. (1977). Generality and necessity in three types of theory about human communication, with special attention to rules theory. *Human Communication Research, 3,* 344–353.

Cushman, D. P., & Whiting, G. (1972). An approach to communication theory: Towards consensus on rules. *Journal of Communication, 22,* 219–238.

Drew, P. (1984). Speakers' reportings in invitation sequences. In J. M. Atkinson & J. Heritage (Eds.), *Structures of social action* (pp. 129–151). Cambridge, England: Cambridge University Press.

Donohue, W. A., Cushman, D. P., & Nofsinger, R. E. (1980). Creating and confronting social order: A comparison of rules perspectives. *Western Journal of Speech Communication, 44,* 5–19.

Edmondson, W. (1981). *Spoken discourse: A model for analysis.* London: Longman.

Galbraith, J. (1973). *Designing complex organizations.* Reading, MA: Addison-Wesley.

Lewis, D. (1979). Scorekeeping in a language game. *Journal of Philosophical Logic, 8,* 339–359.

Nofsinger, R. E. (1988/1989). "Let's talk about the record": Contending over topic redirection in the Rather/Bush interview. *Research on Language and Social Interaction, 22,* 273–292.

O'Keefe, B. J., & Delia, J. G. (1982). Impression formation and message production. In M. E. Roloff & C. R. Berger (Eds.), *Social cognition and communication* (pp. 33–72). Beverly Hills, CA: Sage.

O'Keefe, B. J., & Shepherd, G. J. (1987). The pursuit of multiple objectives in face-to-face persuasive interactions: Effects of construct differentiation on message organization. *Communication Monographs, 54,* 396–419.

Pearce, W. B., & Cronen, V. E. (1980). *Communication, action, and meaning: The creation of social realities.* New York: Praeger.

Pomerantz, A. (1984). Pursuing a response. In J. M. Atkinson & J. Heritage (Eds.), *Structures of social action* (pp. 152–163). Cambridge, England: Cambridge University Press.

Pomerantz, A. (1988/1989). Constructing skepticism: Four devices used to engender the audience's skepticism. *Research on Language and Social Interaction, 22,* 293–314.

Reichman, R. (1985). *Getting computers to talk like you and me: Discourse context, focus, and semantics (an ATN model).* Cambridge, MA: MIT Press.

Sanders, R. E. (1987). *Cognitive foundations of calculated speech: Controlling understandings in conversation and persuasion.* Albany, NY: SUNY Press.

Sanders, R. E. (1989). Message effects via induced changes in the social meaning of a response. In J. Bradac (Ed.), *Message effects in communication science* (pp. 165–194). Newbury Park, CA: Sage.

Sanders, R. E., & Cushman, D. P. (1984). Rules, constraints, and strategies in human communication. In C. C. Arnold & J. W. Bowers (Eds.), *Handbook of rhetorical and communication theory* (pp. 230–269). Reading, MA: Addison-Wesley.

Schegloff, E. A. (1988/1989). From interview to confrontation: Observations on the Bush/Rather encounter. *Research on Language and Social Interaction, 22,* 215–240.

Tracy, K. (1982). On getting the point: Distinguishing "issues" from "events," an aspect of conversational coherence. In M. Burgoon (Ed.), *Communication Yearbook 5* (pp. 279–301). New Brunswick, NJ: Transaction Press.

Tracy, K. (1984). The effect of multiple goals on conversational relevance and topic shift. *Communication Monographs, 51,* 274–287.

Von Wright, G. H. (1971). *Explanation and understanding.* Ithaca, NY: Cornell University Press.

CHAPTER 11

A Synthetic Perspective on Goals and Discourse

Gregory J. Shepherd
University of Kansas

Eric W. Rothenbuhler
University of Iowa

There is something ironic about verbal interaction. It is both wonderous in its diversity and exceptional in its sameness; both frustrating in its ease of failure and mundane in its everyday successfulness. That is so, at least in part, because discourse is individually goal-driven yet socially structured. As scholars of discourse, then, we are confronted by a tension that we must theorize. This chapter addresses various aspects of this tension and offers some thoughts about reconciling it in our theories of discourse.

Invoking a notion of "goals" to explain features of discourse has become increasingly popular, for straightforward reasons. As witnessed by the chapters in this volume, it is a useful approach to problems that have not been satisfactorily solved by other methods. Invoking goals as an explanation of discourse also jibes with common presumptions about the nature of the social actor. Most of us share beliefs that people are willful actors, that discourse is one of the most purposive of forms of social action, is fundamentally intentional, and that discourse, therefore, is well understood as goal-driven: Discourse is shaped by the fact that its speakers have goals and make choices.

But it is no less true that discourse is fundamentally structured, ordered, and patterned. It is from this empirical truth that many theories of language derive. For example, Searle's (1969) speech–act theory and Grice's (1975) conversational maxims address, in a sense, the predictability of discourse, its pattern, structure, and order. The genuine success of these theories depends on the predictability of discourse that is embodied in its orderliness.

It seems, then, that we have two readily apparent features of discourse and two corresponding bodies of theory and research. Discourse appears to us as a highly volitional form of social action, usefully explained by reference to the goals of interactants. Discourse appears to us also as a structure, that is, as an instance of social order: Relatively independent of the actors and the situation, samples of discourse exhibit patterns that can be explained as specifications of general social rules and structures.

THE TENSION

The way in which we, as scholars of discourse, have primarily addressed the double aspect of discourse—its individually goal-driven and socially structured nature—is as a pair of alternatives. This has been made manifest in divisions of labor that lead, in turn, to false arguments. We have divided ourselves in the academy into camps. For example, we divide into camps of psychologists and sociologists. The former take as their primary territory the investigation of human behavior from an internal, individualistic, and, at least since the cognitive revolution in psychology, relatively voluntaristic point of view. Sociologists, on the other hand, lay claim to investigations of human behavior from a more external, collectivistic, and more deterministic point of view. Within departments of communication studies, we have made similar divisions (not surprisingly, given such departments' historical reliance on the fields of psychology and sociology for theoretical and research paradigms). Most of us consider ourselves to be either psychologically oriented individualists (humans are willful, intentional, action-oriented creators of discourse) or culturally oriented collectivists (society or culture structures, patterns, and orders communication). We then, of course, engage in entertaining but rarely fruitful debates over the primacy of our respective orientations: cognition versus culture; nature versus nurture; traits versus situations, and so on.

These arguments occur in spite of the fact that most of us will say, when asked, that human action, in general, and discourse, in particular, cannot be anything but a complex synthesis of these and other features. What we do, how we interact, and the things we say must always be voluntary, creative, and therefore unpredictable while simultaneously being determined, repetitive, and therefore predictable. But seldom have our theories attempted to grasp the two aspects of this simultaneity simultaneously; rather, we treat the horns of the dilemma as alternatives, moving back and forth between the positions.

We seem better able to philosophize than to theorize this tension; it shows up in our speculative reflections but not in our research work. Many of us, for example, can appreciate Wittgenstein's (cited in Scruton, 1981) perception of:

. . . a fundamental demand that human utterance be answerable to a standard of correctness. This standard is not God-given, nor does it lie dormant in the order of nature. It is a human artifact, as much the product as the producer of the linguistic practices which it governs. This does not mean that an individual can decide for himself what is right and wrong in the art of communication. On the contrary, the constraint of publicity binds each and all of us; moreover that constraint is intimately bound up with our conception of ourselves as beings who observe and act upon an independent world. Nevertheless, it is true that there is no constraint involved in common usage other than usage itself. If we come up against truths which seem to us to be necessary, this can only be because we have created the rules that make them so, and what we create we can also forgo. The compulsion that we experience in logical inference, for example, is no compulsion, independently [sic] of our disposition so to experience it. (p. 280)

This tension is captured in another form by MacIntyre in discussing the ways in which human behavior *must be* both predictable and not predictable. The sum of MacIntyre's (1981) position is this: "It is necessary, if life is to be meaningful, for us to be able to engage in long-term projects, and this requires predictability; it is necessary, if life is to be meaningful, for us to be in possession of ourselves and not merely to be the creations of other people's projects, intentions and desires, and this requires unpredictability" (p. 99).

It is easy to see the ways in which the philosophical positions of Wittgenstein and MacIntyre speak directly to the fundamental tension of discourse. Wittgenstein philosophized discourse as something that is both voluntary and determined as well as something that was both producer and product. MacIntyre suggested the appeal of invoking a notion of goals to understand discourse. Such an invocation is appealing, in part because we believe that discourse accomplishes things: We produce discourse in order to accomplish certain goals (long-term projects, in MacIntyre's terms), and the successful accomplishment of those goals depends, in part, on the production of relatively predictable discourse. It is here, perhaps, that we are confronted with the rub of theorizing discourse that may be absent from our attempts to philosophize the same.

If one follows out the line cast by MacIntyre, it becomes apparent that it cannot be simply discourse (i.e., the talk itself) that is relatively predictable, but if goals are to be an explanation of discourse, they must be predictable as well. But goals are individual things, are they not? How, then, can the individual phenomena of goals be predictable? If our goals are unique in the sense that they are associated with us rather than with someone else in a given situation—if they offer ways in which we stay in possession of ourselves, as MacIntyre put it—how can they be a source of the trans-individual, trans-situation patterns we observed in discourse? Can we explain the observable patterns of discourse through our invocation of individual goals? At best, it seems difficult. It would seem to require we explain commonality by reference to uniqueness, a constant by a variable. We may try the trick by refering to the "typicality" of goals, but doing so ultimately produces unsatisfactory theorizing. If goals are things that belong fundamentally to the individual, if we really do "have" them as we say, and if they then are the basis for real choices that we make, how can there *be* typical goals? From whence does the typicality come? We cannot logically say that it derives from without, from something existing across actors and independent of them. In that case it becomes a form of determination of the actor, not a choice that has been made; it is a response, not a volition. Typicality of goals, then, is symptomatic of a form of determination, or at least of limits on choices.

In sum, we cannot think of goals as fundamentally individual in nature while also thinking of them as typical in some way—or can we? MacIntyre urged us, in a sense, to simply accept this "fact" of human behavior: It simply is always partly predictable and partly not. But such acceptance makes theorizing human behavior, in general, and discourse, in particular, very difficult, as we try to point out in the next section of the chapter.

TYPICAL THEORETICAL CHOICES

One of the fundamental questions we face in our study of discourse that arises from the tension we outlined earlier is this: How do we go about explaining the patterns that obtain in conversational interaction consistent with our commitment to the willfulness of individuals? The structural and functional patterns we observe across conversational interactions are the outcome of actions taken by the individuals involved. If those individuals are willful, then we can not explain that they were "caused to emit the speech behaviors" we observe. Rather, they must have chosen to engage in the actions we observe. If patterns are to result from choices, then there must be some pattern in the choices themselves. How, then, do the choices of willful individuals come to be patterned?

When confronted with this problem, theorists typically make one of two choices, both of which entail sacrifices of theoretical power; and empirical generality.

Some theorists forward rational models that emphasize the individual goal seeker at the expense of a social, structuring force in discourse. Thus, they locate goals in individuals but, recognizing the need to account for orderliness and patterns (the apparent typicality of goals and interaction patterns), posit the social world as a constraining force on the individual. For example, Fish (1978, pp. 248–251) wrote of a sign "that is affixed in this unpunctuated form" to the door of the Johns Hopkins University Club: "PRIVATE MEMBERS ONLY." He noted the range of responses he received from his students when he asked them what the sign meant, including, "Only those who are secretly and not publicly members of this club may enter it," and "Only genitalia may enter," which, he said, is the most popular reading, perhaps because of its Disney-like anthropomorphism. Fish went on to note, however, that eventually one student would state the obvious: "But you're just playing games; everyone knows that sign really means 'Only those persons who belong to this club may enter it.' " And Fish agreed, of course; everyone does know. Fish used this illustration primarily to make a point about the contextual nature of language and meaning: Because messages always appear in a context, their meanings are relatively unambiguous. Assuming that messages have not been artificially contextually displaced (and the receivers of those messages are members of the "language community"), their meanings are, necessarily, rather unequivocal. And so it is clear that the implicit theory of meaning here is that meaning is in contexts, that is, that an individual's reading is constrained by the situation of the text.

Alternatively, Fish's illustration might also suggest that everyone understands the meaning of PRIVATE MEMBERS ONLY as it appears on the clubhouse door because everyone understands the "goal" or intent that underlies the message. This is the view of Jacobs and Jackson (1983) in their work on conversational coherence. These authors argued that conversational coherence is grounded in a process of making intentions known: "the sense of an utterance—its coherence—is to be found in its relations to some goal"; "incoherent utterances are those which have no apparent goal, or which ignore apparent goals behind other utterances, or which pursue goals in an irrational manner" (p. 65).

But how is it that we come to even have a chance at knowing the intent that produced PRIVATE MEMBERS ONLY or the goals that are tied to coherent discourse? Fish, and many others, of course, might point to situational factors that constrain our reading of the message; Jacobs and Jackson (1983) seem to have pointed to something different but analogous. They wrote: "Coherent discourse must be shown to be the orderly output of practical reasoning about goals, constrained by institutionally defined means of *achieving* those goals" (p. 51). That is, to Jacobs and Jackson, conventional forces work to constrain the means by which goals might be achieved (e.g., the discourse structures in which goals might be pursued, or societal norms of appropriateness, politeness, and the like). Thus, both Fish's sign painter and Jacob's and Jackson's coherent conversationalist are "constrained" by forces that are external to them in the production of their messages, and readers of the sign and hearers of the conversation are similarly constrained in the interpretations they might make by external forces (e.g., contextual factors).

These, then, represent common ways in which builders of "rational" theories or models account for orderliness and patterns in message production and interpretation. Although individuals are voluntaristic, willful, and intentional, they are *constrained* by social forces that are external to them. This, in a sense, represents an attempt to attenuate a reductionist bent in such theories.

We find this, however, to be an unsatisfactory solution to the fundamental tension we have been addressing. Although it is evident enough that we can explain some of what people do by reference to their individual goals, or to what they are seemingly consciously trying to do, notice that we are essentially explaining only a unit act by reference to the wants or goals of a unit actor. This is *not* explaining discourse. What makes explaining discourse different from explaining unit acts is the trans-unit pattern that characterizes discourse and distinguishes it from simple, single utterances. It is precisely this trans-unit character that must be explained if we are to say that we have explained discourse. Discourse, and its ability to help us achieve goals, is something that occurs in patterns across units, across acts, and across individuals. We cannot explain discourse—as distinct from the things people say—by reference to some pure notion of the individual goals of the actors involved, for one primary reason: the goals of individuals cannot explain trans-individual patterns unless they themselves are trans-individually patterned. Secondly, referencing individuals' goals as an explanation fails to identify what is unique about what we study. In referencing individuals' goals, it seems that we set about explaining discourse by the same logic we might use to explain eating, sleeping, or chewing gum. It is precisely blind to what makes discourse unique: its simultaneous internal and external, individual and collective nature.

A second way in which theorists may confront the tension between the goal-seeking individual actor and the patterns, orderliness, and typicality of discourse is to reverse favor. Some theorists locate goals outside the individual and thus are able to account for patterns, order, and typicality; but, recognizing the need to account for the range and diversity observed in human interaction, they posit individual differences as a constraining force on a structuring, social world. Such an approach is evident in the recent work of O'Keefe and Shepherd (e.g., O'Keefe, 1984; O'Keefe & Shepherd, 1987, 1989; Shepherd & Trank, 1986).

These authors have recently argued for a "rational goals analysis" of situations, in which various aspects of a context or situation are considered, and the "natural goal configuration" of that situation is then determined. This uncovering of the "natural goal configuration" is employed, in part, to examine the influence that social–cognitive development has on the extent and ways in which interactants pursue the goals comprising that configuration in the situation. In this way, these authors might be seen as trying to avoid the inherent weakness of purely rational models. Again, by placing goals outside of individuals, in situations, it becomes potentially possible to account for trans-unit patterns in communication. Nevertheless, to many of us there is something odd about locating goals in situations rather than in individuals. As one anonymous reviewer put it, "*People* have goals, situations do not." But authors such as O'Keefe and Shepherd might simply be seen as turning the culture-as-constraint argument on its head and positing a kind of individual-as-constraint notion instead. That is, goal configurations are seen by these authors, in a sense, as existing naturally in situations, but the perception and pursuit of such configurations is constrained by individual-level phenomena—individual differences in sensitivity to these forces.

We believe this is one way in which theorists may favor the social-structuring force but bow to individual force by considering the latter as a constraint on the former. Individual differences, either as traits (e.g., Snyder's [1974] self-monitoring variable) or developmental level (e.g., construct differentiation, Crockett, 1965) work to constrain the extent of determination by the social world that is external to individuals. This represents an attempt, in a sense, to attenuate a certain deterministic bent in such approaches.

But, of course, seeing individuals as "mere constraints" on situations is as unsatisfactory as seeing situations as "mere constraints" on individuals. We think humans are willful, intentional, and action-oriented creatures. Countless cognitive theories have shown us the value of considering humans as such. One only needs to think of the cognitive critiques of behaviorism, both empirical and theoretical, to appreciate the rationality of the individual actor (see, e.g., Kiesler, Collins, & Miller, 1969, pp. 142–152). We want our theories of discourse to account for reasoned action and to be responsive to the individual and perhaps idiosyncratic goals of interactants; But perhaps we can accept that persons do things for reasons (a la the rational models of Fishbein, 1980, and Jacobs & Jackson, 1983, for example) but reject the notion that each of those reasons is necessarily wholly voluntaristic.

Ultimately, we believe, the solution to this problem (or the relief from this tension) can only come through redefinition and reconceptualization of taken-for-granted terms of relationship in social theory. In the final section of the chapter, we consider questions of "action" and "order," as we address the relationship between these fundamental concepts in terms of the individual, the collective, the internal, and the external.

THE ACTION/ORDER PROBLEM

This tension we have been addressing in the study of goals and discourse has its counterpart in sociological theory. There, an analogous tension is referred to as "the action/order problem." Briefly, that "problem" can be summarized as follows. It is self-evident that societies are, in one sense, particular sorts of aggregations of acting individuals. But they are not just actions; there must be pattern to those actions. If action were random, there could be no coordination, no interaction, no groups, communities, or societies. Action must, then, be ordered.

The problem with the statement, "action must be ordered," is that it implies that humans are primordially monadic actors and that they can only be formed into a society by the imposition of some form of external order. An alternative is the statement, "order must be enacted." The problem with this is that it implies that societies are somehow transcendental orders waiting to be enacted. Both have an element of truth in them, but both are incomplete, just as notions of individual goals constrained by situations and situational goals constrained by individuals are semitruths.

Recently, Alexander (1982–1983, 1987) has suggested that social theories have erred in seeing action and order as dialectically related, that is, as lying at opposite ends of a single dimension, defining each other in their opposition. We find merit in this claim. Like Alexander, we contend that order and action are not opposite in any sense. Indeed, each requires the other, and together they provide the defining terms of discourse. Discourse is simultaneous action and order. Action without order is randomness, and randomness cannot be discourse. But, order without action is stasis, and neither can stasis be discourse. Yet, we believe that our theories of discourse have been primarily theories of pattern, typicality, order, and, ultimately, stasis, *or* of choice, creativity, idiosyncracy, and, ultimately, randomness.

No theorist, of course, posits a theory of discourse as randomness—randomness would seem to necessarily defie theorizing. Rather, as noted earlier by example, some theorists favor the explanation of individual action and so forth in their theories but posit situational constraints in an attempt to account for patterns and such, thereby avoiding the folly of theorizing randomness. But such theorists see order and action as opposites, the former imposed on the latter. As such, they are contradictory terms and cannot be logically synthesized. Theorists that posit action constrained into order have opened up a residual category in their theories in an attempt to fix them. But, they have done so by violating the logical structure of those theories. It is as if they argue that "people are free . . . except sometimes" or that "people are rational . . . except when they are not." They have theorized action but not order. Order can only be explained in such theories by positing a deus ex machina called "external constraints," and this is really no explanation at all.

Similarly, of course, no theorist poses a discourse theory of absolute stasis—lack of variance is no more explainable than is random variance. Rather, again as noted by example, some theorists favor the explanations of patterns and whatnot but posit individual differences and the like as constraints on such patterns to avoid the folly of theorizing stasis. Theorists that do, however, are liable to the same critique as those just discussed: Action and order are seen as opposites, though these latter theorists choose to theorize order at the expense of action. Such theorists have devoted their attention to what exists in the situation as it can be intersubjectively verified and would be shared by us all. Then, becoming uncomfortable with the predominance of order and the determinism it implies in their theories, they ultimately violate their own logic by positing individual differences: "what we perceive is culturally or socially determined . . . except sometimes"; "the situation dictates our behavior . . . except when it does not."

Perhaps it seems as if we are being overly harsh in our judgments, for one might argue that, essentially, we have a simple division of theoretical labor taking place; that some communication theories are built to explain the variance we observe in our day-to-day interactions, and others are built to explain the commonalities we perceive. But, such an argument misses our central point: As we began suggesting in the first section of this chapter, creation of a theoretical division as a response to the tension we have been addressing is ultimately detrimental to the study of discourse. We can best develop a satisfyingly complete theory of discourse only by refusing to dichotomize action and order.

Following Alexander's (1982–1983, 1987) argument about the development of social theory, we argue that theories of discourse have tended to collapse action and order into a single dimension, perceive that dimension as defining a theoretical dilemma, and construct explanations that favor one end over the other. We have tended to see the individualistic, the subjectivistic, and the voluntaristic as all being relatively closely identified, as having reference to phenomena that are "internal" to people, and as being terms belonging to theories of action. We have also tended to see the collectivistic, the objectivistic, and the deterministic as being relatively closely identified, as having reference to phenomena that are "external" to people, and as being terms belonging to theories of order. We have tended to see these clusters of terms as being mutually exclusive and as setting up a single dilemma that theories must resolve by choosing one end over the other. We argue that by seeing action and order as distinct, we will gain important flexibility in our thinking and, at some point in the future, greater power in our theories of discourse.

If, as we have already contended (and following Alexander, 1982–1983, 1987), it is wrong to see action and order as lying on opposite ends of a single dimension, then they must be separate questions. Our theories must ask both where does action come from and where does order come from? Presuming that there are at least two possible types of answers to each of these questions, we find ourselves with two dimensions that can be crossed to create a four-cell system. This is exactly what Alexander argued vis-à-vis sociological theory, and we feel that the argument applies equally well to discourse theory.

Origins of Action

Consider the origins of action. The two dominant types of answer to the question, "Where does action come from?" are (a) action is principally internally motivated, and (b) action is principally externally motivated. In other words, most theories tend to see action as either explainable by reference to the actor's internal states (as represented in the work of Jacobs & Jackson, 1983, for example, as reviewed earlier), or by reference to the actor's situation (as represented in the work of O'Keefe & Shepherd, 1987, for example, as discussed earlier). The theories that offer explanations of action by reference to *both* internal and external phenomena are rare; those that do it without assigning priority of one over the other are almost nonexistent. Alexander's position, and our own, is that this is unfortunate: an a priori privileging of one type of action explanation over another prejudges the empirical situations we may want to analyze and thus limits theoretical generality and flexibility. The only a priori judgment that can be sustained is the assertion that social life is complicated and that a full explanation of any action is going to require both internal and external reference.

The one aspect of social life that most requires explanations that reference both internal and external origins of action is discourse. Discourse is clearly always both internally and externally motivated. Discourse is the very act of articulating the internal and external, the ego and the alter, the self and the situation. (We mean to call to mind the double meaning of articulation here, regarding speech and the act of uniting by forming a joint.) Ricoeur (1976) argued something similar:

> Being-together, as the existential condition for the possibility of any dialogical structure of discourse, appears as a way of trespassing or overcoming the fundamental solitude of each human being. . . . My experience cannot directly become your experience. An event belonging to one stream of consciousness cannot be transferred as such into another stream of consciousness. Yet, nevertheless, something passes from me to you. Something is transferred from one sphere of life to another. This something is not the experience as experienced, but its meaning. Here is the miracle. The experience as experienced, as lived, remains private, but its sense, its meaning, becomes public. Communication in this way is the overcoming of the radical noncommunicability of the lived experience as lived. (pp. 15–16)

If communication requires the bringing together of self and other, then where this does not occur we should also not find communication. Consider this example (from Boswell, 1982):

> "The great hitter, Don Miguel Cuevas, kept a notebook on every pitcher in Cuba. He wrote down every pitch he ever saw," said the gentle Torpedo [Adres "Papo" Liano]. "So one day the pitchers stole his book and it was passed all over the country until every pitcher had read what Cuevas had said of him. It did not help at all. Cuevas knew everything about us, but had written down nothing whatsoever about himself." (p. 93)

Cuevas' notebook was not meant as communication but as record keeping. It was written in the same general codes that are familiar to all speakers of the language and all players of the game, but it didn't speak to them of Cuevas. It could not work as communication, for there was no communicative intent embedded in it. It might report something, but it was not a report of the intentions of a communicator.

If communication is, by definition, the bringing together of self and other, a bridging or melding of internal and external worlds, then our explanations of discourse must also reference both features. If we leave out a reference to internal or external motivations, we cannot have explained discourse. We may have said something about something that is part of the process of communicating (such as providing an expectancy-value explanation for the utterances people make), but we have not explained discourse. In the same vein, if we are going to illuminate discourse by reference to goals, then we must see that goals in interpersonal interaction arise from both internal and external sources, that is, from both the individuals involved and the situations they are in. If communicative action is a kind of engine, it is both internally and externally combustive.

Origins of Order

Consider now the question of what gives rise to order. Where do the patterns we observe come from? The two most common types of answers to this question (excluding reference to a deity) are (a) that order arises from the aggregations of individual actions and (b) that order arises from sui generis collective phenomena, from something relatively independent of the individuals and actions that exhibit the pattern we want to explain. A paradigm case of the former is classic free-market price theory. There is an order of interaction, a pattern, established by the balance among the number of people offering a commodity for sale, the number of people buying, and the price established by that relation. It is a perfectly determined three-variable, three-equation system. The resulting order can be entirely predicted, in a "pure market," by simply knowing the counts and distributions of individual actions taken. If one individual switches from being a buyer to a seller, that changes the price of the commodity. If the price changes, so will the balance of buyers and sellers. Another example of this approach to order—one that sees order rising from the aggregation of individual actions—might be seen in the small-group decision-making model of Davis (1973), which attempts to account for the decisional outcomes of group deliberations solely on the basis of individual group members' initial preferences for certain outcomes and a decision scheme structure that combines those initial preferences into a final group decision.

A paradigm case of collective order, on the other hand, is Durkheim's category of "social facts." These are phenomena such as norms, symbols, and rituals that each individual experiences as a unique subjective force but that derive from and belong to the collectivity. No one of us has the power to change a norm or symbol or ritual. If one member of a community were to decide not to obey a norm, that would not result in a change of the norm as the price would change if one member of the market chose to buy rather than sell; it would result in that member of the community being punished. The norm is a collective ordering phenomenon; neither its form nor its power is dependent on an aggregation of actors.

Language also works as a collective order. Each individual comes into a world that already has a language, and each individual eventually leaves that world. This coming and going does not change the language the way the coming and going of buyers and sellers changes prices in free-market theory. The language is a social fact; it is collectively possessed (and collectively possessive), and it provides order to what concretely appear to be individual actions. It does so relatively independent of the individuals involved—thus, de Saussure's (1915/1966) distinguishing of *langue* as the system of language from *parole* as the spoken language. *Langue* is a collective phenomenon, whereas *parole* is an individual one.

Now, as part of his call for multidimensionality in social theory, Alexander argued that the only a priori judgments that should be made about the origins of order are, as in the case of action, that every theory should be prepared to consider orders that derive from both individual and collective phenomena and to do so without assigning priority. Again, we feel that such is especially true of discourse, which is unlike other social phenomena in the extent to which it obviously depends on both individual and collective ordering principles. The noises we make constitute communication only to the extent we order them according to both individual and collective patterns. Individual ordering principles will include our individual wants, personas, situational reactions, accounting of the other individuals in the situation of the moment, and so on. Collective ordering principles will include rules, roles, social structures, relationships, languages, and so on. If behaviors fail to call on or articulate (again, in that double sense) both individual and collective orders, they cannot constitute discourse.

As Ricoeur (1976) put it:

> *Langue* is the code—or set of codes—on the basis of which a particular speaker produces *parole* as a particular message. To this main dichotomy [in Saussure's work] are connected several subsidiary distinctions. A message is individual, its code is collective. . . . A message is intentional; it is meant by someone. The code is anonymous and not intended. In this sense it is unconscious . . . in the sense of a nonlibidinal structural and cultural unconscious. More than anything else, a mes-

sage is arbitrary and contingent, while a code is systematic and compulsory for a given speaking community. (p. 3)

CONCLUSION

In sometimes roundabout fashion, we have tried to build a two-headed argument in this essay. First, we have tried to make a definitional point: The tension we have continually pointed to between individual goals and social structure as related to discourse is really no tension at all. For too long, we have considered such concepts as action and order only in opposition to one another, when we should have been taking them as the defining terms of discourse. The rules, norms, systems, and structures of language do not become discursive until they are given action by human interactants. Discourse puts action to order. But if a social fact such as language is a kind of nothing until it is put into action, so is action a kind of nothing unless it can be seen as an acting of something: the speaking of a language, the adherence to a norm, the honoring of a symbol, the achievement of a goal. In this way, the doings of the self become meaningful for the other; they become something that we can agree is an action, not just a behavior. And at this point, of course, they also gain the potential to be communicative.

In essence, to engage in discourse is to perform. As a performer, the discoursing individual is both creator and conduit; the performer has both a role and an interpretation to perform. The role is the collective and shared aspect of the performance; the interpretation is the individual and creative aspect. Both are required for the accomplishment of discourse.

The second head of our argument has been more analytical than definitional: Given the simultaneous internal and external, individual and collective nature of discourse, we can sensibly invoke a notion of goals to explain such a happening only by giving broad analytical consideration to the term "goal." Goals cannot be expected to satisfactorily explain discourse if they are seen as having only internal, or only individual, or only external, or only collective origins. Goals must be seen and theorized as arising from all of those sources. Furthermore, any singular goal ought to be thought of and theorized as possessing internal, external, individual, and collective qualities. Other writers have recently addressed some of the same issues that we have raised in this essay but have tended to feed "the fundamental tension" by approaching it from a methodological orientation (notably, see the "levels of analysis" treatment this fundamental tension receives in the collection by Berger & Chaffee, 1987). We are arguing more than that there are different levels and perspectives on the issues of communication theory and more than the methodological point that theories that encompass more than one level or perspective are more general than others. We are arguing that communication theories *must*, by the nature of the logic of that which they analyze, address the coming together of individual and collective patterns and of internal and external experience. Theories that link goals and discourse may provide particularly fertile ground for synthesizing these terms.

REFERENCES

Alexander, J. C. (1982–1983). *Theoretical logic in sociology* (Vols. 1–4). Berkeley: University of California Press.

Alexander, J. C. (1987). *Twenty lectures: Sociological theory since World War two.* New York: Columbia University Press.

Berger, C. R., & Chaffee, S. H. (1987). *Handbook of communication science.* Newbury Park, CA: Sage.

Boswell, T. (1982). *How life imitates the world series.* Middlesex, England: Penguin.

Crockett, W. H. (1965). Cognitive complexity and impression formation. In B. A. Maher (Ed.), *Progress in experimental personality research Vol. 2* (pp. 47–90). New York: Academic Press.

Davis, J. H. (1973). Group decision and social interaction: A theory of social decision schemes. *Psychological Review, 80,* 97–125.

Fish, S. (1978). Normal circumstances, literal language, direct speech acts, the ordinary, the everyday, the obvious, what goes without saying, and other special cases. *Critical Inquiry, 4,* 625–644.

Fishbein, M. (1980). A theory of reasoned action: Some applications and implications. In M. M. Page (Ed.), *1979 Nebraska symposium on motivation* (pp. 65–116). Lincoln: University of Nebraska Press.

Grice, H. P. (1975). Logic and conversation. In P. Cole & J. Morgan (Eds.), *Syntax and semantics: Vol. 3. Speech acts* (pp. 41–58). New York: Academic Press.

Jacobs, S., & Jackson, S. (1983). Speech act structure in conversation: Rational aspects of pragmatic coherence. In R. T. Craig & K. Tracy (Eds.), *Conversational coherence: Form, structure, and strategy* (pp. 47–66). Beverly Hills, CA: Sage.

Kiesler, C. A., Collins, B. E., & Miller, N. (1969). *Attitude change.* New York: John Wiley & Sons.

MacIntyre, A. (1981). *After virtue: A study in moral theory.* Notre Dame, IN: University of Notre Dame Press.

O'Keefe, B. J. (1984). The evolution of impressions in small working groups: Effects of construct differentiation. In H. E. Sypher & J. L. Applegate (Eds.), *Communication by children and adults: Social cognitive and strategic processes* (pp. 262–291). Beverly Hills, CA: Sage.

O'Keefe, B. J., & Shepherd, G. J. (1987). The pursuit of multiple objectives in face-to-face persuasive interactions: Effects of construct differentiation on message organization. *Communication Monographs, 54,* 396–419.

O'Keefe, B. J., & Shepherd, G. J. (1989). The communication of identity during face-to-face persuasive interactions: Effects of perceiver's construct differentiation and target's message strategies. *Communication Research, 16,* 375–404.

Ricoeur, P. (1976). *Interpretation theory: Discourse and the surplus of meaning.* Fort Worth, TX: The Texas Christian University Press.

Saussure, F. de (1966). *Course in general linguistics* (trans. W. Baskin, Trans.). New York: McGraw-Hill. (Original work published 1915)

Scruton, R. (1981). *From Descartes to Wittgenstein: A short history of modern philosophy.* New York: Harper & Row.

Searle, J. R. (1969). *Speech acts*. London: Cambridge University Press.

Shepherd, G. J., & Trank, D. M. (1986, November). *Construct system development and dimensions of judgment*. Paper presented at the annual meeting of the Speech Communication Association, Chicago, IL.

Snyder, M. (1974). Self-monitoring of expressive behavior. *Journal of Personality and Social Psychology, 30*, 526–537.

Appendix: Transcript Notation

Transcription is the process of presenting face-to-face interactions in a written form. The level of detail at which interactions are presented can vary enormously. At one extreme, a transcript might include only a rough rendering of the words spoken; at the other, a transcript could include peculiarities of pronunciation and vocal stress, the occasions and lengths of pausing, the timing of multiple speakers and the degree to which their utterances were adjacent or overlapping, the inhalation and exhalation of breath, the concomitant gaze patterns of interactants, the specific timing of applause, and so on.

A researcher's general theoretical framework and specific purposes will affect what level of detail will be deemed most appropriate (see Craig & Tracy, 1983, for a discussion of the trade-offs involved in transcribing at different levels of detail). Because of the different motivating concerns of researchers, a number of distinct transcription systems have developed. Each of the systems has particular features that merit attention. For instance, the system refined by Gumperz and colleagues (Gumperz, 1982a, 1982b) is particularly sensitive to vocal stress patterns. Perhaps the most widely used system is the "conversation analysis" transcription system (Schenkein, 1978; Atkinson & Heritage, 1984). Initially developed by Gail Jefferson, it has become a preferred transcription system for many discourse researchers. This system of notation is the one used by authors in this book who transcribed in detail. The most common notations are explained here; more detailed explanation and examples of this system can be found in Atkinson and Heritage (1984) or in Schenkein (1978).

Notation	Meaning
[[	Utterances that begin simultaneously.
[ ]	Marks the beginning and ending of overlapping utterances.
=	Indicates that two contiguous utterances have no time interval between them.
(.)	Short untimed pause within an utterance.
(1.6)	Pauses within and between utterances timed to tenths of a second.
((pause))	Untimed intervals heard between utterances.
:	Marks the extension of the sound or syllable it follows.
.	Indicates an intonation that falls and stops.
,	Marks a continuing intonation.
?	indicates a rising intonation.
-	Indicates a halting abrupt cutoff.
!	Marks an animated tone.
↑↓	Marks the direction of an intonation shift.
word	Indicates a word said with emphasis.
WORD	Indicates words said louder than the surrounding talk.
o o or	
* *	Indicates passage that is quieter than surrounding talk.
> <	Marks an utterance said more quickly than the surrounding talk.
(hhh)	Audible aspirations.
(.hhh)	Audible inhalations.
( )	Indicates transcriptionist doubt.

REFERENCES

Atkinson, J. M., & Heritage, J. (Eds.). (1984). *Structure of social action: Studies in conversation analysis.* Cambridge, England: Cambridge University Press.

Craig, R. T., & Tracy, K. (Eds.). (1983). *Conversational coherence: Form, structure and strategy.* Beverly Hills, CA: Sage.

Gumperz, J. J. (Ed.). (1982a). *Language and social identity.* Cambridge, England: Cambridge University Press.

Gumperz, J. J. (1982b). *Discourse strategies.* Cambridge, England: Cambridge University Press.

Schenkein, J. (Ed.). (1978). *Studies in the organization of conversational interaction.* New York: Academic Press.

Author Index

Subject Index